The Failure of Free Market Economics and the Future of New Zealand

CHRIS NOBBS

A catalogue record for this book is available from the National Library of New Zealand

ISBN 978-0-473-28856-3

Design by Smartwork Creative, www.smartworkcreative.co.nz
Cover painting by Gerda Leenards
Typeset in Minion Pro
Printed by CreateSpace, an Amazon.com company
Available from www.createspace.com/7345663

Table of Contents

About the Author

Chris Nobbs grew up in New Zealand. Following graduation from the University of Auckland he has enjoyed a wide-ranging career as a research scientist at the University of Cambridge, as a consultant and administrator at the OECD Environment Directorate, as economist to the Government of Victoria's salinity control programme, and as co-director of an Australia-wide social research consultancy. His book *Economics, Sustainability, and Democracy: Economics in the Era of Climate Change* was published by Routledge in the UK and in the US during 2013. He currently lives in Auckland.

Preface

The economic reform programme introduced in New Zealand in 1984 and pursued in subsequent decades, has probably been the greatest manmade misfortune in New Zealand's history outside of two world wars. It was the expression of an extremist form of free market economics that originated in the work of US economist Milton Friedman, and developed by his colleagues, at the University of Chicago. This style of economics was promoted in New Zealand by over-zealous Treasury officials, adopted by naïve politicians, and implemented by those same Treasury officials. Despite some moderation in the implementation of these free market policies in recent years, this style continues to determine the tenor and impulse of New Zealand economic and political life. It is necessary finally to tell the emperor he has no clothes. It is time for New Zealanders to commence reclaiming the ground that has been lost in recent years, and begin to choose a better future.

The purpose of this book is to show how these free market economic policies and their encompassing neoliberal political attitudes have failed to solve New Zealand's core economic problems; have created damaging social consequences; have demonstrated a seriously unbalanced attitude to international trade; and are inadequate – not to say already obsolete – in providing the context for solving the new problems that New Zealand society faces in the twenty-first century.

The case to be presented rests on the notion that there is something distinct about being a New Zealander, and about New Zealand society, which we are prepared to defend and promote. The book does not speak to those who believe in a globalised perspective in which the course of civilisation is to be determined by economic markets in which self-interest is the sole motivating factor. The claim made here is that a broader span of values should determine the type of economics we embrace. The importance of market exchange and of international trade are taken for granted. However it is contended that there are surpassing matters of justice and fairness that are not part of neoliberal thinking, and which require a broader ethical view than that provided by free market economics. One dollar one vote is not the limit of our imaginings or our wishes. In concert with this approach the emphasis in the present book is on the political ideology that drives and continues to drive government policies, rather than on rivalry amongst various political parties.

The book concerns the political philosophy of liberalism. It is a philosophy that puts primary emphasis on individual freedom – the ability of individuals to carry out their own projects in an environment of tolerance towards others doing the same. Liberalism is premised on a view that individuals are rational, independent agents, and each of equal value. Even so the idea is a complex one, and can be interpreted in different ways, as we shall see. So we need to be clear about the terminology to be used here. In this book we will refer to the variant of liberalism that attained ascendancy in the latter decades of the twentieth century as 'neoliberalism' (or 'libertarianism'), and its economic manifestation as 'free market' (or 'laissez-faire') economics. We will refer to the variant of liberalism that it replaced as 'new liberalism' (or 'welfare liberalism') and its economic manifestation as the 'mixed economy' (or 'Keynesian economy'). Interpreted into its economic context, neoliberalism is defined by *Collins English Dictionary* as 'a modern politico-economic theory favouring free trade, privatisation, minimal government intervention in business, reduced public expenditure on social services, etc'. We will accept this definition as our own, and contrast this with the mixed economy which favours a more receptive attitude to government participation in economic management.

Free market economics and the economics of the mixed economy can be described as alternative 'paradigms': two different models by which we can order our thinking about economy and society. The emerging twenty-first-century problems of climate change and the increasing scarcity of natural resources force us to reconsider the adequacy of these two paradigms, and the relevance of a third which emphasises the future sustainability of New Zealand economy and society within a finite global ecological system.

It is hoped that this book will engage the interest of a wide spectrum of New Zealand citizens. The arguments to be presented are powerful ones and solidly based. It is not to be suggested that all readers will agree with everything that is said, but it is hoped that, at least, the arguments will be understood. The arguments demand a response from those who would deny them. If we value democracy as we should, it is important that we speak out and engage in discussion and debate in order to take wise decisions about New Zealand's future.

The book is divided into three parts: the first deals with the performance of the New Zealand economy in the pre- and post-reform eras and some of the economic and social consequences of those reforms; the second deals with overseas trade in general and the currently proposed Trans-Pacific Partnership in particular; and the third considers the major twenty-first-century problems of climate change and natural resource depletion. If in the future New Zealand is to be a sustainable and democratic society with a high level of well-being, substantial changes in policy will be required. The final chapter suggests directions in which some of these changes might lie. In each part of the book a discussion is provided of the main theoretical ideas that have been used to support and oppose neoliberal policies. Relevant economic concepts are explained as the story unfolds. A detailed bibliography and set of endnotes is included in order to validate the factual claims made, to give proper weight to the arguments presented, and to provide an opportunity for readers to follow matters elsewhere. Little is lost from the essential narrative if these are ignored on first reading.[1] Wikipedia provides a valuable source of information on events, definitions, and facts of all descriptions relevant to this book.

The neoliberal agenda – as it has been applied in New Zealand – has been described above as extremist. There are several arguments that might be presented to justify this characterisation, some of which will emerge as we proceed. Here is one. In classical Greece, the philosopher Plato recounts a dialogue that supposedly took place between the philosopher Socrates – in prison and recently condemned to death for corrupting the minds of the youth of Athens and for impiety towards the Gods – and his friend Crito. It is a deep conversation about justice and injustice, and the rights and duties of citizens in relation to the state. It is a dialogue that across the centuries has inspired philosophers, lawyers, and those interested in rhetoric, politics and civil society to debate these matters on the foundation of Plato's recorded dialogue. And so to 1987 when British Prime Minister Margaret Thatcher, doyenne of neoliberal visionaries, asks rhetorically: '... who is society?' and replies: '... There is no such thing!' This is an example of the extremism that we must now confront.

---

1 A more technical presentation of many of the ideas that underlie this book can be found in the author's *Economics, Sustainability and Democracy: Economics in the Era of Climate Change*, published by Routledge in 2013.

Acknowledgements

I wish to acknowledge the generosity of Gerda Leenards in allowing the use of her painting *Dusky Blue* for the cover of this book. I thank Dexter Fry of Book Design Ltd, Birkenhead, for his skills, Eva Chan who edited my manuscript, and Clive Hilliker who prepared the figures. I also wish to thank publishers Routledge (Taylor and Francis Group) for permission to reproduce Figure 2, and Professor Ronald Inglehart for permission to reproduce the charts in Figure 3. In the course of preparing this book I have enjoyed many stimulating discussions and received valuable advice – not all of which I have taken – from a wide range of people: friends, colleagues, and specialists in several fields. I thank them one and all.

Part I

NEW ZEALAND NOW

1

Free Market Economies

The Global Financial Crisis 2007–08

The global financial crisis (GFC) of 2007–08 was the world's most significant economic crisis since the Great Depression of the 1930s and a transformational event for economies around the world. Untold billions of dollars were wiped off the value of assets not only of banks and financial institutions, but also off the assets held by individuals and families in pension funds and investment accounts. In the year following the crisis industrial production slumped by over 10 per cent in major economies, and by over 20 per cent in some (including Korea, Japan). The Organisation for Economic Co-operation and Development (OECD) estimated that the crisis would increase unemployment in Member countries by over eight million. In the wake of the GFC the global economy has since remained sluggish, with low levels of investment and economic growth, unemployment at historical highs, and debt levels in some countries approaching the intolerable.

Although the immediate cause of the GFC was the financial failure associated with sub-prime housing loans in the US, the preconditions for the crisis had been building up over previous decades. The story has been told in many books and journals.[1] In its final report of 2011 the US Financial Crisis Inquiry Commission concluded that not only was the crisis avoidable, but that it was characterised by widespread failures in financial regulation and supervision, corporate governance and risk management, excessive borrowing, risky investments and lack of transparency, a government ill prepared for the crisis, and a systemic breakdown of accountability and ethics. As the Commission report noted: 'What else could one expect on a highway where there were neither speed limits nor neatly painted lines?'[2]

There are many threads of explanation of the causes of the GFC, but one unites them all. If the GFC demonstrates one thing it is the disastrous failure of the then-ascendant free market economic paradigm to adequately describe the global economy and promote policies to manage it. (Many would also argue that it demonstrates that economists do not learn the lessons of history.)

In the decades following World War II, the Western nations of Europe, North America and Australasia enjoyed a period of prolonged peace, stability and economic growth. This is commonly attributed to the application of principles of macroeconomic management set out by British economist John Maynard Keynes. These policies involved an active though still limited role for government in guiding the economy, particularly through government's use of taxing and spending powers, in order to maintain full employment. Linked to Keynes' ideas about managing the economy was the view, widely held at the time, that it was a proper role of government to ensure the basic well-being of citizens by providing adequate access to public goods such as education, health and social services. This approach to economics went by the name of the 'mixed economy' and its motivating philosophy 'new liberalism' or 'welfare liberalism'.

In the 1970s an alternative paradigm of political philosophy dubbed as 'neoliberal', and in its economic manifestations as 'free market' or 'laissez-faire' or 'libertarian', swept all before it. This approach, associated particularly with Chicago University economist Milton Friedman, advocated unfettered markets, free trade, the strict limitation of the role of government, the use of monetary policy as the means of economic regulation, low taxes, the curtailment of social provision, and the redefinition of 'full employment' away from the Keynesian idea that implied the active engagement of all the resources of the economy, to one which emphasised merely the number of people prepared to work at the going wage. The motivation behind these policy changes was the idea of that they would provide maximal freedom for individual economic activity. This emergent style of economic thought was seized upon in the US and the UK by President Ronald Reagan (1981–89) and Prime Minister Margaret Thatcher (1979–90) respectively, in Australia by Prime Minister John Howard (1996–2007), and in New Zealand by Finance Minister in the fourth Labour government (1984–90) Roger Douglas. However this transformation in policy thinking was not restricted to the relatively wealthy capitalist democracies, and countries such as South Africa, China, and those of Eastern Europe after the collapse of the Soviet Union, all embraced some form of libertarian economic theory and policy prescription. It is a style of economic theorising that continues to dominate policy thinking in many countries and in international economic organisations such as the International Monetary Fund (IMF) and the World Trade Organization (WTO).

It is therefore not surprising that following the GFC there has been a resurgence of interest in Keynesian policies of economic management, due to the continuing high levels of unemployment and low levels of interest rates, and the failure of monetary policy to restore health to many economies.[3]

Free Market Economies: Policies

The promise held out by the free market approach to economic policy was that freed from the restrictions of government, private enterprise and entrepreneurship would provide the engine to drive an increase in economic growth. This idea was based on the assumption that because government activities were not subject to the discipline of the market, they were *ipso facto* less efficient than the same activities carried out privately. It was further assumed that the benefits from this entrepreneur-led growth would trickle down through the economy to provide higher levels of employment, higher wages for workers, and lower prices for consumers. According to this approach, attempts by government to manage aggregate *demand* – particularly through the use of tax policy – in order to ensure full employment as Keynesian policies had done previously, was merely to cause inflation, without substantial effect on the level of employment. The key economic variable was now to be the money supply, the quantity of which would be adjusted in accordance with the scale of the economy, and through the use of monetary policy any inflationary tendencies would be inhibited and unemployment stabilised at its 'natural' level.

In this view of economic management, the only effective policies for moving the economy to levels of unemployment less that the 'natural' level – and to the higher levels of economic output that such a move implied – were policies that acted on the *supply* side of the economy, and in particular the supply of labour. Overall, policies would be launched to emphasise the privatisation of public assets, the deregulation of markets (and in particular the labour market), the reduction of taxes (particularly on the rich), and the scaling back of social entitlements. What was remarkable about this change of policy direction during the 1980s and 1990s – apart from its content – was the speed with which its prescriptions moved from academic debate to application in the real world: a speed described by one observer of the international scene as 'positively frenetic'.

The most prominent public assets slated for privatisation were banks and other financial services[4], energy provision (electricity, gas), telecommunications, transportation, and water and sewerage provision. Some privatisations were only partial, with assets either 'corporatised' in public-private partnerships and required to act as commercial ventures, or retained in public ownership but with private sub-contracting. Statistics reveal that the revenues raised by governments over 1977–99 from the privatisation of public assets were substantial, for example: Japan $198bn from 14 deals, UK $153bn from 169 deals, and Italy $106bn from 80 deals. In terms of total revenues raised from privatisations as a proportion of gross domestic product (GDP), it is the Anglo-Saxon countries that stand out, with New Zealand topping the global table.[5]

Deregulation was applied in transportation (air, rail, shipping), telecommunications and banking. This included the removal of restrictions on non-national flag carriers in airlines and shipping, the permitting of competitive bidding for government contracts, and the streamlining of private investment approvals through environmental assessment procedures. Two markets of central importance in deregulation were the labour market and financial markets. In the labour market, supply side policies involved increasing the flexibility of wages and working conditions, and encouraging labour mobility and retraining. These policies were typically implemented by reducing the tenure and security of employment, removing neutral umpire systems for setting wages and replacing them with enterprise-level bargaining and individual work contracts, and circumscribing the power of trade unions.

The second critical area of deregulation was that involving financial markets and financial intermediaries (typically banks, insurance companies, pension funds). In this the US led the way, under the guidance of Alan Greenspan, Chairman of the US Federal Reserve and staunch free market advocate. In 1982 legislation was passed to deregulate the savings and loan industry; in 1999 key sections of the Glass-Steagall Act of 1933 – passed in the wake of the Great Depression and designed to limit speculation – were repealed; and in 2004 debt limit controls on investment banks were relaxed. The steps taken to deregulate the financial markets caused surges of funds into the money markets which resulted in asset price bubbles as early as 1990, but it was not until 2007 that the apocalyptic consequences of these moves were made manifest in the global financial crisis of that year.

Of great significance have been the international economic aspects of deregulation. These included the abolition of exchange controls, the introduction of floating exchange rates, the reduction of tariff barriers and other national protective measures, the freeing up of international capital flows, as well as the opening up of financial intermediaries to international competition. These measures were at the heart of the process of globalisation of the world's economies that took place over these decades. And it is not fortuitous that the free-trade-oriented WTO was established in the high summer of these neoliberal policies.

The third prong of the neoliberal policy makeover was the reduction in taxation on companies and high income earners, together with reductions in social welfare provision which became less accessible and more conditional, and with greater penalties for non-compliance.[6]

Free Market Economies: Outcomes

Although these free market policies were applied in different OECD Member countries at different times and with different degrees of rigour, there are some generalisations as to their consequences that stand out. Here we abstract from the effects of the GFC by excluding data from 2007–08 and more recent years or by referring to them separately.

GDP growth. Between the decade of 1970–80 (typified by Keynesian policies) and 1990–98 (typified by free market policies), GDP growth per capita fell in 18 of the 24 OECD Member countries, including in all the largest economies.[7] It rose only in Australia, Denmark, Ireland, Luxembourg, Turkey and New Zealand (in this case from a very low base, from 0.5 to 0.7 per cent). From the decade

1980–90 to 1990–98 the weighted average trend rate of GDP per capita growth for the 24 OECD Member countries fell from 2.1 per cent to 1.8 per cent, and fell again slightly over the period 2000–07.[8]

Unemployment. A comparison of the average standardised unemployment rates in 21 OECD Member countries in the years 1980–89, 1990–99 and 2000–06 in comparison with a base period of 1973–79 shows that in only one, the US, did the average unemployment rate fall in each subsequent period. In the great majority of cases, in comparison to the base period, the decades of the 1980s and 1990s show a major upward surge in average unemployment, reaching maxima that were in some cases double the rates of 1973–79, and even three times the rate in Spain and Sweden. In the majority of these countries the average rate of unemployment declined in the period 2000–06, but not to the low levels recorded during 1973–79. Only in the cases of the Netherlands and Ireland was the average unemployment rate lower over 2000–06 than over 1973–79. For Austria, Germany, Japan, Luxembourg and Switzerland, the average unemployment rate continued to rise over all subsequent periods from 1973–79.[9]

Income inequality. In the two decades from the mid-1980s until the onset of the GFC of 2007–08, inequality of disposable income increased in 17 of the 22 OECD countries for which data is available. Across the OECD the standard measure of inequality – the Gini coefficient (0 = everyone has the same income; 1 = one person has all the income) – stood at an average of 0.29 in the mid-1980s, but by the late 2000s this had risen by almost 10 per cent to 0.32. Only Turkey, Greece, France, Hungary and Belgium recorded no increase or small declines in their Gini coefficients over this period.[10] In some countries with free market policies the share of gross income going to the top 1 per cent of earners over these years increased substantially: in the US from 8 to 17 per cent, and in Canada and UK from 8 to 13 per cent. No such rise is seen in the statistics from the social democracies of France and the Netherlands, which were not drawn so tightly in to the free market circle.[11]

Comparison of regimes. A comparison of the two policy regimes shows no evidence that mixed economies, with a more accommodating and inclusive attitude to the welfare of their citizens, have fared any the less well economically than free market regimes. An examination of the relationship of government spending to economic growth in 18 OECD Member countries across the period 1960–85 rejected the hypothesis that government expenditures reduced economic growth, and indicated areas of social expenditures which tended to increase it.[12] Peter Lindert in a sweeping study of individual OECD Member countries from the late eighteenth century to year 2000 concluded that 'contrary to the intuition of many economists and the ideologies of many politicians, social spending has contributed to, rather than inhibited, economic growth.'[13] Economic historian Robert Skidelsky carried out a comparison of the Keynesian and post-Keynesian eras and found superior economic performance in the former period on a range of variables with the exception of inflation where there was no significant difference.[14] Development economist Dani Rodrik studied economic growth spurts (which take place over several years) in a wide variety of countries between 1957 and 1992. While such spurts are not uncommon, in less than 15 per cent of cases was the spurt associated with economic liberalisation. As Rodrik concluded: 'the vast majority of growth accelerations *do not* take place in the context of standard economic liberalisation programmes' (author's italics).[15] Recent economic modelling studies have shown a significant and large negative relationship between inequality and economic growth, a relation that is present only in democracies.[16] A wide-ranging review of empirical literature from a sociological perspective concluded that 'there is very little evidence that welfare states produce inefficiencies on such a scale that the accumulation of wealth is jeopardized.'[17] An empirical study of 182 countries over 1950–2004 confirmed a positive relationship between government spending and economic growth, excepting for those countries of very low income.[18] Even the IMF –

traditionally a bastion of free market orthodoxy – recently published research showing that income inequality leads to slower economic growth.[19]

What this body of work demonstrates is that even in terms of economic output, a mixed economy approach to economic policy is not inferior to a free market approach, and to almost all evidence appears superior. It points too to the fact that free market economics has failed in its central claim of enhancing economic growth. No one believes in 'trickle down' economics any more.[20] Economist J K Galbraith described it as the horse-and-sparrow theory: 'If you feed the horse enough oats, some will pass through to the road for the sparrows'[21]. Given the increase in inequality and the resultant loss of personal power and freedoms that this implies, there seems no good reason to continue this baleful approach to economic policy. Furthermore, research has shown that the growth rate of GDP per capita has little relation to levels of personal happiness in the longer term, a subject to which we return in Chapter 9.

New Zealand as a Free Market Economy: Processes

Economist Geoff Bertram in his description of the evolution of the New Zealand economy over the twentieth century identifies three distinct eras.[22] The first, the era of 'grass monoculture' (extending from the 1880s to the 1930s), was characterised by the dominance of the 'backbone' industries of pastoral production and livestock-derived commodities. The second era of 'insulation and industrialisation' (from around 1935 to the 1970s) followed the Great Depression, and was characterised by a continuing reliance on export earnings from pastoral products, but also by state protection of and support for emergent manufacturing and construction sectors, and by income-redistribution mechanisms characteristic of a Keynesian and welfarist economy. Subsequent to World War II this was an era of full employment and increasing levels of wealth and income.

In 1967–69 New Zealand experienced a downturn in earnings

from wool. In 1973 the UK joined the European Economic Community (EEC) and New Zealand lost its privileged status as an exporter to the British market. And the New Zealand economy suffered further blows with the two oil price shocks in 1973 and 1979, which raised costs across the whole economy. These events provided strong incentives for the third National government under Prime Minister Muldoon (PM 1975–84) to pursue an economic strategy that was more self-reliant, particularly in relation to New Zealand's dependence on foreign energy. Thus was ushered in a 'think big' programme of government-initiated energy and industrial projects which were also associated with a wide range of economic controls, and through which the Muldoon government became increasingly unpopular. It was the election of David Lange's Labour government in 1984 that marked the introduction of the free market 'shock therapy' approach to economic reform under Ministers of Finance Roger Douglas (1984–88) and David Caygill (1988–90).[23] And this was a programme pursued unremittingly by the National Party government when it returned to power in 1990 and over the subsequent decade, under Finance Ministers Ruth Richardson (1990–93) and Bill Birch (1993–99).

Thus the third economic era in New Zealand's twentieth-century experience identified by Bertram involved a 'swing to services and the arrival of neoliberalism' (dating from the 1980s and through to 2000). This swing followed the surge of free market policies that emphasised the uncompromising exposure of all aspects of the economy to the workings of market forces, and the reduction in the role formerly played by government. Economically this led away from an emphasis on the traditional exports of tradable commodities, to the de-industrialisation of the New Zealand economy, to a new emphasis on the services sector including in particular tourism and education, and to the emergence of new elites associated with the new highpoints of the financial economy.

In describing the course of what we might call the 'neoliberal era' in New Zealand (1984 to the present), it too can be divided into three phases, of which that from 1984 to 1999 can be considered the first. The return of the Labour Party to government under Prime Minister Helen Clark in December 1999 inaugurated a second phase, which continued until Labour's defeat at the polls in November 2008. In that time and particularly in its earlier years, the Labour government acted to reverse some of the laissez-faire actions of its predecessors, including the repeal and replacement of National's unpopular Employment Contracts Act, the renationalisation of the struggling Air New Zealand following its privatisation in 1989, and the creation of the state-owned bank Kiwibank and the KiwiSaver retirement savings scheme. However, it is fair to say that the overall architecture of the free market programme remained in place.

The third phase commenced with the return of the National Party to power under Prime Minister John Key in the November 2008 election, and continues to the present time. Bill English became Deputy Prime Minister and Minister of Finance, and Tim Groser Minister of Trade and Minister for Conservation (until January 2010). This government has continued to pursue a neoliberal and business-favouring agenda, in reducing top personal income tax rates while increasing the level of the goods and services tax (GST), capping employer contributions to KiwiSaver, watering down the New Zealand Emissions Trading Scheme, continuing the privatisation of public resource companies under a 'mixed ownership model', and promoting the Trans-Pacific Partnership (TPP) free trade agreement. This has also been a period of substantial challenge for government in responding to the effects of the GFC and the Christchurch earthquakes of 2010 and 2011.

In reviewing the overall programme of reform dating from 1984, the 2010 *New Zealand Official Yearbook* described it as: 'floating the exchange rate, abolishing control on capital movements, ending industry assistance, removing price controls, deregulation across a number of sectors of the economy, corporatising and privatising state-owned assets, and labour market legislation aimed at facilitating more flexible patterns of wage bargaining. During the last decade there has been fine-tuning in policies, rather than major reform.'[24] From what has been described previously in relation to OECD Member countries, these policies have a familiar ring. The extra twist in New Zealand's case was that in the period 1984–99 the policies were carried out with such extreme vigour and comprehensiveness that the New Zealand reforms were hailed internationally as 'an extraordinary experiment', and as 'one of the most notable episodes of liberalisation that economic history has to offer'.[25,26]

Apart from being hailed as the darling of neoliberal theorists and politicians elsewhere, what has New Zealand actually gained from these reforms? There are some things that can be counted as gains over the reform period: a greater openness to the rest of the world, new attitudes to innovation, creativity, entrepreneurship, and more generally a move away from social conservatism. But such changes were open to New Zealand to gain without free market shock therapy. The argument of this book is that the extremist reform programme implemented in New Zealand has not only not produced what it promised, but has had damaging consequences for the nature of New Zealand society, and is irrelevant to the major problems of the twenty-first century now confronting New Zealand. In the remainder of this chapter we look at New Zealand's economic record against the background of that already described for OECD Member countries.

New Zealand as a Free Market Economy: Outcomes

GDP growth. In a 2013 paper on the subject of living standards in New Zealand, the Treasury noted that 'New Zealand's average GDP per capita growth for the last six decades has been poorer than all other OECD countries. New Zealand's GDP per capita ranked third among OECD countries in 1950 and 22nd in 2009 (of the 34 OECD Member countries currently).'[27] In 1999 Australian economist Bob Gregory compared the outcomes of the free market reform process in New Zealand with those of Australia, the UK under Margaret

Thatcher, and the US under Ronald Reagan. Whereas GDP per capita in the four countries was almost identical over the years 1960–65, and the upward trend continued for the three comparison countries over the surveyed period to 1997, the trend line for New Zealand has been flat from 1985 to 1997. As Gregory commented: 'New Zealand has been the worst performer by a very large margin ... thirteen years after the reform process began New Zealand has lost one and a quarter years of GDP per person relative to Australia (and the US) and the loss continues to grow.'[28]

Unemployment. Unemployment in New Zealand as a percentage of the working-age population was well below 2 per cent over the period 1945–80, then rose steeply to peak at 11 per cent in 1990 before declining to under 4 per cent (2004–07) and then climbing back to over 6 per cent in the wake of the GFC. The average unemployment rate over 1986–2005 was above 7 per cent.[29]

Income inequality. A study contracted by the Treasury to describe changes in income distribution during the period 1981–96 concluded: 'Income inequality rose in the 1980s and the 1990s regardless of how income is measured ... Income rose most substantially in the late 1980s, but continued to increase more slowly during the 1990s ... Income inequality did not fall during the economic expansion in the 1990s. This provides some evidence that it was driven by structural changes to the fabric of the economy or society'[30]. Over the period 1988-2007 income inequality as measured by the Gini coefficient increased substantially whether measured by market income, disposal income (market income plus government income support payments less direct tax payments), or final income (disposal income plus government health and educational expenditure less indirect tax payments). The coefficient for disposable income rose very substantially from 0.30 in 1988 to 0.38 in 2007, according to recent New Zealand calculations.[31] The income gap between the richest and poorest has been growing faster in New Zealand than in any other OECD country apart from Sweden since the 1980s, and currently the richest 10 per cent of citizens earn ten times more than the poorest 10 per cent.[32]

Poverty rates in New Zealand have increased for all age groups since the mid-1980s, and most substantially for children. The Children's Commissioner estimated that in 2006–07, 230,000 or 22 per cent of New Zealand children were living in poverty: that is, in households with incomes below the 60 per cent of median income poverty line after taking housing costs into consideration.[33] The Commissioner's Expert Advisory Group on Solutions to Child Poverty estimated the number of deprived children at 270,000 in 2012.[34] Deprivation rates in New Zealand are lower than the OECD average, higher than in most Western European countries, but lower than in the poorer countries of Eastern Europe.

Commentaries. What have economists and commentators had to say on the subject of the New Zealand free market reform programme? Evans and co-workers writing in 1996 asserted their satisfaction with the reforms, noting that 'After decades of policy errors and investment blunders, New Zealand appears to have finally diagnosed its predicament appropriately and is on a trajectory to maintain its economy as a consistent high performer among the OECD.'[35] Governor of the Reserve Bank Donald Brash in giving the Fifth Annual Hayek Memorial Lecture at the Institute of Economic Affairs in London in 1996 grandiloquently declared: 'The revival of New Zealand's economy in the last few years follows one of the most remarkable economic liberalisations of modern times.'[36] Other economists, not so close to those bearing responsibility for the programme, were less impressed: Keith Rankin doubted whether the New Zealand economy had achieved the miracles ascribed to it[37]; Tim Hazledine called the reform programme a failure[38], as did Paul Dalziel. Writing in 2002 Dalziel commented: 'the New Zealand experiment did not succeed, despite achieving greater microeconomic efficiency in some industries and obtaining its intermediate objectives of price stability and fiscal balance.'[39] Geographers Willie Smith and Hayden

Montgomery in 2004 contended that: 'the trends evident in New Zealand agriculture since 1984 pre-existed the reform period and that the apparent success of the reforms evident at a national scale have not addressed or removed the fundamental problems which face New Zealand agriculture, just as they do modern agricultural systems elsewhere.'[40] The reality that transpired was that the two years of sharp economic growth over 1993–94 that had so impressed Evans and Brash were followed by falling growth for the next four years: the two years of growth appearing to be no more than the normal cyclical economic expansion after earlier years of recession.[41] The Australian economist Bob Gregory in summarising his 1999 study of New Zealand (referred to above) concluded: 'Indeed it is perhaps difficult to believe that the outcomes could have been worse if there were no reforms at all.' He was surely on track when he pointed out that there was a fundamental need to understand what happened in New Zealand under the reform programme as: 'the country with the greatest rate of reform experienced the worst economic outcomes'.[42] Extremism, perhaps in all things, has its own inexorable costs.

The issue has been taken up more recently by Tim Hazledine and John Quiggin who explored the difference in experience between Australia and New Zealand in the two decades following the introduction of the free market reforms.[43] This is a particularly interesting study because both countries were subject to free market pressures, but their policy responses were different: in Australia policy makers took the path of 'gradualism and consensus' whereas in New Zealand the approach was 'crash or crash through'. With the perspective provided by the additional years that had passed since Gregory's study of the two economies, it was clear that there was to be no miracle transformation of New Zealand's economic performance just around the corner, and that although there were emerging signs of convergence in economic performance, Australia has opened up a 33 per cent gap in GDP per capita with New Zealand. Hazledine and Quiggin in exploring the reasons for the differing performances between Australia and New Zealand, found no evidence to substantiate the commonly quoted reason that New Zealand's poor performance was due to the chaos of the preceding Muldoon years. In that epoch both countries had similar policies, and if the New Zealand economy was indeed liberated from chaos by the coming of laissez-faire, then its performance should have outstripped that of Australia. These authors point rather to the fact that New Zealand politicians and Treasury, in introducing their reform programme, were not applying economic 'normal science' but an ideologically-based model of market merit and government failure for which there was only rudimentary evidence.

The damage done to the New Zealand economy and society by the decades of neoliberal reform policies was readily avoidable. It is true that in the years following World War II New Zealand's was a cosseted economy, finally exposed to the winds of self-reliance by the UK joining the EC and the collateral loss of trading privileges. It is also true that this was an era when 'globalisation' became a word in common currency, with expanding international trade spurred on by increasing prosperity and improvements in information and communications technology, and new market opportunities for New Zealand around the world. And it is also true that New Zealand could have reaped many of the benefits of this new open era without the costs heaped upon it by neoliberal extremism. This is shown by the relative success – described above – of those OECD economies that maintained more 'mixed' economic regimes. And it is reinforced by the possibilities of more pragmatic approaches to policy that might have been adopted by New Zealand, as outlined by economist Brian Easton, amongst others.[44]

Across the wide range of capitalist democracies, free market policies in place for more or less three decades have not delivered on their key promise of increasing economic growth. Trickle down has not occurred. Unemployment and economic inequality have increased.

Why then do the proponents of the free market persist in promoting policies with such failed outcomes? Chapter 2 will open a window on this question. Meanwhile we might reflect that it is not the first time in history that such folly has been manifest. It calls to mind the satirical tale of eighteenth-century French philosopher Voltaire who tells the story of the young Candide who, with his tutor Dr Pangloss, undertakes a series of adventures in the course of which the two are shipwrecked at sea in a violent storm, then reach the shores of Lisbon, which is immediately hit by a violent earthquake, tsunami and firestorm in which many thousands are killed. Arrested for heresy and set to be tortured and killed, the pair manage to escape when a further earthquake hits the city. Dr Pangloss is captured by pirates and enslaved as an oarsman in a galley, which is where Candide next encounters him. Despite Candide's concerns about the meanings of all that has befallen them, Dr Pangloss maintains his undeterred optimism that 'All is for the best in this the best of all possible worlds'. Dr Pangloss lives.

2

Liberalism, Economics, and Ethics

Classical Liberalism

English philosopher John Locke (1632–1704) is commonly considered the founder of liberalism as a political philosophy. In developing his political theory Locke envisaged an initial situation in which individuals lived in a state of nature governed by natural law that required, because all persons were equal and independent, that 'no one ought to harm another in his life, health, liberty or possessions'. To ensure adherence to this law it would be necessary for members of the community to come together and agree some means of arbitrating disputes, so that all could live in peace and security. Locke surmised that the community of individuals would need to elect some form of legislature, which would govern on behalf of all and with their consent. Any laws established would be on the basis of equality and for no other purpose than the good of the people. Because Locke stressed the idea of liberty of the individual, the scope of government would be strictly circumscribed. The ultimate restriction on the power of government would be that those elected were answerable to the will and determination of the majority. Locke also placed a considerable emphasis on the matter of private property, and spent much effort in justifying the private appropriation of common lands and their fruits – a debate that continues among philosophers to this day.

The idea of limited government was also emphasised by Adam Smith (1723–90), whose notion of the 'invisible hand' appeared to show that individuals acting in their own self-interest in unfettered market transactions provided the best guarantee for the welfare of society as a whole. And by the middle of the eighteenth century, merchant traders in England and on the Continent were agitating for the removal of government restrictions on overseas trade with the catch-cry of '*Laissez-faire!*' (French 'Let be!'). These three claims, for limited government, unfettered domestic markets and free international trade, provided the core economic motifs of classical liberalism.

The type of economic theory to which these claims gave rise was spelled out in the early nineteenth century by French economist Jean-Baptiste Say in his 'law of markets', which contended that the bringing to the market of one good provided the income for the purchase of other goods in other markets, or in other words, supply creates its own demand. Say's Law implies that although there could be temporary over- or under-supply in an individual market (say, in the market for bread), these would be rapidly eliminated, assuming that prices could respond flexibly to the level of supply. However taking markets across the economy as a whole, Say's Law implies that there will be no general glut of commodities and no lack of demand in aggregate for them. And consequently, in the important market for labour there would always be full employment, because – provided wages were flexible – everyone who wishes to be employed at the going wage, would be. In such an economy the role of government would be restricted to ensuring personal security, raising armies for national defence, and determining the rules under which the unfettered markets would operate.

New Liberalism (Welfare Liberalism)

Jeremy Bentham (1748–1832), lawyer, philosopher and social reformer, in his influential book *Introduction to the Principle of Morals and Legislation* promoted his 'principle of utility', or 'greatest happiness principle'. For Bentham, the actions of individuals were to be judged according to 'that principle which approves or disapproves of every action whatsoever, according to the tendency which it appears to have to augment or diminish the happiness of the party whose interest is in question …'. In this calculus, the interest of the community as a whole is 'the sum of the interests of the several members who compose it', and government actions conform to the principle of utility 'when in like manner the tendency which it has to augment the happiness of the community is greater than any which it has to diminish it.' Although Bentham was a great believer in individual freedom, he brought to it the idea of a positive role for government in achieving overall social well-being, to be measured in terms of 'utility'.[1] This approach to political philosophy, known as utilitarianism, is evidently distinct from the classical liberal view, even if both focused on achieving the goal of individual freedom. It can readily be seen too that it is the utilitarian view of economics, in which benefits (positive utility) are weighed against the costs (negative utility), that lies at the base of the technique of cost benefit analysis by which alternative actions open to government may be compared.

Philosopher and political economist John Stuart Mill (1806–73) was both a liberal and a utilitarian, although he extended the bounds of Bentham's utilitarianism in several directions. Personal freedom should be as unrestricted as possible, and in actions involving only the self 'the individual is sovereign'. Market exchange was, Mill believed, an other-regarding act, and government intervention was admissible for the prevention of fraud and the adulteration of food, and for the protection of workers. As for government, the first element of good government was, according to Mill, 'the virtue and intelligence of the human beings composing the community'. Education in its broadest sense was therefore key. Mill was convinced of the salutary and educative effect of the public participation of private citizens in political processes: 'He is called upon, while so engaged, to weigh interests not his own; to be guided, in case of conflicting claims, by another rule than his private partialities; to apply, at every turn, principles and maxims which have for their reason of existence the common good ...'[2].

By the early years of the twentieth century, this utilitarian perspective had become well established in economics and politics. Alfred Marshall (1842–1924), professor of economics at Cambridge University and elder statesman of economists across the English-speaking world, took the view that it was the task of economics to focus on the needs of ordinary people, as these were concerned with survival and health, and because 'all should start in the world with a fair chance of leading a cultured life.' Utilitarian (that is, 'new liberal') ideas such as those of Mill and Marshall were current in the Liberal governments of the UK prior to World War I, and reached their high point after World War II in the legislation that established the UK National Health Service and the Universal Child Benefit in 1948.

Earlier, the stock market crash of October 1929 had heralded the economic slide into what became known as the Great Depression: to that time the deepest economic slump in the history of the Western industrialised nations. Its most severe effects lasted from 1929 until 1932, although these were not fully dissipated until the coming of World War II. The Depression severely affected many countries, most particularly the US, the countries of Western Europe, Canada, Australia and New Zealand, although few if any escaped its influence entirely. Between 1929 and 1932, industrial production in the US fell by 45 per cent, GDP contracted by 28 per cent, unemployment rose from 3 to 22 per cent of the workforce, and more than 5,000 local and regional banks closed their doors. With this huge contraction in economic activity imports to the US shrank significantly, and as the flow of credit to debtor countries dried up, the effects of the downturn were transmitted around the world. Whatever the causes of this painful global downturn, most contemporary economists' policy prescriptions were based on Say's Law: namely that given time, the self-adjusting powers of the market would work themselves through the system, and wages and prices would adjust downwards to establish a full-employment equilibrium. The longer the Depression continued, the less convincing this explanation became. In retrospect it was clear that neither the economists nor the soothsayers of the time fully understood the phenomenon they were witnessing, and many economic policies were ineffective in responding to it.

It was the central insight of British economist John Maynard Keynes (1883–1946) to propose that in such depressed conditions the price mechanism was unlikely to function smoothly, and therefore supply would not be brought into equality with demand as Say's Law had proposed. In the important labour market, wages would be hard to adjust downwards and the supply of labour would not necessarily equate to the demand, and full employment would not be achieved. And in the financial markets, because people would hoard money for precautionary and speculative motives, interest rates would remain high and investment curtailed. In such circumstances, Keynes argued, government intervention would be required to stimulate spending and increase aggregate demand for goods and services in the economy and thus lead back to full employment.

At this point it is worth noting that, generally speaking, the major goals of macroeconomic policy are held to be ensuring full (or near to full) employment, price stability, and the avoidance of fluctuations in these quantities. The two main policy levers available to government to achieve these goals are fiscal (tax) policy – relating to government revenues and expenditures – and monetary policy – involving the money supply and the interest rate. (As far as the international economy is concerned, trade policy might be considered as a third lever.) The 'business cycle' is the phrase used to refer to the observed phenomenon that over time economic activity (measured by, say, GDP) appears to fluctuate up and down around a trend line. These sequential periods of expansion and contraction, described as 'cycles', can give rise to significant changes in the level of output and employment and the need for government to respond appropriately: hence the reference to 'countercyclical' government policy. Keynes' emphasis was on the use of fiscal rather than monetary policy, in a countercyclical manner.

Keynesian policies gradually became adopted in Britain as the 1930s progressed, but the effects of the Great Depression were not fully alleviated before the onset of World War II. Keynes' policy of putting people to work by spending government money was enthusiastically endorsed in the US by President Roosevelt, against the widespread opposition there of libertarian economists and other conservative interests. Roosevelt's 'New Deal' policy was epitomised by the creation of the large-scale Tennessee Valley Authority, which undertook the construction of hydroelectricity dams, fertiliser plants and flood control works in order to provide employment and economic development in an area particularly hard hit by the Depression.

In the decades following World War II the nations of Europe, North America and Australasia experienced a prolonged period of prosperity with low and steady rates of unemployment and inflation, and long-run growth in real GDP, commonly attributed to the success of Keynesian policies. However by 1970 the so-called Keynesian 'Golden Age' was drawing to a close. There were two major reasons for this: on the one hand the large budget deficits built up by the US government in paying for the war in Vietnam were contributing to inflation, and on the other the oil price shocks of 1973 and 1979 – due to the OPEC oil export embargo and the Iranian revolution respectively – had caused a downturn in employment and economic activity. This combination of inflation and recession (dubbed 'stagflation') was one unfamiliar to the Keynesian analysis, and one with which economists in general were not well prepared to deal. The diagnosis of stagflation called forth a new treatment for a new malaise. Although latter-day Keynesian economists had some proposals to make, an alternative analysis of the economy that had been emerging over preceding decades at the University of Chicago, particularly from the work of economist Milton Friedman, captured professional and public opinion.

Neoliberalism (Libertarianism)

Friedman worked from a classical economic perspective. He was sceptical of the Keynesian claims that disturbances in the economic system were primarily caused by disturbances in the real economy of goods and services, and that government should respond to these primarily through the use of fiscal policy. Friedman wished to re-emphasise the important role of money in the economy, and his approach became known as 'monetarism'. He took the view that the economy had a natural rate of unemployment (estimated to be around 6 per cent in the US), to which the economy fundamentally inclined. His analysis suggested that whereas in the short run increases in the money supply to the public can have significant effects in increasing employment and aggregate demand (by causing people to spend more), in the longer run such increases would not affect the real economy of goods and services at all, but lead only to higher inflation of wages and prices at the natural rate of unemployment. Thus the stagflation of the 1970s was seen from this perspective as having two causes: the shock administered to the economy by the rise in oil prices which restrained output growth, and excessive growth in the money supply which caused inflation. This led Friedman to propose that the monetary authorities should adopt a rule whereby money supply growth would be systematically expanded (or contracted) in line with the trend rate of growth (positive or negative) in the economy. In this case economic equilibrium would be maintained automatically at the natural rate of unemployment and a specific level of inflation.

Some other classically-inspired economists, chief among whom Robert Lucas (also at the University of Chicago), pointed to inconsistencies in Friedman's analysis, and commenced to develop alternative ideas which would express the theory with greater rigour than Friedman had achieved. What emerged was a radical form of monetarism (dubbed 'new classical macroeconomics') which took monetary policy well beyond the bounds envisaged by Friedman, and which dominated academic debates in macroeconomics in the 1970s and 1980s. Although these ideas were high fashion in some academic economic circles in this era, they were the result of advanced mathematical calculation and only loosely connected to observed behaviour and empirical research. In focusing on market behaviour, Lucas proposed that all individuals act with great rationality, so that they do not make systematic errors in their market forecasts.

This approach yielded surprising results. One was that not only was fiscal policy ineffective (as Friedman believed), but that monetary policy was also. Another result was that financial markets in particular – the markets for bonds, shares, currencies and the like, in which a great deal of information is available to participants – are super-efficient in their use of information. No one can outperform the market. Ergo, stock market bubbles cannot exist. The activity that Keynes had compared to that of a 'casino' had been transformed theoretically by this new breed of economists into one of mankind's most rational activities. (Here clearly we have another of the sources of the stream that led to the global financial crisis of 2007–08.)

If as proposed by the new classical economists, Keynesian demand management policies cannot permanently increase the level of output beyond that implied by the natural rate of unemployment, and monetary policy is equally ineffective, then in order to move the natural rate of unemployment to lower values and increase economic output, government policies would need to concentrate exclusively on 'supply-side' (rather than 'demand-side') policies that would shift the economy's aggregate supply function outwards. Thus what started out as a modest attempt to provide a more adequate theoretical foundation for Friedman's monetarism became a self-consistent theory in its own right, monetarist in impulse, but representative of an extreme re-interpretation of classical economics in which the economy is permanently in equilibrium, unemployment is fixed at the natural rate, money is neutral, and because fiscal and monetary policies do not work the role of government in the economy is limited to increasing output and decreasing the natural rate of unemployment through the workings of Say's Law: that is, through supply-side policies. The child had devoured its parent. Such was the confidence and optimism – even hubris – among economists of the time that Lucas was awarded the Noble Prize in economics in 1995 for his work. Friedman had already received the Nobel Prize in 1976 for his much more substantial contributions.

How Did Neoliberalism Gain Its Political Ascendancy?

The rapid ascendancy of neoliberal economic ideas to the status of orthodoxy, not to say dogma, among Western governments and international organisations in the later decades of the twentieth century was remarkable: commonly economic change is rather slow to emerge as argument and counter-argument contend in what is a difficult area of research and measurement. Several influences can be perceived as contributing to this rush. The first, as we have seen, involved the need to find appropriate economic policies to respond to the phenomenon of stagflation. Another was undoubtedly the post-war reaction in the Allied democracies to the emergence of totalitarian states on both the political left and political right – communism in the USSR and Nazism in Germany – and concerns for the robustness of the liberal democracies in confronting them.

This concern was expressed particularly by the Austrian economist and political philosopher Friedrich von Hayek. In 1944 he published a short tract, *The Road to Serfdom*, in which he criticised the 'welfarist' tendencies that had emerged in British liberalism, and argued for a return to a more 'classical' view of individual freedom. Hayek considered that all societies employing central planning by government would inevitably end in tyranny. (He thought that Sweden, a social democratic state at the time, would inevitably become communist.) His book made little impression in England, but enjoyed great success in the US, and went on to sell over a quarter of a million copies and was translated into many languages.[3] In 1962, Friedman published his own political tract, *Capitalism and Freedom*, which attacked the Keynesian policies of the US government of the day led by President John F. Kennedy. Friedman's book was even more successful than Hayek's, and was later included in the *Times Literary Supplement* list of the hundred most influential books since World War II. Both books became canonical texts for the emergent political movement of neoliberalism or, as is said in referring to its economic manifestations, 'market fundamentalism'.

On the theoretical front, the nascent neoliberal ideology found substantial support in the philosophical ideas of Harvard University philosopher Robert Nozick, whose 1974 book *Anarchy, State and Utopia* promoted a political philosophy of extreme individualism based on a comprehensive view of individual rights. These rights were so comprehensive, Nozick believed, that the individual had no responsibility for others in society apart from voluntary acts, and only unfettered market transactions voluntarily entered into were permissible means of exchange. Only states with the most minimal of powers could be justified. Taxation of earnings was on a par with forced labour. Judged as a political tract, the book enjoyed remarkable success at the time. Among philosophers on the other hand, his ideas have received little support.[4]

Another major influence was the process of globalisation. In the large, this process can be seen as the intensification of worldwide economic and social relationships: a process that gathered pace in the latter decades of the twentieth century spurred on by advances in transport, telecommunications and the internet. It is a process with many facets: economic, in terms of the rise of multinational companies and the expansion of international trade; political, in terms of increased integration, as in the EU, and in the power of international organisations; ecological, in relation to the global nature of environmental problems such as climate change and loss of biodiversity; and cultural, in terms of increased tourism, migration, and the dissemination of languages, TV sports programmes and soap operas. From a neoliberal perspective, economic globalisation is seen as an unfolding process of freer and freer worldwide exchange untrammelled by government. Economic globalisation envisaged thus, as a natural and inevitable process, provided neoliberals with an opportunity to advance their political philosophy that was not left wanting.

The rise and proliferation of neoliberal-inspired 'think tanks' provided perhaps the greatest impulse in favour of free market economics in the later years of the century. Hayek, even as a young man, had envisaged the creation of a society of liberal scholars that would meet regularly and publish materials designed to promote the restatement of liberal principles along classical (Lockean) lines. In 1945 he had his opportunity when, after delivering an address at Zurich University, a group of Swiss bankers and industrialists agreed to provide support for such a society. The first meeting was held in the village of Mont Pèlerin above Geneva, and was attended by a number of libertarian economists (including Friedman and others from Chicago), together with philosophers and journalists. And so the Mont Pelerin Society was formally inaugurated. Membership of the Society has risen over the years to some hundreds including, according to its website, 'high government officials, Nobel prize recipients, journalists, economic and financial experts, and legal scholars from all over the world'.

Hayek was also instrumental in encouraging Englishman Antony

Fisher to found the Institute of Economic Affairs (IEA) in London, the goal of which would be to disseminate an understanding of classical liberalism and free market economics. This it did through meetings and conference, and more particularly by inviting libertarian thinkers and practitioners to write monographs and reports in advocacy of a wide range of policy issues. Hayek and Friedman were both contributors to this stream. The success of the IEA in capturing the broad political agenda of the British Conservative Party during these years was remarkable, and is graphically recounted by Richard Cockett in his book *Thinking the Unthinkable*.[5] Sir Keith Joseph, former UK Minister of Housing, became a regular visitor during the 1960s, as did Margaret Thatcher in the 1970s. (A British MP from 1959, Thatcher became leader of the Opposition Conservative Party in 1975 and Prime Minister in 1979, a position she held uninterrupted until 1990.) Reflecting on this circumstance, Friedman was later to comment: 'Without the IEA, I doubt very much whether there would have been a Thatcherite revolution.'[6]

Buoyed by the success of the IEA, Fisher extended his vision to that of creating a worldwide network of libertarian think tanks. He was instrumental in setting up the Fraser Institute in Vancouver in 1977, the International Center for Economic Policy Studies in New York in 1977 (now the Manhattan Institute for Policy Research), and the Pacific Research Institute in San Francisco in 1979.[7] In Australasia the Centre for Independent Studies was inaugurated in Sydney in 1976. In 1981 Fisher created the Atlas Economic Research Foundation as a non-profit organisation to assist and promote the establishment of a network of libertarian think tanks around the world. As its website proclaims: 'The Atlas Economic Research Foundation is a nonprofit organization connecting a global network of more than 400 free market organizations in over 80 countries to the ideas and resources needed to advance the cause of liberty.'[8] Friedman himself maintained a long-term interest in the success of the Atlas project.

We may well speculate on the reasons for the success of this self-assertive movement. For those involved it may have included elements of moral or political conviction, fashion, and/or opportunism. One important opportunity would undeniably have been for those with money and wealth to capture the political agenda to their own advantage.[9]

New Liberalism Now

In 1972 Harvard philosopher John Rawls published *A Theory of Justice*, which it is probably fair to say has become the yardstick against which other ethical positions are measured in economic-political discourse in democratic countries. In his book Rawls explores the principles of justice that ought underpin the basic structure of a liberal society. Like Locke he appeals to a hypothetical argument about what members of a community would be prepared to agree to under certain circumstances. But unlike Locke, who argued directly to the set of rules or form of government that individuals would be prepared to contract to, Rawls sets up a thought experiment in which parties as 'free and rational persons concerned to further their own interests' must agree the terms of their association from an 'original position of equality'. The key element in this process is that the individuals are required to agree terms from behind a 'veil of ignorance': they understand political affairs and the principles of economic theory, and they know the basis of social organisation and the laws of human psychology; but they do not know their own place in society, their personal assets, abilities or intelligence, nor do they know the particular circumstances of their own society.

Rawls argues that the outcome of such a deliberative process would be expressible in terms of two principles of justice. These he formulated as: '(1) Each person to have an equal right to the most extensive total system of basic liberties compatible with a similar system of liberty for all (equality of basic liberties principle); and (2) Social and economic inequalities are to be arranged so that they are both (a) to the greatest benefit of the least advantaged, consistent with the just savings principle (the difference principle), and (b) attached to offices and positions open to all under conditions of fair equality of opportunity (equality of opportunity principle)' (bracketed text added) [10] Priority is to be accorded to the first principle over the second, so that all citizens are assured of equal basic liberties, including civil and political rights. Within the second principle, priority is given to (b) over (a) so that conditions of fair and equal opportunity are guaranteed to all. Rawls' difference principle, we observe, does not require that the distribution of income and wealth be equal, but that it should be to everyone's advantage: differences in income and wealth are acceptable provided the superior prospects of those with more are to the advantage of those with less. It is evidently a strongly egalitarian principle. (Rawls' 'just savings principle' referred to in (2) (a) expresses how much each generation would be prepared to save for the next generation in relation to what they would feel entitled to claim from the previous one.)

Rawls claims that his principles are equivalent to the 'maximin decision rule' of choice in conditions of uncertainty. This is a rule which specifies that a decision should be taken in the light of the worst that could happen: one should attempt to maximise the minimum payoff. The equivalence between the two principles arises, Rawls contends, because they are the same as those 'a person would choose for the design of a society in which his enemy is to assign him his place'. Importantly, what is being chosen in Rawls' thought experiment is in essence a one-off choice about how society is to be organised and operate, not choices relating to personal day-to-day decisions. In this regard, the maximin rule has considerable appeal in relation to the major twenty-first-century decisions that will be required of states in their responses to climate change and natural resource scarcity. Rawls advances three arguments in favour of why such a maximin rule would be chosen under the veil of ignorance. First, as the participants have no knowledge of their own circumstances and social position, future outcomes for them are highly uncertain, and it would not be possible to make the calculations of costs and benefits that a utilitarian approach would require. Second, under the maximin rule 'the rejected alternatives have outcomes that one can hardly accept': that is to say that under the difference principle everyone gets an acceptable supply of primary goods, whereas under a utilitarian principle that maximises expected utility across society as a whole, this is not guaranteed. Third, the participant 'cares very little, if anything, for what he might gain above the minimum stipend': that is to say that the additional possible gain from choosing an alternative rule is not balanced by the increase in downside risk.

Rawls' primary concern is with the determination of the rules of justice to which participants in the original position are prepared to contract. Justice as he sees it emerges from fair process. He envisages a just constitution as securing the liberties of equal citizenship, and a political process conducted as far as possible in terms of just procedures for choosing governments and enacting legislation. He sees the functions of government as including not only the maintenance of the basic kinds of 'social capital', but also functions which try to ensure 'equal chances of education and culture for persons similarly endowed' and which provide a social minimum to families which 'guarantees a certain level of well-being and honours the claims of need'. Once a suitable minimum is provided, Rawls suggests that 'it may be perfectly fair that the rest of total income be settled by markets and the price system, assuming that it is moderately efficient and free from monopolistic restrictions, and unreasonable externalities have been eliminated.'[11]

Philosopher and economist Amartya Sen developed an approach to economic development with similarities to that of Rawls. However Sen rejects Rawls' difference principle as inadequate because it gives insufficient concern for the ability of individuals to convert resources available to them into personal well-being. (A disabled person may not be able to do many things that an able-bodied person can with the same bundle of goods, for example.) If a theory of justice has a genuine concern for freedom, then the ability of individuals to convert goods into well-being must take centre stage. Whereas Rawls' theory focuses attention on the characteristics of the good provided, for Sen this is less important than the *capabilities* it gives rise to for the individual, and which allow the person to function in various fruitful ways. As individual freedom is important, the idea of capability comes closer to expressing value in terms of individual well-being than do descriptions of goods' characteristics. Thus for Sen it is the individual's set of capabilities which provides the measure of freedom to choose different types of life (to do and to be) and which contributes most directly to well-being.[12] Another distinction is that whereas Rawls proposes a very egalitarian view of what is just, Sen's focus is on providing for each individual a minimum threshold of capabilities – an approach referred to as 'sufficientarian' rather than egalitarian. Sen's approach has proved of considerable practical importance in providing the grounding for human development indices used by the United Nations Development Programme (UNDP), and in recent years a series of conferences and publications have been devoted to developing his theory and its practical applications. Martha Nussbaum is another philosopher who has given an account of human capabilities that parallels, and which to a large degree converges with, Sen's account. Her approach finds its source in Aristotle's notion of *eudaimonia* (well-being, flourishing) and the qualities required as a basis for achieving a flourishing life.[13]

Two Concepts of Justice[14]

The foregoing has surveyed the two main strands in the development of current liberal philosophy: the neoliberal strand running from Locke to Hayek, Friedman and Nozick, and the new liberal strand running from Bentham and Mill to Rawls, Sen and Nussbaum.[15] These strands provide two very different approaches to management of the macroeconomy, particularly with regard to the acceptable role of government.

Whereas *macroeconomics* is concerned with economy-wide aggregates such as national income, economic growth, unemployment, the price level, and inflation, *microeconomics* is concerned with such issues as individual markets, firms, the organisation of production, resources and technology, as well as consumer behaviour and welfare: matters which directly impinge on issues of justice. Here too the two strands of liberal philosophy provide very different understandings of how economic life should be organised, and of what should be considered as fair or just. Let us examine the matter in a little more detail.

The market is the centrepiece of the liberal economic system. In a market the forces of demand and supply generated by competing buyers and sellers determine the price and quantity of the good exchanged. In the ideal market of orthodox economic theory, buyers and sellers are considered to have perfect knowledge of their opportunities (so that a single equilibrium price can be identified), no single buyer or seller can influence the market price (so that there are no monopoly or monopsony influences), and buyers and sellers are free to enter or leave the market as they desire (so that there is no coercion). In these circumstances 'perfect competition' is declared to exist in the market, and as the good exchanged will go to those buyers to whom its value is highest, the market is declared 'efficient' (or 'Pareto efficient'). The goal of orthodox economic theory is that all markets in the economy be perfect and therefore efficient. But matters do not stop there. The important thing to note is that this understanding involves not just matters of fact, but also matters of ethics: it involves judgements about what is right or wrong, good or bad.

First, we can see immediately that the theory says that monopoly and coercion are bad. Second, it says that efficiency is good. Furthermore we need to recognise that the market actually performs two functions, namely: to *allocate* resources among competing uses –

that is, to say how much resources goes into the production of bread, houses, automobiles and so on; and to *distribute* the final products of economic activity among individuals in society – that is, to say who gets what. So that in this respect too the market inescapably involves matters of ethics in relation to what is considered just or fair. And finally, if we were to dig a little deeper into how orthodox economic theory assumes that individuals behave in market transactions, we would see that they are assumed to act from purely selfish motives. Economic rationality as selfishness. This too raises ethical issues but of a somewhat different sort. It is imperative to ask therefore how the differing views of liberalism deal with matters of justice and fairness arising from market transactions.

Most people would agree that to allocate resources efficiently is a good idea. What distinguishes the neoliberal approach to economics is that this idea is elevated to the status of central dogma: efficiency is all, 'fairness' is what the market provides. Justice is having what I am entitled to. 'Distributive (or social) justice' has no meaning. This is the major thrust of Robet Nozick's book, as we have seen[16]; it is the claim of Margaret Thatcher which we recorded in the Preface. Hayek expressed it this way: 'the term is intellectually disreputable, the mark of demagogy or cheap journalism which responsible thinkers ought to be ashamed to use because, once its vacuity is recognised, its use is dishonest'.[17] The new liberal view, on the contrary, while recognising the importance of efficiency in markets, recognises in addition that the pure market outcome may not in fact be the best one for society, and that the 'social optimum' also depends on the distribution of the economic product. As a consequence, government will have a role in ensuring that each person has a 'fair' chance in such things as self-improvement and personal health and well-being (with 'fairness' possibly being determined in a manner which Sen and Nussbaum might approve, for example).

There is a further moral strand exposed by neoliberalism's focus on market mechanisms. In recent years there has been a remarkable increase in the range of social transactions which have fallen under the thrall of market allocation. Political philosopher Michael Sandel in a recent book gives many examples of the phenomenon.[18] In the US, places previously allocated in accordance with the ethic of queuing are increasingly being replaced by allocation on the basis of the market ethic of willingness to pay (assuming individuals can pay) – in airport security, doctors' appointments scheduling, and the use of freeway express lanes, for example. The economic justification offered for such changes is that they increase individual freedom, and that access to the service goes to those who value it most highly. But when a group of child-care centres in Israel was experiencing difficulties with parents coming late to pick up their children and imposed a fine on late pick-ups, late pick-ups increased. The moral norm of obligation (and the justification for the fine) had been transmuted into the payment of a fee for service. In Switzerland, a small mountain village was chosen as a possible site for the storage of the country's radioactive waste. Economists who conducted a survey of the village prior to the decision being taken found that a slight majority said that they would accept the facility. When the economists proposed that the villagers receive an annual compensatory payment, support for the facility halved. Pride in civic commitment on behalf of the country had been reduced in the citizens' eyes to a bribe. In such day-by-day ways does the ideology of the market undermine the existing web of social norms that make up the fabric of society. This is not to say that all change is bad, but that there are imminent dangers in the thoughtless replacement of existing social mechanisms by others based purely on market principles. The nature of the danger was well recognised in the nineteenth century by John Stuart Mill, who of his own time warned: 'A neighbour, not being an ally or an associate, since he is never engaged in any common undertaking for joint benefit, is therefore only a rival. Thus even private morality suffers, while public is actually extinct.'[19] We will come across other examples of this phenomenon as we proceed.

It is a central claim of the present book that the neoliberal approach to economics is too narrow and too demeaning ethically to provide an adequate foundation for civilised democratic life in the twenty-first century. By focusing on the technical criterion of market efficiency, the libertarian view of economics conceals important ethical issues. This has the effect of placing economics (and thus the way we think about the economy) in a social vacuum. Such an approach is both intellectually inadequate and practically dangerous. The approach is intellectually inadequate because it is not possible to disassociate economic decision-taking from ethical issues: to avoid moral commitment is itself a moral commitment; to distinguish between Friedman as economic analyst and Friedman as political advocate is not possible. Furthermore the libertarian view ignores the fact that the market is a socially constructed institution and that the idea of 'efficiency' only has meaning within the institutional context that society has chosen to give it. The approach is a dangerous oversimplification practically because by attempting to remove ethical considerations from economics it blindsides public debate about the role of the economy in relation to social purposes, and renders economics the fiefdom of technicians and specialists rather than citizens; it reduces the concept of civilised life to the mechanics of production and consumption; it implies that ethics beyond personal selfishness are unnecessary – if so in economy, why not elsewhere in life? – and it ignores the reality of the power that money gives. The following chapter will give examples of how these issues have emerged in New Zealand life in the wake of the neoliberal policy reform programme.

British Prime Minister Margaret Thatcher in advocating her neoliberal economic policies often used the phrase 'There is no alternative' (abbreviated to the slogan 'TINA'): it being supposed that the embracing of free markets, free trade and economic globalisation was the best and only way for economies to develop. The proposition was, and remains, false. As we have seen by examining the historical evolution of liberalism, laissez-faire economics is not the product of some inevitable evolutionary process akin to a law of nature, but the construct of the minds and motives of individuals, promoted through political processes. There were always alternative economic voices to be heard by those willing to listen. In his 1987 film *Wall Street*, Oliver Stone has the main protagonist, stockbroker Gordon Gekko, extol the virtues of the free market: 'Greed, for lack of a better word, is good. Greed is right. Greed works. Greed clarifies, cuts through, and captures, the essence of the evolutionary spirit.' We deny that such should express the limit of our economic, political and social aspirations.

3

Consequences of Neoliberalism in New Zealand

Privatisation, Privilege, and the New Elite

Neoliberal policies employed by successive governments in New Zealand have led to the substantial privileging of business interests at the cost of other sections of society. Here are some of the means by which this has been achieved and what this implies for New Zealand society.

Privatise public assets on favourable terms. Following the introduction of the economic reform programme in 1984 the New Zealand government undertook a wave of privatisations of state enterprises over the years 1985–99. This was the most sweeping de-governmentalisation programme imposed on any liberal democratic economy in the world, and one in which the total of revenues received as a proportion of GDP was the highest of any country in the world.[1] The headlong rate at which state assets were set on the course to privatisation, described at the time as a blitzkrieg, the all-embracing nature of the changes, and the diversity of outcomes in individual cases, suggest that an overriding reason for the programme was the pursuit of a free market ideology unrelated to economic good sense. Many public enterprises became 'state-owned enterprises' (SOEs) which, under the requirements of the State-Owned Enterprises Act 1986, were required 'to operate successfully as a business, as profitable as those not owned by the Crown': that is, they were to be subject to the 'efficiency only' criterion. This step was usually, but not always, a prelude to privatisation.

The era of the 1980s and 1990s was a heady period in New Zealand, reminiscent of the American Wild West in which opportunism was rife, big deals were done, and claims and counterclaims proliferated.[2] Entrepreneurs became heads of SOEs and bought companies when they were privatised.[3] Fortunes were made, and some lost.[4] In the roll-out of the programme, most of New Zealand's largest state enterprises came under the hammer, including Telecom, the Forestry Corporation of New Zealand, Contact Energy, Bank of New Zealand, Petrocorp, the State Insurance Office, Air New Zealand, the Post Office Bank, Auckland International Airport and New Zealand Rail.[5] The overall privatisation programme has been described elsewhere, from a number of points of view.[6]

We would be remiss, however, if we did not give something of the flavour of those times. In 1993 New Zealand Rail was sold as Tranz Rail for NZ$328.1m to a group of investors the main members of which were: Fay Richwhite, a New Zealand-listed company (31.8 per cent); Wisconsin Central, an American rail company (27.3 per cent); Berkshire Fund, a US investment group (27.3 per cent); and Alex van Heeren, the owner of Huka Lodge (9.1 per cent). Tranz Rail listed on the stock market in June 1996. Critical reports were made of the privatised company's lax safety standards, inadequate maintenance, asset stripping and insider trading. When these investors sold their Tranz Rail shares they were able to reap NZ$370m, mainly tax free. In 2003 a bid by Toll Holdings to take over the company valued it at NZ$231m. In May 2008 the government agreed to buy back Toll's rail and seas transport assets for NZ$665m.[7] Such a chaotic sequence of events was not unique in those years. As for those responsible for implementing the privatisation programme, they appear either to have displayed incompetence on their own account, or to have responded to a lack of concern on the part of their political masters, or both.

Just how cynical this lack of concern for the economic well-being of citizens could be was revealed by the 1994 decision by the Privy Council in the case of Telecom vs Clear Communications Ltd. This dispute arose over the interpretation of a section of New Zealand's Commerce Act 1986. The Privy Council concluded on the basis of the New Zealand legislation before it that the recently privatised telecommunications monopoly 'had the legal right to extract monopoly profits from its customers unless the Minister of Commerce chose to exercise his or her executive discretion to intervene and regulate prices': what this meant in the case of the electricity distribution networks can be seen by the 29 per cent disclosed accounting rate of profit for Vector Ltd in 1997, and United Networks' disclosed return on equity of 235.3 per cent for 2000 and 346.8 per cent for 2001.[8] As for the provision of electricity itself, the 2009 report of the New Zealand Commerce Commission determined, on the basis of the same Act, that the largest four suppliers into the wholesale market – Contact, Genesis, Meridian and Mighty River Power – had a substantial degree of market power, and 'have used that power to increase prices considerably above the competitive level for substantial periods during 2001, 2003 and 2005/6'. The report continues with breathtaking aplomb: 'It appears that the periods of high prices simply reflect generators lawfully using substantial market power to maximise profit, rather than being the result of anti-competitive behaviour'. The effects on consumers of this retail market power were not investigated by the Commission.[9] These are examples of what is euphemistically called 'light-handed regulation' (see further below).

As the above makes clear, the government provided direct opportunities for businesses to profit. Within a lax regulative environment, businesses too can be proactive in increasing their own advantage. It was evident in retrospect that commercial interests and their advisors were adept at finding and exploiting legal loopholes in shoddy regulatory provisions, at creative accounting in the valuation of privatised assets, and at granting themselves substantial salary increases based on international comparisons – while at the same time holding employee wages down.

The privatisation programme was brought to a temporary halt with the election of the Labour Government under Helen Clark in 1999, and this stay remained in place until the return of the National Government under John Key in 2008. Key gave an undertaking that there would be no further privatisations until his second term, if re-elected. With a second term in place from 2011, privatisations of state assets recommenced, albeit under a different model of 'mixed ownership' in which companies are partly owned by the Crown (the current proposal being not less than 51 per cent) and partly owned by private investors. This is the model under which the four energy companies Mighty River Power, Meridian Energy, Genesis Power and Solid Energy New Zealand are being privatised, and the government reducing its majority stake in Air New Zealand. As for the notion of mixed ownership, it does raise some problematic issues of its own which will need wise management.[10] However, the fundamental question is the extent to which citizens can put trust in the government's statement of 'greater than 50 per cent ownership' or whether this is merely a temporary sop to public opinion, to be abrogated in due course.

In 2010 Treasury insider John Wilson provided a paper to the New Zealand Treasury in which he gave an outline history and assessment of the privatisation experiences of nine privatised New Zealand companies.[11] Wilson sets out five general objectives of privatisation, and we consider them in turn.

(1) 'Putting businesses under full pressures of private capital markets, and thus making them more efficient'. As an idea this has merit. However the assumption that in the real world privatised enterprises are necessarily more efficient than public ones is false.[12] Several important instances of what are often government-run enterprises, water and power utilities and rail networks for example, are natural monopolies[13] – that is why they were run by the government in the first place (in New Zealand as in many other countries). In such cases, and particularly in small countries like New Zealand, privatisation does not solve the efficiency problem: management of the enterprise by government is merely exchanged for government administration of the enterprise's prices, or in New Zealand's case by government management of the market. This is one reason why there has been such drawn-out contention over energy pricing in New Zealand following privatisation. Furthermore, in a sane world government exists to deliver not only economic efficiency but also well-being. That is to say that market efficiency is not by necessity the only relevant criterion in determining the adequacy of a government performance in its enterprises, neoliberal ideology notwithstanding. (This theme will be taken up in detail later in this chapter in relation to media privatisation in New Zealand; and general arguments in relation to the 'common good' will be discussed in Chapter 6.) Even so, suppose for the moment that efficiency is to be the sole criterion: the very different experiences of privatisation of New Zealand's public enterprises, some of which were reintroduced into public ownership and remained successful (for example Air New Zealand, Ports of Auckland), shows the very conditional nature of the original objective.

(2) 'Reducing the exposure of the government balance sheet to risky debt-financed assets'. It is not clear what the substantive content of this objective is intended to be. Any investment in an asset involves acceptance of a risk against future performance. All large economic enterprises use debt as a means of financing projects that

are planned to yield benefits in the future (in addition private firms can use shareholder equity, and governments can use tax receipts). Furthermore, governments can often borrow money at preferential rates which reduces financial risk exposure relative to private investment. However if this objective intends that governments should only undertake low-risk investments, then so be it. It is not an argument against government enterprise as such. The main force of the proposition appears to be the ideological one directed against the *idea* of government enterprise. In this regard it is worth pointing out that the development of the internet, of nuclear power, and the discovery of the structure of the genetic code and the basis of genomics, were all government-sponsored projects.

(3) 'Removing the capacity of the businesses to seek government aid in bad times, thus promoting better business management (to avoid that risk) and reducing risks to government fiscal outcomes'. The assumption underlying this objective is that there are no 'bad times' in which it might be appropriate for the government to support either its own undertakings or those of the private sector with money derived from taxes. The assumption is belied by the evident fact that the government does give or loan money to *private* enterprises under a range of circumstances, most notably perhaps in the recapitalisation of the partially-privatised Bank of New Zealand to avoid its collapse in 1990. If such aid is legitimate in order to ensure the stability of the financial system, then there are other circumstances under which it may be warranted too. Privatisation does not remove the capacity of private businesses to seek government aid. It is a source of some irony that one argument used by the Key government to justify its continuing asset sales programme is to aid the rebuilding of Christchurch in the wake of the 2010 and 2011 earthquakes. Such action speaks to the justification of government holding substantial and varied capital assets in order to provide adequate aid in critical circumstances in the future. Once again ideology appears to have lost sight of good reason. (The issue of New Zealand's holding of strategic

assets is considered further in Chapter 9.)

(4) 'Promoting the development of local capital markets, and/or encouraging a broad ownership of shares in the community'. Privatisation will indeed promote the development of local capital markets. However the idea that privatisation encourages broad ownership of shares is a deceptive one. When an enterprise is in government ownership, each citizen and taxpayer can rightfully be considered as an equal participant and owner of the assets, and of the profits and losses, of that enterprise. To privatise the enterprise is to shift ownership of the assets from New Zealand citizens in general to individuals and companies around the world with disposable income or accumulated wealth. Why should that be considered meritorious? (The issue of the ownership of New Zealand assets is considered further in Chapter 8.)

(5) 'Using the sales proceeds for higher priorities, typically to reduce government debt'. The first phrase of this proposition contains substance, particularly where the proceeds are used to finance nationally important infrastructure. The second phrase begs two questions: Why the fascination with government debt (which is modest) rather than the country's debt as a whole? And why is privatisation the best means of raising the necessary money? As to paying off debt, Douglas (now Sir Roger Douglas) admitted at the time of the 1990s privatisation frenzy: 'I am not sure we were right to use the argument that we should privatise to quit debt ... We knew it was a poor argument but we probably felt it was easier to use politically'.[14]

Even within the context of his own free-market criteria Wilson found the record of privatisations to be patchy. He found that the Crown did not receive 'consistently poor prices' for its sales. He found some evidence of efficiency improvements, but what this meant was more a question of 'whether commercial players responded effectively to commercial incentives' than whether monopoly profits were being reaped. The approach of light-handed regulation was found to be 'optimistic'. The transfer of skilled workforce overseas appeared to be 'more the result of competitive pressure than private ownership'. In adopting such a self-referential approach to assessing the privatisation programme, other concerns were swept to the periphery if not out of sight: the level of service provided by the privatised entities was of note only in the case of Tranz Rail; the significance of foreign ownership was worthy of discussion only in the case of Auckland International Airport. In admitting the public perception of privatisation in New Zealand was negative, Wilson pleads that proper opinion sampling would be required to identify the reasons for this. However the fact that no such government-sponsored poll can be referred to in the year 2010 carries its own commentary. Writing at about the same time as Wilson, but from a broader perspective on the social costs and benefits of the privatisation programme, economist Bill Rosenberg summarised it as 'an appalling experience'.[15]

There can be no general presumption in favour of the privatisation of state assets. Privatisation can be a useful step in increasing economic efficiency and social well-being, but that needs to be decided on a case by case basis. The wholesale privatisation of New Zealand government assets in a poorly regulated environment on the basis of ideological presumption was, and remains, both reckless and irresponsible.

Introduce or perpetuate 'light-handed regulation' of business. 'Light-handed regulation' is the idea that private entrepreneurs operating in markets, relieved of supervision by government, are capable of self-regulating market behaviour. It has been an integral part of the government's neoliberal economic approach. The argument in justification is that if business people do not behave adequately their reputations will suffer, or in more significant circumstances they will incur fines or in extreme circumstances be sent to gaol. However as governments regulate for social purposes (where they acknowledge any) and private firms emphasise private profit, there will always be a disjunction in motives whereby private interests seek to minimise their regulatory responsibilities in order to lower their costs. In New Zealand light-handed regulation has been all too obviously a contributing factor to the Cave Creek platform collapse (1995), to failures in rail safety (1984–2000), the leaky building syndrome (1994–2005), the Pike River Mine disaster (2010), and failures in the investment advice industry, to point to some of the better known examples.[16] Such failures became so apparent and urgent during the 1990s that with the election of the Clark Labour government in 1999 some re-regulation was introduced in the finance, telecommunications and electricity sectors, and in workplace safety.

Is light-handed regulation still an issue? The deaths of 29 workers in the forestry industry in the last 6 years say emphatically that it is. And it remains a live issue in relation to the implementation of any Trans-Pacific Partnership agreement (Chapter 5), and the conduct of the Overseas Investment Office (Chapter 8), to point to further areas of relevance.

Provide an advantageous tax system. New Zealand is a generous place for those lucky enough to have discretionary income or accumulated wealth. There is no capital gains tax that might be levied on financial gains achieved from the ownership of bonds, shares, property or precious metals. Estate duty on inherited money or property was abolished in 1992. The highest rate of individual income tax has been halved since the 1980s (from 66 per cent to 33 per cent in 2010), and business income tax on profits almost halved over the same period (from 48 per cent to 28 per cent). Businesses pay no payroll tax, no social security tax, and no health care tax apart from the minimal accident compensation tax. A goods and services tax (GST) was introduced in 1986, which now stands at 15 per cent on goods and services sold. This tax places an additional burden on lower income households relative to those with higher income, as the former are obliged to spend a greater proportion of their income on essentials than are the latter. And financial services are exempt from paying GST. Oh and yes, wealthy migrants to New Zealand can receive a tax waiver on foreign-sourced income for four years.

Consequences. The foregoing puts a little flesh on the statistical bones of the inequality examined in Chapter 1. A detailed survey of high incomes in New Zealand based on income tax evidence shows that the share of income going to the top 0.1 per cent (one in every thousand) of income earners experienced a sharp doubling between the early 1980s and the decade following 1988, from 1.25 per cent of national income to 2.5 per cent. The share of national income going to the top 1 per cent of income earners moved from about 5.5 per cent to 8.5 per cent. Percentage changes in Australia over these years were more restrained.[17] Such income data are likely to underestimate the true situation due to the ability of high-income earners to reduce their tax liabilities.[18] As J K Galbraith observed some years ago: 'Executives who speak most warmly about the stern rule of the market usually have excellent control over the income that they get themselves.'[19] In 1993 Sir Roger Douglas lectured government on what he saw as its appropriate and diminished role: 'Governments would do best by keeping in mind the interests of taxpayers and consumers – the small people – not those of producers and special-interest groups.'[20] With the hindsight of 20 years, we can only applaud his concern, but he would probably not appreciate the irony.

The practical consequences of rising income inequalities in New Zealand are several, and are referred to at various points in this and other chapters. Here we wish to emphasise the fact that the neoliberal policies discussed in the foregoing have given rise to a new, or at least transformed, elite based on privatised public wealth and other favourable treatments given to business interests.[21] But with wealth goes power, and in a neoliberal environment it is of substantial concern for society as a whole as to whether, and by what means, such power is exercised.

The New Zealand Business Roundtable (NZBR) was founded in 1985 as an early private sector advocate of the neoliberal reforms of the fourth Labour government, and was led throughout its time by former

Treasury official and libertarian economist, Roger Kerr. It produced a number of policy papers and reports from a libertarian perspective designed forcefully to influence public views and government policy. The New Zealand Institute on the other hand arose following the 2003 'Catching the Knowledge Wave' conference sponsored by the University of Auckland, as a less doctrinaire, but nonetheless free market oriented, alternative to the NZBR. In 2012 these two organisations merged into a single entity, The New Zealand Initiative, heralded as 'the country's newest libertarian think tank'.[22] The New Zealand Initiative counts within its membership the CEOs of 38 of New Zealand's most substantial companies.[23] New Zealanders who value democracy should see this merger as a chilling development. This is because in a small democracy such as New Zealand there are few, perhaps no, alternative centres of countervailing power, which a vibrant democracy requires. It is a sign that New Zealand under the neoliberal banner is in danger of becoming a kleptocracy of a power and business elite. Those companies represented in The New Zealand Initiative that value democracy should be encouraged to provide equivalent funding for the support of non-neoliberal think tanks.

Government as the Servant of Business

A consequence of the neoliberal reform programme has been to alter substantially the economic landscape in favour of private business interests. It has also led to the consolidation of neoliberal ideas among a moneyed and mainly corporatist elite, which suggests a powerful ability to influence government policy in its favour. This ability is augmented by the 'revolving door' process of hiring whereby individuals move between roles as legislators and regulators and roles in the industries affected by that legislation and those regulations, or in private consultancies, and vice versa. Such interchanges build up a shared understanding and outlook on policy issues across government and business which seeks to co-legitimise both. There are also consequences for government itself.

The reduction in the scope of things that government does under a neoliberal regime, and the rise in importance of private enterprise, means more and more that government success is measured by business success rather than the promotion of the well-being of citizens generally. Government, if it wants to be re-elected, must show evidence of a successful economy and pander to the business community to achieve it. And in response business may well be more prepared to support compliant political parties with donations.[24] (The Electoral Finance Act 2007, designed to limit chicanery from electoral financing in the wake of the 2005 election funding controversy, was repealed as unworkable following the subsequent election in 2008. The Act has yet to be replaced.) It is not that government ministers and elected officials should not seek to bring prosperity and jobs to New Zealand, but that governments are in danger of forgetting why they were elected, namely to serve the interests of all their constituents. The issues involved in free trade (Chapter 5), in climate change (Chapter 7) and in resource management (Chapter 8) give point to this fact. In observing this trend across many capitalist countries in the globalising world, economist Noreena Hertz describes it thus: 'by giving corporate wishes such priority, by defining themselves solely in terms of economic success, by supporting international institutions that value economic interests above all else, governments are in danger of becoming the puppets of business.'[25]

The Media in New Zealand

Judge Raymond Finkelstein QC in his 2012 report of the Australian Independent Inquiry into the Media and Media Regulation explored in detail the rationales offered by philosophers, politicians, lawyers and journalists for the indispensability of free speech and a free press in democratic societies.[26] These rationales he identified as: the search for truth; the enhancement of democratic discourse ('what is essential is not that everyone shall speak but that everything worth saying will be said'); self-fulfilment and autonomy (enabling the individual to live at choice); and the fourth estate (the assignment to the press of a central role in safeguarding democracy). Whatever the rationale, it was recognised that free speech is not absolute (for example with regard to inciting violence, protecting individuals against false or misleading statements, and the like). In review Finkelstein concluded that there is almost universal agreement on the importance of a free press for the vitality of democracy, and while there may be some qualifications to be made on the various rationales offered, 'together they form a compelling case'. There is also agreement that the media wields considerable power, and 'with such power comes responsibility'.

In New Zealand, broadcast radio and television were from their origins (in 1925 and 1960 respectively) provided by the state as a public service. In 1975 a second non-commercial television channel was introduced, and in 1976 commercial operation of radio began.[27] In the reforms of the late 1980s the Broadcasting Corporation of New Zealand was dissolved, its commercially based radio operations sold to private investors, and its non-commercial assets New Zealand Public Radio (which became Radio New Zealand Ltd) and TVNZ (Television New Zealand Ltd) became separate SOEs which needed to 'compete commercially and return dividends to the Crown', thereby downgrading their public service function. Funding from government for 'public good' broadcasting content across television, radio and new media platforms would henceforth be channelled through an autonomous Crown entity called the Broadcasting Commission or 'NZ On Air'.

The commercial media market in New Zealand is currently dominated by four players.[28] APN News and Media is an Australian and New Zealand public company which owns the *New Zealand Herald*, *Herald on Sunday*, (and up until December 2013 the *New Zealand Listener*), a substantial number of radio stations, as well as having outdoor advertising interests. Fairfax Media is an Australian company focused on print media, and owns the leading newspapers the *Dominion Post* in Wellington, the *Christchurch Press*, as well as the majority of other daily newspapers with circulations greater than 25,000 (excluding the *Otago Daily Times*). MediaWorks owns TV, radio and interactive media outlets in New Zealand including TV3, Four and C4 and 10 radio networks. In 2007 the Australian private equity group Ironbridge Capital gained full control of MediaWorks and the company was delisted from the New Zealand stock exchange. In June 2013 the company was placed in receivership with substantial debts and subsequently sold to MediaWorksHoldings Limited, a syndicate of banks and equity companies, many of which were holders of MediaWorks debt. Finally Sky TV provides pay-to-view television to about 850,000 subscribers and through the Prime channel delayed free-to-air sports programmes. In addition, TVNZ operates TV One, TV2, the pay channel TVNZ Heartland, and TVNZ Kidzone. As a possible 90 per cent of TVNZ's revenue comes from commercial activity (advertising and merchandising)[29], it raises the question as to whether TVNZ should also be considered as part of the commercial media market. (Maori Television, on the other hand, is wholly funded by the New Zealand government to advance the understanding and development of Maori culture and language.) In terms of overall coverage, APN and Fairfax are the major players in the print arena, having over 40 per cent of the universe, while in television MediaWorks has about 45 per cent of the metropolitan audience aged 18–49, and TVNZ about 30 per cent.

The central question is whether the media as they exist in New Zealand are capable of providing the media environment that a healthy society and democracy requires. The necessary characteristics were identified by Judge Finkelstein as a freely accessible, open and diverse media landscape, and one that encourages vigorous debate and the interaction of ideas, particularly in relation to the public interest. There are cogent reasons why New Zealanders should doubt the adequacy of its media environment. First, the primary motive of any commercial television channel or radio station is to generate profit for its owners. Most revenues come from advertisements. There is therefore inevitably pressure on managers not to bite the hands that feed them and to 'shield advertisers from views they do not like, to avoid complicated or expensive stories, and to avoid content that does not attract the maximum possible audience at any given time'.[30,31] Nor is publicly-owned TV that accepts advertisements immune from such pressures. Second, owners of commercial media operations have an interest in influencing the content of their media outlets, either to protect their own organisations or to promote their own views. Third, commercial television has a strong tendency to centralise its operations in order to reduce costs, thus squeezing out local and regional participation and perspectives: consider for example the recent demise of the New Zealand Press Association and its replacement by three news services, all Australian owned. (Book publishing in New Zealand has likewise suffered from marginalisation by overseas owners.)

In 2011 the Key government decided not to renew funding for TVNZ7 – New Zealand's last commercial-free public interest television channel established by the previous Clark government. Despite an appeal by over 60 media academics to the relevant Ministers[32], the channel ceased transmissions on 30 June 2012. In justifying his decision, the Minister of Broadcasting Jonathan Coleman said: 'Sinking money into a public broadcasting infrastructure which continues to suck up money in the long-term doesn't make sense ... It's important to fund the content, not some monolithic public broadcaster'.[33] If we ignore the pejorative 'monolithic', the Minister is wrong on both counts: maintaining and enhancing democracy is a public obligation and was never costless; and it is not the content that is in need of funding but the idea. The amount saved by this miserable action amounted to NZ$15m per year, or less than NZ$3.50 per person.

Funding previously going to TVNZ7 was redirected by the government to NZ On Air, which was left to carry the weight of 'public service' broadcasting in New Zealand. Despite its merits, this is patently something that NZ On Air is incapable of doing. A major reason is that it too is subject to the government's commercial criteria, and can only make programmes that the commercial broadcasters are prepared to transmit. A particularly significant loss has been that of searching documentaries.[34] As Mark Jennings, head of News and Current Affairs at MediaWorks' TV3 explained to Radio New Zealand's Mediawatch host Colin Peacock on being quizzed as to why TV3 was scrapping its current affairs programme *The Vote*: 'The hard reality of it is that those programmes have not rated well enough ... The audience ... is too small for a commercial television station to continue with it'.[35] A second reason is the narrow remit given NZ On Air. In the Broadcasting Act of 1976 its general purposes were identified as: '(a) To maintain and develop broadcasting, as a system of human communications, to serve the people of New Zealand; (b) To obtain, produce, commission, and broadcast a range of programmes which will inform, educate, and entertain; (c) To ensure that programmes reflect and develop New Zealand's identity and culture ...'. When NZ On Air was set up under the Broadcasting Act of 1989, only the anodyne third of these purposes survived.

This shoddy view of 'public good' broadcasting should satisfy no New Zealander. UNESCO defines public service broadcasting thus: 'Neither commercial nor State-controlled, public broadcasting's only *raison d'être* is public service. It is the public's broadcasting organization; it speaks to everyone as a citizen. Public broadcasters encourage access to and participation in public life. They develop knowledge, broaden horizons and enable people to better understand themselves by better understanding the world and others.'[36] It is important that government ministers and other politicians find the intestinal fortitude to make better provision for genuinely free and open public broadcasting, including the use of social media, if they are to avoid undermining not only New Zealand's democracy but their own legitimacy.

New Zealand's Gordian Knot

New Zealand's number one macroeconomic problem has always been to try to ensure that earnings from exports were sufficient to pay for necessary imports and to service repayments on existing overseas debt. We should therefore examine the issue in detail.

Historically this balance of payments problem was managed through the use of controls on imports and foreign exchange. In the period following World War II New Zealand entered a period in which it could just about manage to balance its overseas payments books year by year. However Britain's joining the EC and the oil shocks of 1973 and 1979 administered severe blows to New Zealand's economy and overseas payments position, and this was exacerbated by the 'think big' programme of large-scale infrastructure projects associated with the Muldoon era, which required substantial levels of imports. As a result, New Zealand's balance of payments on current account headed deep into negative territory and has remained there ever since. In four of the five years 1969–73 the balance was actually positive, but over the latter part of the decade it fell to an average of about negative NZ$650m, and plunged to a low of negative NZ$4,049m in 1986 before climbing back to negative NZ$2,945m a decade later.

A deficit on current account in any one year indicates that New Zealand has received a flow of imports greater than the value of its flow of exports and has thereby registered a debt in relation to the rest of the world. This debt needs to be covered in some way. In New Zealand this has mainly been done by overseas borrowing. Regular borrowing to cover current account deficits has meant that New Zealand's stock of debt to the rest of the world has built up over time. Overseas borrowing is not necessarily bad: all countries borrow to finance important projects. The inflow of investment funds provides companies in New Zealand with the potential to make investments in productive assets (buildings, machinery, technology, human expertise) that would not otherwise be possible. What is critical however, is that such funds be invested sufficiently productively so that the loans or other investment can be repaid out of generated income or profit.

In the years following 1984 New Zealand's economy was effectively thrown open to investment from the rest of the world, and New Zealand experienced a huge influx of foreign funds. Although the country continued to rely on overseas debt finance, the great majority of this inward flow of funds was foreign direct investment (FDI): investment conferring ownership rights in New Zealand companies. (See Appendix 1 for definitions of terms.) In 1984 the stock of inward FDI stood at less than10 per cent of GDP before soaring in 1998 to 60 per cent of GDP (a percentage more than double the values for other developed countries such as Australia, Canada and the Netherlands). Since the year 2000 the stock of inward FDI has fluctuated, and in 2012 stood at 48 per cent of GDP or NZ$99,142m. On the other hand New Zealand's outward stock of FDI rose from just 2 per cent of GDP in 1984 to 10 per cent in 1998 and has hovered above this level since that time.[37] The New Zealand economy is therefore very reliant on foreign capital and is highly exposed to changes in the international investment climate: a circumstance that is exacerbated by the fact that much of New Zealand's overseas debt is short term.[38]

Net investment income paid overseas each year (mainly dividend payments on foreign-held equity in New Zealand companies), which had been trending upwards following the crises of the 1970s, took another large jump upwards after 1984, and has moved erratically around an average of about 5.8 per cent of GDP since that time. New Zealand's net international investment position (NIIP) (which combines both the international debt and international equity positions) deteriorated steadily from the mid-1970s to the early 1990s after which it has steadied, ranging around 70 per cent of GDP since that time. (As at March 2012 New Zealand's NIIP liability stood at 72 per cent of GDP or about negative NZ$148,713m.[39]) New Zealand's NIIP is less as a percentage of GDP than those of the currently problematic economies of Europe such as Greece, Portugal, Ireland and Spain, but is greater than those of Poland, Slovakia and Romania and almost double those of Turkey, Mexico, Indonesia and Kazakhstan. These statistics indicate two things: first that New Zealand has, through increasing GDP and the sale of public assets, been able to cover the increase in overseas obligations resulting from the surge in FDI; and second that the FDI itself has facilitated no improvement in New Zealand's overall debt position. And this circumstance has arisen after more than two decades of wholesale privatisations and the 'open door' policy towards foreign investment.

Two explanations are commonly proposed to explain New Zealand's failure to improve its overseas debt position: low productivity and low domestic savings. Workforce productivity is clearly a critical consideration for any economy, as higher productivity means more output per unit of effort and provides a clear pathway to higher prosperity and living standards. For many decades New Zealand workforce productivity growth has been low, averaging about 1.9 per cent per year over the period 1978–2012. Relative to other OECD countries, New Zealand's productivity growth has suffered a slow but steady decline over this period and currently stands at 20 per cent below the OECD average. This weak growth has been identified as a key reason why New Zealand's GDP per capita is so low in comparison with other OECD countries. In trans-Tasman comparison, current New Zealand workforce productivity is about 38 per cent less than that in Australia, and is less for all industry sectors except for services (electricity, gas, water and waste), rental and real estate, and professional science and technical.[40]

Over the period 1985–2000 New Zealand's workforce productivity did show some uplift, but this has not been sustained and current levels are now less than in the pre-1984 period.[41] Despite the surge and continuing stream of inward FDI, economy-wide data show no indication that it has made a contribution to overall productivity growth. Perhaps this is not surprising, as evidence from studies globally on the productivity benefits of FDI remains equivocal.[42,43] This is not to say that there may not be other positive or negative spillover effects from inward FDI – such as from training and demonstration effects, from product quality improvements, or from R&D activities. However the main conclusion remains that New Zealand's free market policies of recent decades have neither reduced the country's poor productivity growth nor contributed to reducing its overseas debt.

What has been Treasury's response to this situation? More of the same. Treasury's recommended domestic policy settings for overseas investment continue to be those of open doors and no restrictions, namely to keep investment screening to a minimum (if at all), avoid direct incentives, create a generally attractive business environment, and in the international sphere to promote free capital flows in international forums and reduce additional costs of capital flows. The government's Business Growth Agenda of 2012 continues these themes in the domestic economic arena.[44] It is a recitative with which we are by now familiar.

There are nonetheless available alternatives. One set has been cogently argued by economists and policy analysts Rick Boven, Dan Bidois and Catherine Harland. As they point out, New Zealand exports are currently concentrated in commodities, low-productivity activities which have grown globally much more slowly than trade in value-added and technology-based products and services. Thus expansion of agriculture, forestry and horticulture will not be adequate to increase current GDP per capita significantly. Successful small countries have become so by focusing on innovation, and on high-value differentiated products in the export sector, and this is where New Zealand should focus its efforts in improving workforce productivity and GDP per capita.[45] In contrast to the hands-off and unsuccessful Treasury approach, this alternative is a more targeted, managed approach in which the government plays an important role in the reallocation of resources from low to high productivity, and domestic to export, sectors. Another fruitful approach to increasing workforce productivity is likely to be by increasing the distributional equity in society, as was noted in Chapter 1.

A similar message has been delivered by the report of the 2013 House of Representatives Inquiry into Manufacturing, which enumerated a number of practical steps that could be taken to encourage manufactured exports.[46] The report was endorsed by the New Zealand Manufacturers and Exporters Association, with CEO John Walley declaring that 'The report underlines the importance of manufacturing to the future of New Zealand; manufacturing is not an optional extra ... Everything in the report is doable given the political will.'[47] Promoted by the opposition parties in parliament, the Inquiry was labelled a political stunt by the government, which refused to make it official.[48]

Another quite different set of possibilities for improving the balance of payments is for New Zealanders to consume less (and thereby import less), and save more (thereby providing additional domestic funds for investment rather than relying so heavily on foreign funds). To this end the New Zealand Treasury in 2010 called on a high-level Savings Working Group (SWG) to advise it on how to increase national savings. (Over the last 25 years New Zealand net household savings as a percentage of household disposable income has averaged minus 2.5 per cent: the lowest rate in the OECD and 10 per cent lower than the OECD median.[49]) In its final report the SWG noted: 'Clearly there are serious questions to be asked about New Zealand's economic policy and how we got into this mess. Why was it not better designed and managed, and more focussed, coordinated and strategic?'[50] Well might they have asked. The SWG agreed with the Treasury analysis that an increase in savings was an essential component in reducing the economy's international vulnerability, and recommended a number of 'urgent actions' to increase national saving. Specific measures included higher productivity and performance from the state sector as an 'immediate priority': this would be the government's contribution to savings, namely getting more work from its workforce with no increase in expenditures. Other recommendations included improving management and increasing the transparency of the Crown's balance sheet, the downward adjustment of some taxes associated with interest and dividend income, the continuing move from taxing income to taxing consumption, and changes to KiwiSaver to make it more attractive to would-be investors.[51]

Despite the incisiveness of the SWG analysis, we should be in no doubt as to the ideological context within which the invitation from Treasury to the SWG was made and the response from the SWG received: a context that validated some responses to the savings issue but invalidated others. In this regard the terms of reference to the SWG specifically excluded any consideration of taxes on capital gains or land (as means of raising increasing savings in the hands of the government), or of any economic sectoral issues in relation to savings. The report of the SWG emphasised the importance of households increasing their savings irrespective of income decile[52], of the government increasing the efficiency of the public service, but gave only passing mention to the issue of the accumulation and use of business savings (profits) despite the Reserve Bank in its submission to the SWG believing that trends in these were likely to be at least as important as changes in household savings. Tax evasion by multinational companies received no mention at all. Thus is opportunity held hostage to ideology.

The general conclusion that we take from this consideration of New Zealand's economy in an international context is that it continues to suffer a serious structural problem, and one that has not been alleviated by three decades of free market policies. In the annals of personal psychology there is a belief that to persist in the same behaviour with the expectation of a different outcome is likely to be unrewarding, if not pathological. It is time for a paradigm change.

Democracy

If you lose the ability to buy necessities at your local dairy store when it closes down it is evident immediately. The loss of more abstract goods of value, such as elements of democracy, are less visible, but they are losses just the same: and they are losses that can have profound consequences for individuals and for society as a whole.

It was Robert Dahl, political scientist and respected scholar of twentieth-century democracy, who pointed out that the evidence accumulated over the twentieth century demonstrates that all enduring pluralist democracies are associated with predominantly capitalist economies.[53] The converse however is not true. Fascist Germany had a capitalist economy but was repressive with regard to citizenship and rights; Chile, following the 1973 *coup d'état* that deposed popularly elected President Salvador Allende was a military dictatorship despite installing a free market economy; Saudi Arabia, China and post-Soviet Russia are all capitalism-oriented but non-democratic regimes. The moral to be drawn is that capitalism does not ensure democracy, and if democracy is to survive and flourish it needs its own attention and husbandry. There is also, as Dahl points out, an ongoing tension between the market capitalist idea of 'one dollar one vote' and the democratic idea of 'one person one vote', which ensures that the relationship between the two is always open to debate and renegotiation. However Dahl observes that in no democratic country does a market-capitalist economy exist without some government regulation and intervention to rectify its more harmful effects.[54]

Dahl sets out five criteria that he believes a modern democracy should meet for its members: effective participation, equality in voting, enlightened understanding, control of the agenda, and inclusion. How well does New Zealand measure up since 1984? Author and commentator Gordon McLauchlan, in explaining the title of his book *The Big Con*, proclaimed: 'The Big Con began with the stealth campaign in 1984 by a powerful core of Labour politicians, covert converts to fundamentalist economics, who won office without ever disclosing an intention to impose a laissez-faire economic policy on New Zealanders. It was an act of deception probably unparalleled in our history.'[55] There can be little quarrel with the essence that statement. It was an ignoble blow to all those in New Zealand who cherish democracy. (McLauchlan continued in his book by berating the National Party for similar behaviour in the 1990 election.) In 2005 the National Party, then in opposition – or more precisely the right wing of that party colonised by ACT Party backers whose members aspired to bring National's leader Don Brash to power in the election of that year – repeated the dose. The treatment is described by Nicky Hager in *The Hollow Men*.[56] With such conduct abounding in the core of major political parties, there can be no 'enlightened understanding' as Dahl would require, and 'effective participation' is undermined. 'Equality in voting' and 'inclusion' become meaningless rituals. Adequate democracy finds no safe harbour here.

Given this conduct, one is impelled to search for reasons. One may be found perhaps in the increasing ranks of young professionals drawn into politics as a career rather than emergent from grass-root involvement in civic and local life; another no doubt in the increasing sophistication of political promotion based on social psychological research and emanating particularly from the US. A third emerges from the neoliberal paradigm itself. In anaesthetising public morality in the conduct of markets and government, it gives licence to those involved in commercial and political life to act by ignoring it. This is the licence that Gordon Gekko takes.

Governments' loss of moral purpose and responsibility to citizens generally is also shown by their disregard of the result of citizen-initiated referenda, most recently in relation to the proposed partial privatisation of Meridian Energy, Mighty River Power, Genesis Power, Solid Energy and Air New Zealand, which was rejected by two thirds of the 45 per cent of the total number of enrolled voters (1.3

million voters) who participated.[57] More egregious has been the 2013 refusal by the government to adopt the major recommendation of the Electoral Commission review of the MMP voting system, namely to abolish the one electorate seat threshold for the allocation of list seats.[58] The Office of the Ombudsman has been overstretched and underfunded for years, according to reports.[59] As a consequence it is not surprising that the electorate has been engaging less and less.

Turnout at New Zealand general elections has been in decline. After a steady level of turnout averaging 87.7 per cent over the six general elections from 1960 to 1975, turnout rose to a peak of 93.7 per cent at the 1984 election. Since that time the trend has been steeply downwards, with turnout dropping to an all-time low of 74.2 per cent in 2011. The 2013 local body elections also recorded their lowest turnout ever of around 45 per cent.[60] Surveys of public opinion in the years following the introduction of the reform programme showed that although a large majority of people valued the democratic system, they also felt themselves disempowered in relation to government: 85.4 per cent believed they had little control over the actions of politicians; 61.6 per cent believed they would get nowhere by talking to government officials; and 67.4 per cent felt that the government would not respond to public opinion. The level of dissatisfaction with the public service increased from 52.3 per cent in 1985 to 71 per cent in 1998.[61] A decline in membership of political parties has corresponded with declines in church attendance, sports club affiliations and a decline in volunteers for community organisations, attributed at least in part to the rising individualism in society.[62] While neoliberalism may not be the only causal factor in these social changes, directly or indirectly it is without doubt a major one.

This decline in public participation is not something that New Zealand has suffered alone. It has been recorded and analysed in other countries with neoliberal political agendas, including Britain, Australia and the US. However according to political scientists Ian Marsh and Raymond Miller, the decline in public confidence and trust appear to have had a more profound effect on political life in New Zealand than in either Britain or Australia.[63] In Britain, along with the fall in electoral participation and the decline in public confidence in political leaders, a more insidious and malign effect has also been identified, namely the return of a politics of favouritism and patronage: a trend not unrelated to the subservience of government to business interests discussed above.[64]

The decline in public participation is important as a reflection of the declining health of what is often referred to as 'civil society': the span of voluntary organisations in society independent of government which promote public participation, or as political philosopher Michael Walzer calls it, the 'space of uncoerced citizen action'. Occupying this space are clubs, community organisations, consumer groups, cultural groups, environmental groups, churches, charities, foundations, NGOs, political parties, professional associations, academia, non-profit organisations, support groups, and a myriad of other groupings. Civil society is important because it is the space in which citizens engage, mainly informally, in discussion and interaction, are exposed to new ideas, develop trust and shared values, exercise tolerance, and become more aware of the interconnectedness of society. It is important as the seedbed and nursery of social ideas which can inform political life, and of social norms. Its most profound importance is as the realm in which cooperation, citizenship, justice and service gain their meaning.[65] Declines in the quality of civil society represent damage to democracy and to society as a whole.

Estimates suggest that there are about 97,000 civil society organisations in New Zealand, 90 per cent of which employ no paid staff but rely solely on volunteers, the remaining 10 per cent employing around 100,000 people.[66] There is very little systematic research on such groups that can be called upon. However an example can be given of the baleful effects of neoliberal policy on the conduct of the community and voluntary sector in the health, education and social services areas, recently the subject of public discussion. The neoliberal approach to this and other civil society sectors is based on what is called in free market terminology the 'purchaser-provider model', which employs the market-mimicking mechanism of a contract between the purchaser of a service (the government) and the provider of the service (the community or voluntary organisation). This sets out the various functions that will be carried out by the provider in return for a specified payment by the purchaser. The underlying assumption of this approach is that all parties involved are motivated by self-interest and that competition among potential providers will increase the efficiency of service delivery. The model has led to considerable disillusion and distress in the community and voluntary sector. The threat of losing funding as government priorities change, and of being in competition with other voluntary organisations in the sector for scarce funds, has ingrained a sense of insecurity and risk-aversion with regard to speaking out in advocacy of the groups in society which these organisations support. It is a sense reinforced by gag clauses written in to some contracts, and the clause in the Charities Act 2005 which excludes advocacy as a charitable purpose. Overall the model has led to a muting of the voice of an important segment of informed opinion in public debate and decision making in the areas of health, education and social services.[67]

This manner of degradation of civil society in New Zealand appears to have become pervasive. Take another unrelated example. Universities in New Zealand as elsewhere, under an older dispensation, used to be beneficiaries of the idea of 'academic freedom'. This was an unwritten social contract between universities and the societies that supported them, that in return for their independence and ability to seek out truth, universities in turn would make their findings available for the benefit of society at large. Under neoliberalism's banners of efficiency, competition and financial gain, truth, even as it is sought in universities, has become hostage to commercial advantage. [68]

For John Rawls, a social system is acceptable to individuals in accordance with 'the psychological law that persons tend to love, cherish, and support whatever affirms their own good'; and French sociologist Emile Durkheim drew attention to the social pathology he named *anomie*, which could lead to the fragmentation of individuals' social identities and to anti-social behaviour. In such a context the danger from neoliberalism, particularly in its more extreme forms, is that it exacts competition, fragmentation, atomisation, and the denial of common purposes, all of which are antithetical to social cohesion. A 2014 report from the OECD has warned of the dangers of inequality in creating problems for future social cohesion in Member countries.[69] In recent years the balance between capitalism and democracy in New Zealand has lurched away from social cohesion and the interests of democracy. We need to remind ourselves that democratic practice does not emerge spontaneously, as recent experiences in some Middle Eastern countries, and the behaviour of human groups in crisis situations[70], show. It must be learned, and if it is to be valued and survive, it must be nurtured.

New Zealanders are in the process of having their democracy degraded and taken from them by stealth. Neoliberalism is anti-democratic. Reputable government, prepared to act on the citizen's behalf, is a prerequisite for a stable liberal and democratic society. These are not novel observations, but ones that have increasingly been forwarded in recent years and from various points of view, as the pernicious consequences of neoliberalism have become more apparent.[71,72] Author John Ralston Saul put it like this: 'Government is the only organized mechanism that makes possible that level of shared disinterest known as the public good. Without this greater interest the individual is reduced to a lesser, narrower being limited to immediate needs. He will then be subject to other, larger forces, which will necessarily come forward to fill the void left by the withering of the public good.'[73]

Part II

FREE TRADE

4

'Free Trade' – Theory and Practice

The Meaning of 'Free Trade'

Scottish philosopher and economist Adam Smith argued in the eighteenth century that all countries could gain from trade if each allowed unrestricted trade and specialised in the production of those commodities in which they had an absolute advantage in terms of the labour force productivity. It was the insight of English nineteenth-century economist David Ricardo to see that trade beneficial to each country did not depend on its having an absolute advantage in the production of any commodity, but rather on the much less demanding criterion of comparative advantage.

Ricardo showed that if England produces cloth more efficiently than it does wine, and Portugal produces wine more efficiently than it does cloth, then trade beneficial to both countries can ensue if England specialises in cloth and Portugal in wine, irrespective of whether either country has an absolute advantage in labour productivity for either commodity. By specialising in the production of the commodity that each country produces more efficiently and allowing each commodity to flow freely between the two countries, resources would be liberated with which further commodities could be produced.

This result has proved to be one of the foundational insights in the history of orthodox economic theory, and underlies the belief that most of today's economists have in advocating what is referred to as 'free trade'.[1] Ricardo's result is one about the allocation of resources and economic efficiency, and says that – under its assumptions – more 'stuff', derived from the same resources, is better (recall the discussion of market efficiency in Chapter 2). This is an important result, but also a limited one. Ricardo's result shows that as a consequence of the opening of trade, production will increase and average incomes in each country will rise. But no consideration has been given to the consequences of trade for the existing English wine growers or the Portuguese involved in the cloth industry, nor to any costs involved in structural adjustments to the economy required by the opening of trade. While showing concern for efficiency the Ricardo result takes no concern for the distribution of the costs and benefits within the economies of England or Portugal – that is, for matters of equity. Thus, while there is ample evidence in the modern world to show that in general countries that have economies open to trade are more productive and more prosperous than those that do not, this is a long way from saying that unfettered 'free trade' is always optimal, or 'the best we can do'.

Consider the case where a country's major industry is subject to economies of scale – where the unit cost of production decreases as total production increases – a situation commonly found in industries that employ large amounts of capital equipment such as mining, petroleum, chemicals, steel production. In such cases it would be counterproductive for the country to follow a free trade regime. Again, if markets for goods and services in an agricultural country are less than perfect and crop harvests risky, under some circumstances even autarky (no trade) can be shown preferable to any trade at all. Indeed the further one exposes the idea of comparative advantage to the exigencies of the real world as distinct from the textbook, the more conditional its benefits become: a circumstance well recognised by at least a minority of economists.[2]

And what is meant by 'free trade' anyway? Traditionally, 'free trade' or 'freer trade' has meant the lowering of tariffs on imported goods and of subsidies on exported goods. Nowadays what exactly is to be understood by 'free trade' is not so straightforward. One definition of free trade is *non-discriminatory trade* – trade that places no restrictions on imports that are not equally placed on home products. This criterion at least gives individual states the ability to organise their own internal economic, social, cultural and environmental affairs. However the definition that has gained currency in international trade organisations in the neoliberal era is of trade between importers and exporters unobstructed by government regulations or tariffs – that is, *laissez-faire trade*. This is the definition implicitly employed by the WTO, and underlies the approach taken in recent regional trade agreements such as the North American Free Trade Agreement (NAFTA), and that proposed in the Trans-Pacific Partnership (TPP) agreement currently being negotiated among New Zealand and other Pacific-region countries. We must also be watchful here in our use of words. Supporters of 'free trade' may hope that trade is 'free' in the sense of unobstructed, but it is never free in the sense of costless; and as we have already seen it is not necessarily better than 'less-than-free' trade. Similarly, to describe any impediment to laissez-faire trade as a 'distortion' as its proponents commonly do, is to announce one's ideological preconceptions. One might equally refer to a mathematical curve as a distorted straight line.

The concern in this and the following chapter is not with trade per se, but with the elevation of 'free trade' to the status of dogma. The single-minded pursuit of free trade which has become rife in many countries over the last three decades gives rise to what might be called the 'fallacy of extremism': the belief that if something is good then more of it must always be better. Such a purblind hypothesis can only gain merit from what it chooses to ignore. And an understanding of the role of trade in the history of Western nations must also give us pause.

'Free Trade' and the Evidence of History

The idea of free trade as virtuous is deeply embedded in the psyches of many economists and politicians, and in what has been called the 'official history of capitalism'. This history holds that in the eighteenth century, Britain established itself as the outstanding economic power on the basis of the economic efficiency of its free market and free trade policies, as opposed to the policies of more government-interventionist France: its main competitor on the international stage at that time. This history continues that following the repeal of the protectionist Corn Laws in 1846[3], Britain entered into a long period of economic growth based on non-interventionist policies at home, low barriers to trade, and financial stability guaranteed by the gold standard. This lasted until after World War I when, with the coming of the Great Depression, Britain along with the US and other countries introduced a regime of tariffs in what they considered to be self-protective measures. And as the story continues, following World War II a trade regime of benign government interventionism ensued under the General Agreement on Tariffs and Trade (the GATT), until more laissez-faire policies re-emerged after the 1970s and became enshrined finally in the creation of the WTO in 1994.

This 'official history' is, according to Ha-Joon Chang, a University of Cambridge economist, fundamentally misleading.[4] The historical record shows that Britain in its industrialising phase was an aggressive user of policies to promote its own industries in its own interests, and in the latter part of the eighteenth century its protectionist policies were more obtrusive than those of either France or Germany. In 1721 British Prime Minister Robert Walpole introduced a series of laws designed specifically to advantage Britain's own manufacturing industries. These included the lowering of import duties on raw materials used in manufacturing, abolishing export duties on most manufactures, raising duties on foreign manufactures, and increasing 'bounties' (export subsidies) to some domestic industries.

After the end of the war with Napoleon in 1815, increasingly confident British manufacturers were making demands for freer trade. In response there was in 1833 a round of tariff reductions, but the manufacturers' greatest achievement was the repeal of the Corn Laws. This can be seen either as a triumph of Ricardo's economic theories as the 'official history' proposes, or as Chang claims as an act of 'free trade imperialism' designed to halt the move to industrialisation by countries on the Continent by enlarging the market in Britain for agricultural produce and primary materials. It was certainly seen in these terms by British politicians of the time, and by a number of trade history economists in our own. Other tariff reductions followed in Britain in the latter part of the nineteenth century, and Britain promoted free trade up until the 1930s when, recognising the loss of its manufacturing eminence, it reintroduced tariffs. Preaching free trade as Britain did throughout the nineteenth and early twentieth centuries to less advanced countries like Germany and US was, according to nineteenth-century German economist Friedrich List, like someone who 'kicks away the ladder by which he has climbed to the top, in order to deprive others of the means of climbing up after him'.

Furthermore the historical record shows that the US was even more protectionist in its developmental phase than was Britain. Alexander Hamilton, the first US Secretary of the Treasury (1789–95) was a great advocate of 'infant industry' arguments[5] as a means of protecting fledgling US industries from British exports, by such means as import duties on competing products and where necessary banning certain imports. And Ulysses S. Grant, Civil War hero and US President (1868–76), was reported as saying: 'Within two hundred years, when America has gotten out of protection all that it can offer, it too will adopt free trade'. According to available statistics, in the period from the Civil War until World War II the US was one of the most heavily protected countries in the world. And it needs also to be noted that successive US governments have played a substantial role over a long period in promoting the country's economic development and export potential by supporting agricultural colleges and research institutions since the 1830s, agricultural price and income support policies since the 1920s, and defence research at spectacular levels since World War II.

While Britain and the US may provide extreme examples of protectionist regimes, all now developed countries – with a few exceptions such as the Netherlands and Switzerland – have employed preferential treatment for their industries in their developmental phases. And this is compatible with evidence from our own times, in relation to the development paths of Japan, South Korea, Taiwan and China, for example, all of which pursued paths based on a strong role for the public sector in encouraging and protecting key industries, and investing in human and physical capital.

What the foregoing provides is a lesson in caution. Economics is rife with plausible stories, some of which approximate the truth more closely than others. Another lesson is about the importance of power in determining the course and outcomes of trade negotiations. These lessons alert us to the need to examine scrupulously the legitimacy of the economic assumptions and arguments put forward in favour of, and in opposition to, any trade agreement.

Evolution of the World Trading System

In 1944 the United Nations convened an international conference at Bretton Woods, New Hampshire, to plan the post-World War II international monetary and financial system. The General Agreement on Tariffs and Trade (GATT) was one of three organisations that were established as a result of this conference (the two others being the World Bank and the International Monetary Fund or IMF). The purpose of the GATT was the reduction of tariffs and the promotion of world trade. The text of its Articles was directed to ensuring non-discriminatory trade. It accomplished this through the conduct of a series of ad hoc 'rounds' of trade negotiations among countries that chose to participate; in each round, which might last a few years, an agreed agenda of items was discussed and led to a set of agreements on liberalising trade, particularly through reductions in tariffs.

These GATT rounds concentrated on tariff reductions on merchandise trade: that is, trade in material goods such as automobiles, food, equipment and so on. In its early years the GATT regime was a relatively benign one which left considerable discretion to individual states as to whether or not they chose to join a negotiation round or not and on occasion provided privileged status to less developed countries. In its mission the GATT achieved considerable success, with the world average tariff on manufactured goods falling from 40 per cent to less than 5 per cent from 1947 to the completion of the Uruguay Round of trade negotiations in 1994. Over that period world merchandise trade expanded fifty-fold.

The signing of the Marrakesh Declaration in 1994, agreed by the representatives of 124 governments and the European Union, signalled not only the completion of the Uruguay Round of negotiations under the GATT, but also the transformation of that ad hoc trade negotiating body into the fully-fledged international organisation to be called the World Trade Organization (WTO). The underlying GATT trade principles were retained by the WTO, but the changes wrought by the transformation of the GATT into the WTO had profound implications not only for the nature of trade and trade negotiations but for the world's states and citizens more generally. For whereas the GATT was a treaty under which individual countries retained substantial discretion as to whether or not they became a contracting party to a specific GATT-based agreement, the WTO is an international organisation of member governments, in which all negotiated agreements (and all earlier negotiated GATT agreements and all GATT/WTO agreements to come) are binding on all members, and enforceable. The GATT disputes settlement procedure, one in which panel rulings were adopted by positive consensus, was replaced in the WTO by a supercourt known as the Appellate Body, which oversees the work of all the dispute resolution panels. The decision of a panel – or if appealed, of the Appellate Body – is binding in international law on all parties unless all members (including the member country which won the original decision) vote unanimously to overrule it. A state in contravention of WTO provisions can be subject to suspension of concessions or other obligations including the payment of compensation to the aggrieved party or parties. It is one of the most powerful and wide-ranging of international judicial mechanisms in existence.

In addition, the range of interests of the WTO increased substantially, for whereas the GATT had been mainly concerned with tariffs and trade in merchandise goods, the Uruguay Round went much further, concluding an array of agreements on such matters as agriculture, transport, banking, insurance, health provision, copyright, patents, trademarks, software, plant varieties, food safety, animal and plant health regulations. In several cases these agreements give power to the WTO in pursuit of trade liberalisation to regulate not only 'at border' trade, but to regulate the 'behind the border' conduct of member governments and businesses as well. The goal of free trade promoted by the WTO is not non-discriminatory trade, but laissez-faire trade.

A number of the Agreements reached in the Uruguay Round are of particular relevance to New Zealand and the TPP. The General Agreement on Trade in Services (GATS) was the first international trade agreement to extend the notion of trade in merchandise goods to cross-border trade in services.[6] It is a very wide-ranging and complex agreement. According to Article I (3) those services open to import and export under the Agreement include any service in any sector except 'services supplied in the exercise of governmental authority' where this exception means 'any service, which is supplied neither on a commercial basis, nor in competition with one or more service suppliers'. While it is said that under the GATS governments can exclude specific government-provided services from the Agreement, there is little in the way of case law as yet available for guidance, and there is pressure from international business interests for countries to refrain from claiming exclusions. The major concern with the GATS is that national governments are by stealth losing control of their ability to set their own policies for public services in such areas as health, education and utilities provision (issues that will be taken up again in Chapter 5).

The Agreement on Trade-Related Aspects of Intellectual Property Rights (TRIPS) introduced intellectual property (IP) into the international trading system for the first time. This Agreement sets out the requirements that national laws must meet in relation to copyrights, patents, trademarks, industrial designs, computer software and plant varieties. Requirements are very stringent and subject to WTO arbitration and penalty procedures. The Agreement has been subject to sustained criticism on several grounds, most prominently in relation to the availability and high cost of drugs in less developed countries. Since the formation of WTO, there have been persistent campaigns by industry lobbyists to strengthen existing forms of IP protection and create new ones. (See further Chapter 5.)

The Agreement on Trade-Related Investment Measures (TRIMs) is of particular importance to developing countries, as it introduces limitations on measures they can use in their development policies. Measures that became prohibited include: local content requirements (the use of a certain amount of local inputs in production); trade-balancing requirements (requiring imports to be equivalent to a certain proportion of exports); and exchange restrictions (foreign exchange made available for imports to be a certain proportion of the value of foreign exchange brought in by the firm from exports).

How the Uruguay Round Trade Negotiations Were Conducted

Negotiations in the Uruguay Round extended over eight years (1986–94), and were the most comprehensive set of negotiations on international trade ever undertaken. No one involved in WTO trade negotiations believes they are conducted in accordance with the tenets of orthodox economic theory (despite the employment of the theory to justify the undertaking). On the contrary, almost everyone involved, trade economists, negotiators and diplomats, is agreed that they are conducted on mercantilist terms, vividly described by Nobel Laureate economist Paul Krugman as 'an increase in exports ... is a victory, and an increase in imports ... is a defeat.'[7] We are evidently a long way away from the world of Ricardo in which even a unilateral declaration of free trade is advantageous to the country making it.

In recent years there have been a number of studies of the decision-making processes in international organisations. In the case of the WTO it is generally agreed that the plenary sessions are conducted on the basis of the sovereign equality of nations, formally giving to each nation equal representation, participatory abilities, and decision-making power. Decisions in plenaries are reached by consensus, requiring that no country enters formal opposition to a motion. However smaller countries are often constrained in the use of opportunities provided in this forum. For them a specified trade liberalisation is more important as a percentage of their overall economy, and the internal possibilities for their economies larger, than is the case for larger countries, so that the need to close a deal is more urgent. And conversely, the threat of loss of exports is more compelling for smaller countries too. Thus are larger countries with larger economies already favoured by an open trading system. Furthermore small countries may not wish to get a reputation as being argumentative or obstructive in major international forums by too forcefully arguing there case.

Outside the plenaries, events lie further in powerful countries' favour. This is because the work in caucuses and working groups is convened and orchestrated by the major powers who dominate proposal development and the agenda-setting mechanisms – if for no other reason than the scale of resources they can bring to such tasks – and these become in the process difficult to amend. It is observed that initiatives of weaker countries 'have a habit of dying'. Thus beyond the plenaries a process of invisible weighting according to power and interest replaces the plenary posture of sovereign equality. The consensus would be that the powerful trading blocs, particularly the US and the EC, over the past 40–50 years have used their power to manipulate the negotiating processes in their own interests: a process that has been described as 'organized hypocrisy in the procedural context'.[8]

Nor should the coercion of smaller countries by the larger be seen as a minor or merely sometime matter. Often it involves direct threats by powerful countries to exit negotiations: to take their bat and ball and go elsewhere. In the early 1980s, when the EC and the US were unable to gain the necessary majority support over the objections of many countries for their wish to extend intellectual property protection within the World Intellectual Property Organization, they moved the issue to the GATT and engineered to have their wishes included in the TRIPs agreement in the Uruguay Round. And in the closing stages of the Uruguay Round itself, it became apparent that most developing countries were opposed to the GATS, TRIPS and TRIMs agreements, and were unlikely to sign up to them. US negotiators considered these to be crucial to US interests, and devised a strategy with the EC to overcome developing countries' opposition. This involved wording the draft Agreement establishing the WTO to express the notion that all agreements under negotiation would be bundled as an integral whole and 'binding on all Members' (rather than permitting separate accession as in the GATT). Further wording was included to indicate that for countries that did not accept the Final Act and join the WTO, the US and the EC would withdraw their obligations to these countries under the GATT (1947) commitments. In the event, the US/EC plan was tabled in the name of the WTO Director-General, as the secretariat's draft.[9]

It is no coincidence that the WTO was founded and its interests determined, in the high summer of the neoliberal ascendancy and of what became known as the 'Washington Consensus'. In their scope, intrusiveness, inflexibility and intent, the outcomes of the Uruguay Round and the processes of the WTO can be seen as a climax of the globalising neoliberal agenda. The point is important because the content of the Uruguay Round agreements have been taken as the base level from which all more recent regional and pluri-lateral trade agreements, including the TPP, have been negotiated.

And Who Benefited the Most?

The overall tenor of the Uruguay Round negotiations was one in which countries of the 'North' (the developed countries) were expected to reduce import barriers – particularly on textiles and agriculture which were of major importance to countries of the 'South' (the less developed countries) – while the South would adopt new regulations in such areas as services and intellectual property and patents, which would lead to increased sales opportunities for enterprises of the North in countries of the South. Despite optimistic statements from the WTO about the widespread benefits of the agreements that were concluded during the Round, among independent commentators considerable scepticism existed then, and remains the case.

Following the conclusion of the Round, when the score was totalled on market access concessions made by the North and made by the South, there appeared to be little surplus available to the South. The reductions in tariffs made by the South covered as large a share of their imports as was the case for the North, and their tariff cuts were deeper. Within the Agreement on Agriculture, countries of the North in many cases replaced existing quotas on goods from the South with tariff rates which either minimally reduced or actually increased the degree of protection. As for the matter of negotiated regulations the South appears to have been even more disadvantaged. Many of the regulations agreed upon approximated standards already existing in countries of the North, and any changes necessary would be relatively costless to make. However this was not so for countries of the South, many of which were required to set up new administrative systems to deal with issues ranging from customs valuations to patents and copyrights, and health and plant health requirements. Many less developed countries would find these to be hugely expensive, with no guarantee of ensuing benefits from increased trade.[10]

Estimates made by the United Nations Development Programme (UNDP) suggested that from the Uruguay Round the poorest countries of the world would be heavy net losers, with sub-Saharan Africa set to lose up to $1.2bn. A number of general equilibrium computer-modelling studies projected that benefits from the Uruguay Round would go disproportionately to developed countries, at least in the short run. Commentators external to the WTO described the outcome of the Round variously as 'lopsided', and as a 'bargain that is politically troubling and economically inane'.[11] The long-running and acrimonious nature of the subsequent trade negotiations under the Doha Round, commenced in 2001 and which have yet to be concluded, is no doubt in part a consequence of the unfairness felt by developing countries for their treatment in the Uruguay Round.[12]

Although economic theory is appealed to in international trade negotiations when convenient, it is not the main game, which is about power, both political and economic. The moral to this story from the WTO is that in these days there is little mercy in trade negotiations. Any country engaging in them, particularly if they are negotiating with large and powerful countries, needs to sup with a long spoon. Small countries may gain something, but they will be bargaining under the threat of power, and are likely to have to make disproportionate concessions and receive less than their due. As Joseph Stiglitz, former chief economist at the World Bank and Nobel Prize-winning economist identifies, so-called free trade agreements are not really what they say they are, for if they were they would be only a few pages long. With regard to the TPP in particular Stiglitz counselled New Zealand: 'Most of these free trade agreements are not good deals ... They're managed trade agreements and they're mostly managed for the advantage of the United States, which has the bulk of the negotiating power'.[13]

5

'Free Trade' – the TPP and Other Trade Deals

Liberalising Trade: Finding the Balance

Non-discriminatory trade agreements that involve the exchange of goods and services 'at the margin'[1] raise few policy or political questions. However laissez-faire trade deals in which the negotiated outcomes are likely to pervade many aspects of economic and social life within a country, and which are likely to have long-term and even inter-generational effects, need to be examined in forensic detail. In this regard the proposed Trans-Pacific Partnership (TPP) agreement is not a traditional merchandise-trade-at-the-border agreement but a proposal to restructure the internal workings of individual states in trade-facilitating form. From what is known of it, it has the capacity to alter the life and values that many New Zealanders hold important: values relating to the country's ability to make its own decisions and its own laws, to respond to crises, to determine the use of its own resources, to maintain environmental quality, biosecurity control, affordable health care, and to determine what is to be considered as fair and just. And it is a deal being negotiated in which overwhelming power rests with one participant. In these circumstances it is appropriate that in a democratic country citizens have the right to see and accept any proposed deal before it becomes law.

As already noted the idea of trade between countries is an important and valuable one. However the neoliberal view of ever freer trade is potentially dangerous. Consider the limiting situation in which all barriers are removed and the world has become one large free trade zone. The rules for such a zone (and there would need to be some) would require that each country had the same rules, and these would be dictated by the most powerful countries, such as the US and China. If a nation aspired to be different from other nations in ways that impact on its economy, then the notion of ever freer trade must be restrained at some point: some barriers or safeguards (laws, regulations, understandings of some sort) must be in place or put in place. This is not rocket science. To claim, as many laissez-faire economists do, that all such moves to establish or retain barriers are motivated by trade protectionism and therefore not to be tolerated, is to remain trapped in an ideological straitjacket that sees civilisation as a sub-category of economics. So an adequate approach to trade in general and the TPP in particular must be to find an appropriate balance – which barriers to remove and which to maintain or erect – in order to provide benefits from international trade while preserving other values and ideals which New Zealanders may wish to maintain or regain.

New Zealand has free trade agreements with a number of countries – Australia (the Closer Economic Relationship, or CER), Singapore, China, Hong Kong, Thailand, ASEAN, Malaysia – and it is currently negotiating others – with Korea, India, Russia, Belarus and Kazakhstan, and with the Gulf Cooperation Council.[2] Although we will concentrate our attention on the TPP because of its large scale and current urgency, the issues raised are relevant to all such bilateral and pluri-lateral agreements. The same yardstick might be put over the New Zealand-China Free Trade Agreement, for example. However discussion of the TPP must inevitably be constrained because the negotiations are proceeding behind closed doors and knowledge of its contents is limited. Nonetheless the task of criticism is not without resources. In particular we know that as a baseline all parties accept the content of the GATT/WTO agreements negotiated in the Uruguay Round, and that any further trade agreement will be 'WTO plus'. We know the content of recent regional free trade agreements such as the North American Free Trade Agreement (NAFTA) and the Australia-United States Free Trade Agreement (AUSFTA), and these agreements have been in place long enough for some assessment to be made of their outcomes. Here NAFTA is used as a comparative template for the TPP. In addition, draft chapters of the TPP which deal with some of its more contentious matters have been leaked to the public and also provide starting points for assessment.[3] Whether or not a TPP is finally agreed, or replaced by some other agreement, the issues raised here are of general importance for New Zealand's future.

NAFTA as a Free Trade Agreement

NAFTA is an agreement entered into by the governments of Canada, the US and Mexico, focused on expanding trade between these three countries. As these countries are now all parties to the TPP negotiations, NAFTA is likely to provide the baseline minimum content for any TPP agreement. The NAFTA was signed on 17 December 1992 and came into effect on 1 January 1994 (just prior to the Marrakesh Agreement that created the WTO), and in essence extended a pre-existing free trade agreement between the US and Canada. In particular the NAFTA included provisions concerning foreign investment and trade in services, and later – after the Uruguay Round and the formation of the WTO had been completed – it added provisions on intellectual property. All three of these issues have proved contentious within NAFTA. Political acceptance of NAFTA followed a stormy course in both Canada and the US. The US House of Representatives passed the necessary legislation after vigorous and at times bitter debate. However prior to sending the legislation to the US Senate, President Clinton introduced new clauses: one to protect US workers, and another requiring the US's partners to adhere to environmental practices and regulations similar to those in the US. This 'two bites at the cherry' approach shows power at work, and is one of the constraints under which other countries negotiate with the US.

After 20 years, the outcomes of NAFTA remain the subject of dispute.[4] It is evident that measured in terms of increased cross-border trade and investment, NAFTA has been successful. Quoted US goods exports to NAFTA countries totalled $411.5bn in 2010, up 190 per cent from 1993 (in current dollar terms); US imports from NAFTA totalled $506.1bn in 2010, up 235 per cent from 1993.[5] However such ambitious numbers must be treated with great circumspection as they are not corrected for inflation, and do not reflect the trade in finished as distinct from partly finished goods, nor the losses to trade of intra-country manufacture and sale, nor the indirect costs within the NAFTA countries, nor the extent of trade displaced from elsewhere, nor the effects on levels of employment.

A report from the Carnegie Endowment for International Peace assessed the outcomes of NAFTA for Mexico. It estimated that in the period between 1993 and 2007 Mexico's exports increased 311 per cent in real terms, with non-oil exports increasing 283 per cent. Most of this increase was in manufacturing which saw substantial productivity gains, due in particular to US companies relocating to Mexico. Foreign direct investment mainly from the US tripled but this was almost completely offset by a decline in domestic investment. In consequence, overall growth in GDP per capita over the period averaged only 1.6 per cent (one of the lowest in Latin America), in contrast to the average of 3.5 per cent over the period 1960–79. After an initial spike following the introduction of NAFTA, exports as a percentage of GDP have remained static since 1996, whereas imports have increased and the non-oil trade balance, already in deficit, has continued to decline (the overall trade balance has also been negative throughout the NAFTA period). Over this period Mexico experienced a gain of about 550,000 jobs in manufacturing, but suffered losses of perhaps 2.3 million elsewhere, particularly in agriculture, due to a surge in corn and other grain imports from the US. The manufacturing wages gap between Mexico and the US continues to widen, indicating that local workers have not benefited from the increases in productivity. Poverty has declined somewhat, but in rural areas poverty remains at over 55 per cent, and extreme poverty at 25 per cent. The report's authors refer to Mexico's experience of NAFTA as 'trade without development'.[6] Even strongly pro-NAFTA economists have described Mexican economic growth rates since NAFTA's inception as 'a disappointment'.[7] A twenty-year assessment of the effects of NAFTA on the economy of Mexico published in 2014 points to 'decades of economic failure by almost any economic or social indicator.'[8]

In Canada, criticisms of NAFTA have focused most intensely on the rights given to foreign investors, particularly in their ability to tie the hands of future Canadian governments (a subject of great relevance to the TPP).[9] In the US, economists at the Peterson Institute for International Economics projected that NAFTA would lead to a rising US trade surplus with Mexico which would lead to the creation of 170,000 US jobs.[10] In the event, a huge rise in imports from both Canada and Mexico led to large increases in the US trade deficit and substantial job *losses*, estimated by one group at about one million by 2004.[11] Wage rates in export-oriented sectors of the economy, traditionally higher than the national average, have been replaced by lower rates of pay.

A poll conducted by the respected Pew Research Center in 2010 showed that US citizens were increasingly sceptical about the impact of trade agreements such as NAFTA and the policies of the WTO. Roughly one third of those polled said that free trade agreements had been good for the US, while 44 per cent said they had been bad: the lowest level of support for such agreements in 13 years of Pew polling.[12] An Angus Reid Public Opinion Poll of May 2012 found that US respondents who believed the US should 'renegotiate' or 'leave' NAFTA outnumbered those who believed that the US should 'continue to be a member under the current terms' by four-to-one (55 vs 13 per cent, with 32 per cent 'unsure'), while the same poll found that for Canadians the ratio in favour of renegotiating or leaving NAFTA was nearly eighttoone (62 vs 8 per cent, with 30 per cent 'unsure').[13] Evidently NAFTA is an agreement that raised contentious issues which go to the heart of political and social choices in the countries involved. And despite bland assurances from the New Zealand government, the same is true of the TPP proposals.

The TPP

The Trans-Pacific Partnership (TPP) refers to negotiations among countries of the Pacific Rim, motivated by the idea of increasing laissez-faire trade, and which may lead to a formal agreement among them. At the APEC Leaders Summit of 2002 the governments of Chile, Singapore and New Zealand agreed to enter negotiations towards a Trans-Pacific Strategic Economic Partnership, and in this they were later joined by Brunei. This agreement (the TPSEP or P-4) was signed in 2005 and entered into force in 2006 (and for Brunei in 2009). At the time of signing it was agreed that negotiations over the vexed question of financial services and investment would be deferred for two years. In January 2008 the Bush administration in the US announced that it would join talks with P-4 members regarding the liberalisation of trade in financial services, and in September of that year made known that it would begin negotiations towards full P-4 membership, inviting Australia, Peru and Vietnam to join it in so doing. In January 2009 Barack Obama was inaugurated as US President, and the first round of expanded negotiations, scheduled for March 2009, was postponed until March 2010. In October 2010

Malaysia announced that it had joined the TPP negotiations, and in June 2012 Canada and Mexico did the same. The fifteenth round of negotiations was held in Auckland in December 2012, bringing together the 11 participants. In March 2013 Japan announced that it too would join the TPP negotiations.[14]

Table 1 gives summary information on the relative economic size of the 12 countries involved in the TPP negotiations. The US with a GDP in 2011 of US$14,991bn is first in world ranking of absolute size, while New Zealand with a GDP of US$163bn ranks fifty-third. If the US economy had a size of 100 units, the New Zealand economy would have a relative size of about one unit.

Table 1: Relative Economic Size of TPP Negotiating Countries

Country	GDP (2011) (US$bn)	World ranking	Relative size
USA	14,991	1	100
Japan	5,870	3	39
Canada	1,737	11	12
Australia	1,515	12	10
Mexico	1,155	14	8
Malaysia	288	35	2
Singapore	260	37	2
Chile	249	38	2
Peru	180	50	1
New Zealand	163	53	1
Vietnam	24	56	1
Brunei	16	111	<1

Source: UN Statistical Division, National Accounts Main Aggregates Database, December 2012.

Assessing the TPP

A tabulation of issues to be addressed in the TPP was published by the Peterson Institute for International Economics in 2012, based on a United States Trade Representative (USTR) document released by negotiators in November 2011.[15] This tabulation identified 20 specific issues and 4 cross-cutting ones, and indicated whether or not they were considered as 'mostly behind border' (that is issues addressing 'deep economic linkages which require coherent national regulations'), and whether they were likely to be 'controversial', 'highly controversial', or 'strongly opposed by some' among the negotiating countries. This tabulation highlights two points. First, the proportion of 'mostly behind border' issues is high, indicating the pervasive reach of the TPP into the heart of individual countries' economies and societies. Second, the tabulation shows that there are a number of issues likely to be controversial or highly controversial in the negotiations. In the following sections we discuss behind border issues most controversial from New Zealand's point of view.

Foreign investment: dispute resolution. The leaked draft of the TPP investment chapter posted on the web in June 2012[16] is a document of some 50 typed pages in length, which sets out the terms that would govern investments and financial transfers made between foreign investors and home parties. It includes such things as the definition of 'investor', explanations of what is meant by 'national treatment' and 'most-favoured nation treatment', of the 'performance requirements' required of each party to the investment, and the terms under which 'expropriation and compensation' would be legitimate. The second half of the document, Section B, relates to the proposed investor-state dispute settlement (ISDS) procedure and has provoked very serious concerns.

These concerns refer to the relationship between an overseas investor and the government of the recipient country. First, the definitions of 'investor' and 'investment' are remarkably broad. Second, the draft provides rights to foreign investors, not available to domestic investors, to sue governments outside of national court systems unconstrained by the rights of countries' constitutions, laws and domestic court procedures. It is proposed that arbitration of disputes in relation to the TPP be conducted within the frameworks provided by the World Bank or the United Nations, by tribunals which are constituted of private legal and trade specialists from countries other than those involved in the arbitration. Awards, made by panels of three arbitrators, can be in the form of monetary damages (with interest where appropriate) and/or the restitution of property, and final awards are not appealable to any other legal body. Within the context of what is known of the TPP, and what is certainly true of NAFTA, the disputes procedure exposes recipient country governments to compensation demands from foreign investors where changes in domestic or foreign policy (for example changes in laws or regulations) undermine the 'expectations' of the foreign investors, or go against the 'expected' level of regulatory scrutiny. Thus governments of countries hosting foreign investments under a TPP agreement could be exposed to unlimited monetary and other damages which, in the end, must be met by taxpayers.[17]

It needs to be emphasised too that whereas under WTO rules, disputes procedures take place between states, in the TPP it is proposed that disputes procedures will take place between states on the one hand and corporations on the other, which latter are neither signatories to any international agreements nor democratic in their outlook.

Foreign investment: New Zealand's resource development and environmental quality. The ways in which ISDS issues may arise under the TPP in relation to environmental quality can be illustrated by two cases that have arisen under NAFTA. Both involve US companies and the government of Canada.[18]

MMT is a synthetic chemical containing manganese and used for octane enhancement in unleaded petrol. It has been exported from the US to Canada by the Virginia-based company Ethyl Corporation since 1977. The Canadian government, in response to concerns that MMT may increase hydrocarbon emissions from cars and observations that manganese was neurotoxic at high concentrations, in 1996 introduced legislation banning the import of MMT. In response Ethyl Corporation submitted a claim under NAFTA that the government of Canada had breached its obligations, and sought damages of $201m. As Health Canada investigations were unable to show any evidence of health effects due to manganese in automobile exhaust fumes, the case was decided in favour of Ethyl. The Canadian government thereby repealed its import ban and settled with Ethyl for $13m. This case highlights the question: Who should decide the legitimacy of a country's precautionary approach to the health and well-being of its citizens? It also brings into focus the intimidatory aspect of exorbitant damages claims made by large corporations against governments and how they might be inclined to deal with them. (As a footnote to this case, the EU in 2009 passed a law requiring the phasing out of the use of MMT on the grounds of the risk to human health, and the validity of this law was upheld in 2010 by the European Court of Justice.[19])

In a more contemporary case, the provincial government of Quebec in June 2011 introduced a moratorium on the practice of hydraulic fracturing (or 'fracking') of underground rocks to extract natural gas, so that they could carry out an environmental impact assessment of the practice accused of leaching chemicals and gases into groundwater and into the air. Lone Pine Resources, a Delaware-headquartered gas and oil exploration and production company, had plans and permits to engage in fracking over 30,000 acres of land directly beneath the St Lawrence River. In November 2012 the company served the Government of Canada with notice that it would be submitting a claim to arbitration under Chapter 11 of the NAFTA, 'for the arbitrary, capricious, and illegal revocation of the Enterprise's valuable right to mine for oil and gas under the St. Lawrence River by the Government of Quebec without due process, without compensation, and with no cognizable public purpose.' And the company intends to seek damages in excess of CA$250m.[20]

There are numerous similar situations that could arise in New Zealand which would expose the New Zealand government and taxpayers to claims under the terms of a TPP agreement. These include all issues involving New Zealand government laws or regulations to alleviate air, water, solid waste pollution or the promotion of clean energy, not in place when a TPP agreement would come into force. One might think in terms of the regulation of run-off from dairy farms, the use of pesticides, of emissions from factory chimneys, requirements to install insulation in buildings, for example. Again, consider agricultural water use. Commercial, industrial and domestic water users in New Zealand increasingly have to pay for water they use, but farmers are able to use water sources flowing through their land for free. This arrangement has been criticised by the OECD. If New Zealand were to adopt the OECD recommendation of pricing agricultural water usage at some date after the coming into force of a TPP agreement, overseas investors would likely be able to claim compensation for their financial loss.[21] And again, changes to New Zealand's quarantine and biosecurity laws may fall under the same threat.[22]

On 15 January 2014 WikiLeaks made available a leaked version of the Report from the Chairs for the Environmental Chapter of the TPP, together with a proposed 'Consolidated Text', dated 24 November 2013.[23] These documents reinforce the environmental concerns just expressed. The Consolidated Text has been described as 'vague, weak', and is replete with evasive clauses and caveats. It gives little confidence that environmental values will be given just weight in any TPP agreement. Of matters yet to be resolved at that date, Australia and the US objected to the wording linking trade and climate change, the US did not agree with the Article on trade and biodiversity because it was not a party to the Convention on Biological Diversity, and there was no consensus on how a TPP would accommodate the provisions of existing multilateral environmental agreements (such as the Convention on International Trade in Endangered Species, the Ramsar Convention on Wetlands, and the International Whaling Convention).

Competition: agriculture and the power of the US farm lobby. Currently the United States is New Zealand's third most important individual market for agricultural exports (after Australia and China), with major agricultural exports to the US being beef, dairy products and lamb, and with horticultural products of increasing importance. In return, the US is New Zealand's second-largest source of agricultural imports, behind Australia.

Contestation in the TPP negotiations over dairy issues has been anticipated on both sides.[24] But what can realistically be expected? In January 2010 the US National Milk Producers Federation (NMPF) provided comments to the Office of the USTR concerning the TPP negotiations.[25] The NMPF appealed for the 'total exclusion of all U.S.-New Zealand dairy trade under this TPP'. Their argument was based on the idea that 'we simply cannot compete against the uniquely anti-competitive situation in New Zealand whereby one company there controls over 90 per cent of the country's milk production and more than 40 per cent of global dairy trade in key product areas.'[26] The NMPF estimated that with complete removal of tariffed dairy import quotas, US dairy farmers' revenues would plunge by $20bn over 10 years, and that 'a large quantity of dairy farmers, totalling several thousand of them, mostly smaller and medium family farms, would be forced out of business by the end of this period ...'. In March 2010, 30 US Senators wrote to USTR Ron Kirk making the same claims, and concluding that 'an expansion of U.S.-New Zealand dairy trade would further open the U.S. to these imports while providing little additional market for American farmers in New Zealand and the other Pacific countries.' Signatories to the letter included every Senator, both Republican and Democrat (with one exception), from the six states that provide the majority of dairy production in the US, and included the 2013 Chair of the Senate Agriculture Committee. In May 2010 the American Farm Bureau Federation, the US premier farm lobby group, together with 19 other agricultural producer organisations, wrote to the chief agricultural negotiator at the USTR, and the Under Secretary of the US Department of Agriculture, urging that the Administration not reopen any trade agreements with countries that would become part of the TPP. This move was an attempt to foreclose any reconsideration of dairy quotas already agreed.[27] Notwithstanding the hyperbole associated with vested interest lobbying, this is heavy hitting.

With the entry into the TPP negotiations of Canada and Japan in 2012 and 2013 respectively, and the potential opportunities thus opened, the US dairy industry switched to adopting a more accommodating approach to the negotiations. Nonetheless their key demand remains 'reform of government advantages driving global control' which is spelled out as addressing 'the anti-competitive New Zealand dairy industry structure as a vital precursor to any expansion of U.S.-New Zealand dairy trade by lowering the level of market concentration afforded to one New Zealand dairy company.'[28] Given the emphasis placed by President Obama on US employment in his 2013 State of the Union address and what is known of the manner in which the US conducts trade negotiations, it appears that any gain in access by New Zealand to the US dairy market will be bought at substantial cost to this or other of New Zealand's key interests.

Cross-border services and government procurement: health and access to medicines. The GATS agreement negotiated during the GATT/WTO Uruguay Round and subsequently refined, provides the point of departure for all more recent multi-lateral trade agreements in relation to services. As noted previously, the GATS covers any service in any sector excepting only those services supplied in the exercise of governmental authority where this exception means 'any service, which is supplied neither on a commercial basis, nor in competition with one or more service suppliers'. This, it has been claimed by the

WTO and others, excludes public services from the GATS, and does not require their privatisation. However the GATS agreement does not define 'commercial' or 'competition', and it might well be argued to the contrary that in many cases public utilities such as water and electricity are provided 'on a commercial basis'; and the same might be said of educational and medical services, and even environmental services (such as paid access to national parks). There is however little case law on the matter at present. Monitoring processes involved in the GATS and the stated purposes of its continuing working groups implicitly point to private provision of public services, including health services, as a goal.[29] And this is a goal that has been taken up by pluri-lateral trade agreements such as NAFTA that have followed the GATS. Here we look specifically at the New Zealand government procurement of pharmaceuticals and the forces being brought to bear for change under the TPP.

New Zealand's Pharmaceutical Management Agency (PHARMAC) was established in 1993 with the responsibility of managing the government's expenditure on subsidies for pharmaceuticals used in the community and on the procurement of pharmaceuticals provided to patients for use while in hospital. One of its main roles is to manage the Pharmaceutical Schedule, the list of pharmaceutical compounds and other products that are to be provided to the community on a subsidised basis. PHARMAC's decision criteria for placing items on the Schedule are set out in its Operating Policies and Procedures.[30] By using a system of reference pricing, bulk purchase, and a cost-effectiveness test on any proposal for amendment to the Schedule, PHARMAC has been very successful in keeping the costs of drugs to New Zealanders below those in many other countries. Since its inception, PHARMAC has survived major health system reforms and its decisions have been overruled by government on only two occasions.[31]

A US Embassy cable from Wellington in 2006 made available through WikiLeaks indicates the interest of US in 'pressuring

Pharmac'.[32] In its submission to the USTR in relation to its *2012 Special 301 Report* (of which more below), the Pharmaceutical Research and Manufacturers of America (PhRMA) drew attention to New Zealand and PHARMAC, pointed to their concerns over pending amendment to the New Zealand Patents Act, over government pricing and reimbursement, over the government's Biotechnology Taskforce recommendations (2003), stated that PhRMA member companies were advocating key health policy reforms in New Zealand under 10 different headings, and requested that the USTR place New Zealand on its Priority Watch List.[33] This last the USTR declined to do, but did note in its Report that PhRMA expressed 'concerns regarding, among other things, the lack of transparency, fairness, and predictability of the PhARMAC [sic] pricing and reimbursement regime, as well as the negative aspects of the overall climate for innovative medicines in New Zealand'.[34]

'Big Pharma' is powerful juggernaut. Six of the world's 12 largest healthcare companies are based in the US (Johnson & Johnson, Pfizer, Abbott Laboratories, Merck & Co., Eli Lilly, Bristol-Myers Squib), and each of these has annual revenues of over $18bn (each of the top two have revenues of over $50bn). These are monopolies and oligopolies in product markets, have great power to control markets to their own and shareholders' advantage, and are strongly motivated to increase the rents received from patented products by whatever means available.

According to the non-partisan Center for Responsive Politics, US pharmaceutical companies spent $900m on lobbying between 1998 and 2005, during which time they also donated $89.9m to US federal candidates and political parties.[35] The finessing of laws and regulations by Big Pharma, their widespread manipulations, deceptions, dishonesty and law-breaking are well documented and need not be retailed here.[36] Suffice to note in passing, as doctor and former editor of the prestigious *New England Journal of Medicine* Marcia Angell does, that in the brief period from 2000 to 2003, nearly every major pharmaceutical company went before state tribunals in the US accused of malpractice. The charges included defrauding Medicare and Medicaid by billing at inflated prices, giving kickbacks to providers, anti-competitive practices, and marketing drugs for unapproved uses. Eight of these companies were fined a total of over $2.2bn, and four of these eight pleaded guilty to criminal charges.[37] New Zealanders should be under no illusions that Big Pharma is primarily interested in improving their health.

A leaked US TPP negotiating text dealing with transparency and procedural fairness for healthcare technologies proposes a set of conditions that would undermine PHARMAC's ability to negotiate bulk discounts for medicines, require PHARMAC to give detailed reasons to pharmaceutical companies about purchasing decisions, give these companies rights to appeal PHARMAC decisions, and require PHARMAC to publish the identities of all decision makers.[38] On the contrary, New Zealand is a small country with limited means, and does not need to be told how to run its pharmaceuticals policies for the benefit of its citizens. And if PHARMAC is placed under such attack, might not the Accident Compensation Corporation be a future target?

In November 2012, when asked about the position of PHARMAC in the TPP negotiations, Prime Minister Key could only manage that it would be 'not a good look' if New Zealand made concessions that undermined the status of its drug-buying agency.[39] In August 2013 Key was reported as saying that PHARMAC may not escape unscathed from US pressure during the negotiations but also that the government would not sign up to anything 'not in the country's best interest'.[40] In October 2013 Trade Minister Groser said 'categorically Pharmac is not on the table'.[41] The real question would seem to be: Is half of PHARMAC PHARMAC?

To return briefly to the issue of investor-state dispute settlement. In November 2012 Big Pharma company Eli Lilly initiated formal proceedings under NAFTA against the Canadian government's refusal to grant it a patent for its drug Strattera (used to treat attention deficit hyperactivity disorder, ADHD) on the basis of insufficient evidence. The company is claiming reparations of $100m. This is the first attempt by a patent-holding pharmaceutical company to extend its patent privileges under a free-trade agreement. However in its formal Notice of Intent, Eli Lilly has made it clear that it is not only challenging the invalidation of this particular patent refusal, but the entire doctrine under which the Canadian government determines patent validity.[42]

Intellectual property: copyright, patents. The term 'intellectual property' (IP) covers a range of issues relating to copyright, patents and trademarks. These identify the terms under which creators of an intellectual innovation (an invention, a work of art) can receive financial benefit from their creation and restrict its use by others. Copyrights and patents are commonly granted for a fixed period of time, and after the expiration of this period the innovation enters the public domain and is available to others for copy and reuse without charge. This expanded usage also makes its own contribution to future innovation. The central issue for a country's IP law is to strike the appropriate balance between the wish of the creator to be adequately compensated, and the interests of society in promoting innovation in science and arts more generally through the free use of what has already been created.

The pursuit of augmented intellectual property rights for US individuals and corporations is one of the US's primary trade considerations. To this end the USTR has since 1989 been required under Section 301 of the Trade Act of 1974 to prepare annually a *Special 301 Report* which identifies barriers in other countries' IP laws, names the delinquent countries, and in serious cases initiates the pursuit of sanctions against them under WTO/TRIPS, NAFTA or other trade agreement. The provisions of 'Special 301' reporting have been described by one commentator as 'a public law devoted to the service of private corporate interests'.[43]

Three versions of the US proposals for an IP chapter within the TPP are currently available.[44] The texts require that TPP countries accept the WTO/TRIPS agreement as baseline for IP claims, and calls for even 'more extensive protection and enforcement' of IP rights against the public interest. In what follows we concentrate on the issues of copyright of importance to New Zealand and raised in the US text – namely copyright terms, parallel importing, and IT issues – while noting that issues of patents raise similar concerns.

The current baseline constraints on copying rights found in multilateral treaties are those contained in the WTO/TRIPS agreement, which provides for a minimum copyright term for literary and artistic works based on the life of the creator plus 50 years, and for cinematographic or anonymous works a minimum term of 50 years after the work is made available to the public. In the TPP text the US proposes to extend the copyright term to life plus 70 years for works by individuals, and to 95 years after publication or 120 years after creation, for corporately owned works. However there is no evidence that extending copyright to such lengths of time has any effect in encouraging innovation, and apart from excluding access by others merely provides rents to large media companies and other copyright owners.

A parallel import is a non-counterfeit product imported from another country without the permission of the intellectual property owner. A parallel import restriction on a product means that a manufacturer or distributor can sets different prices for the product in different markets. Without such a restriction industries and consumers can take advantage of lower prices in whatever market to which they have access. This is an important issue for New Zealand, as being relatively isolated and with a small consumer market, pricing decisions taken elsewhere are often to our disadvantage. A study by the Productivity Commission in Australia found that in the case of books, Australian parallel import restrictions made books considerably more expensive and recommended the abolition of the practice.[45] Currently, parallel importing of books is permitted in New Zealand, but since 2003 that of films has not been. The US position vis-à-vis the TPP as far as is known is to prohibit all parallel importing.

Information available suggests that the US is adopting a very restrictive position on IT matters.[46] Included are limitations on the temporary reproductions of copyrighted works (including reproductions of files held temporarily in computer RAM during routine operations); requirements for ISPs to monitor internet activity for copyright breaches; and the patenting of computer software.[47]

In response to the leaked US IP texts, a group of lawyers from the American University Washington College of Law, the Yale Law School and the Northeastern University School of Law provided an analysis of their contents.[48] They observed that the proposed US IP chapter greatly exceeded the imperfect but more balanced provisions codified in the 1994 WTO/TRIPS agreement; that the provisions of the TPP proposals are inconsistent with the current laws in every TPP member country for which public analysis is available including the US itself; and that the proposals are particularly inappropriate for developing countries where the risks and effects of exclusionary pricing by foreign monopolists are most acute. The lawyers concluded that if the US proposals were adopted, they would create the highest intellectual property protection and enforcement standards in any free trade agreement to date, and lead to higher prices and decreased access to a broad range of consumer products in many TPP member countries, with little or no benefit to any TPP member in the form of increased innovation, creativity or local economic activity.

Financial services: market openness and catastrophe risk. The free flow of money capital between countries has always been part of the neoliberal ideal of free trade and a globalised economy, and capital market liberalisation has consistently been one of the suite of IMF policies – the so-called 'Washington Consensus' policies – demanded of distressed countries in return for receiving IMF loans.

And the WTO has, through the GATS, put substantial limitations on individual countries' abilities to control the import and export of capital. In pursuit of the same free trade ideal, New Zealand has dismantled almost all of its mechanisms for the control of capital movements in and out of the country. As a consequence of this lack of financial control, and quite remarkably, the New Zealand dollar has been in recent years the world's tenth most traded currency.[49] As New Zealand requires only modest funds to carry out its proper international business, we may be sure that the majority of these trades are due to international currency hedging and speculation. With such large amounts of money washing in and out of the country in search of short-term profit, the value of the New Zealand dollar is potentially subject to wide fluctuations. This situation exposes the New Zealand economy to dangerous and perhaps catastrophic risk. Any TPP agreement is likely to lock in even further this feckless system of uncontrolled international capital movement to New Zealand's detriment.

The dangers of unregulated capital flows were exposed by the East Asian economic crisis of 1997–98, at that time the most serious financial crisis since the 1930s. Subsequent analyses of the events surrounding this crisis identified a variety of causative influences, but one consistent finding has been the identification of financial deregulation as a major factor in permitting the rapid unsupervised flows of huge volumes of speculative funds in and out of vulnerable countries. And indeed it is widely considered that the IMF's actions exacerbated the crisis.[50] Those Asian countries that escaped the crisis relatively unscathed – such as China and India – were those that had in place, or introduced, regulation of their international financial transfers. Nowadays most countries have floating rather than fixed exchange rates, but this does not remove the very substantial damage that large speculative flows of short-term funds can wreak on small economies.

As a matter of observational fact, there has never been any evidence that the liberalisation of international capital flows contributes to economic development and growth: that policy appears to have been motivated solely by ideological considerations, promoted particularly by the US.[51] In early 2012, over 100 distinguished economists from the TPP negotiating countries sent a letter to their trade ministers warning that if recent US treaties were taken as a model for the TPP, this would unduly limit the authorities in participating parties to prevent and mitigate financial crises. The economists pointed to US and IMF research identifying the importance of limiting short-term capital flows as a possible pre-emptive measure against dangerous asset bubble formation and currency appreciations, and recommending that this ability not be removed.[52] In late 2012 the IMF, in a major ideological shift, issued an institutional statement accepting for the first time the use of direct controls on cross-border capital flows as a means of dampening financial volatility.[53] This statement by the IMF puts it at odds with the US government's position in relation to the TPP, which appears to remain intransigent in its rejection of capital controls.

So what lessons have been learned by New Zealand as a consequence of the accumulated experience of financial crises in recent years? Apparently none: New Zealand remains one of the most financially exposed countries on earth.

Would a TPP agreement provide jobs and economic growth? There is one known and publicly available economic analysis of the estimated economic benefits of the TPP, prepared by a group from the Peterson Institute for International Economics and the East-West Center in the US and published originally in 2012.[54] This study is based on a mathematical simulation model of the world economy split into 24 regions and 18 economic sectors. By making assumptions about the initial states of these economies and the progress and outcomes of the TPP trade negotiations and their implementation it is possible, using the model, to project the course of these economies into the future. As the model is constructed at this high level of generality and involves projections into the medium-term future, many assumptions have to be made in order for the model to make its projections.

The future scenarios envisaged in the study involved the evolution of negotiating 'tracks' extending to the year 2020. The 'Trans-Pacific track' involved the then (2012) nine TPP negotiators – to be joined, it was assumed, in 2014 by Canada, Japan, South Korea and Mexico – and envisaged a progression to a more comprehensive agreement involving all these parties by 2020. (Allied with this, the model also explored a parallel 'Asian track' of free trade agreement which commenced from the existing bilateral trade agreements between Asian countries, and the China-Japan-South Korea agreement, and extended to cover other ASEAN economies as negotiations continued up until 2020.) It was then hypothesised that the two tracks would conjoin into a grand Free Trade Area of the Asia Pacific after 2020. The model calculations yielded positive dollar values for increases in GDP for both the Trans-Pacific track and the Asian track under the scenarios considered.

Despite the mathematical sophistication of the model, its thrust is not very different from that of Ricardo's analysis that was considered in Chapter 4. The model calculates dollar increases in GDP due to the expansion of trade, referring to these as 'welfare gains', without consideration of the collateral costs. Such a description of welfare gains, while being standard economics technique, might more broadly be perceived as disingenuous. (It is particularly these collateral costs that need consideration if any TPP agreement were in the end to show overall benefits for New Zealand.) Furthermore the model as such tells us little about future employment, for the reason that the model assumes that full employment is maintained: to consider employment per se, further assumptions have to be made about the future course of productivity in the various economies.

The economic analysis by the Peterson Institute was reviewed by the New Zealand Institute of Economic Research (NZIER) on behalf of the NZ-US Council, in order to identify the New Zealand component of the Trans-Pacific negotiating track.[55] The NZIER extracted from the model scenarios the value of the TPP for New Zealand as rising over time from US$300m in 2015 to US$1.7bn in 2025, assuming convergence of the two 'tracks' by 2020. These may seem large numbers, but represent just 0.2 and 0.8 per cent of New Zealand GDP as projected by the model. In 2012 the savings achieved by PHARMAC through its drug purchasing policies was US$1.3bn.[56]

Mathematical models of economies are a useful way of organising thought, but beyond that their use is rather limited. The NZIER in their review say of the model: 'It is important to recognise that this is – after all – just a modelling exercise. It won't provide all the answers about the impacts of TPP that interested parties might be seeking. It is not designed to influence negotiators' positions on key aspects of the agreement'. Both the NZIER review and the US authors of the original economic model set out their respective caveats in page-long texts. However in neither case is recognition given either to costs of the TPP as distinct from the benefits, or to the possibility that there might be physical limitations to the natural resources available in New Zealand to be put to achieving the hypothesised benefits.

The problems surrounding such model calculations are exemplified by experience from the AUSFTA negotiations. In the lead-up to AUSFTA the Australian Department of Foreign Affairs and Trade commissioned the Centre for International Economics to analyse the economic impacts on Australia of the likely agreement. They reported an annual benefit of around AU$4bn, largely due to benefits from improved access to the US sugar market. When the agreement was announced and no improved US access to Australian sugar had been negotiated, the Centre prepared a new analysis which showed *increased* benefits, with the loss from sugar more than offset by the inclusion of speculative assumptions about the reduced costs of capital.[57] Four other studies carried out at the same time – by the IMF, ACIL Tasman, the NIEIR and Dr Dee of the Australian National University – found that the AUSFTA would have little or no impact on Australia, or would be bad for the Australian economy. The direst estimate was that AUSFTA could cost the Australian economy up to AU$50bn per annum and 200,000 jobs.[58] In the event, the bilateral trade gap between Australia and US has widened every year since the inception of AUSFTA in January 2005.[59] In 2012 US goods and services exports to Australia totalled US$48bn while imports from Australia totalled US$16bn, a deficit for the year for the Australian economy of US$32bn.[60] The Australian Productivity Commission in 2010 published a research report on a wide range of bilateral and regional trade agreements to which Australia was party, and found that although they can reduce trade barriers and help meet other objectives, their potential impact was limited and that other options may often be more cost-effective. Furthermore, as the Commission noted, current processes for assessing and prioritising such trade agreements lacked transparency and tended to oversell the likely benefits (as has been seen here in the cases of both NAFTA and AUSFTA).[61]

With regard to the TPP, the May 2012 NZIER review of the basic Peterson Institute model suggested that the benefits to New Zealand could be of the order of US$1.7bn in 2025. By the end of 2012 Prime Minister Key was promoting a value to New Zealand of US$2.9bn by 2025, although it was unclear how that number was arrived at. Subsequent analyses by the Peterson Institute which included both Japan and South Korea as negotiating countries augmented the estimated value to New Zealand to US$4.5bn, including US$3.1 in income gains direct from trade, and US$1.4bn in indirect effects of FDI. These figures appear to underlie Trade Minister Groser's October 2013 supposition of US$4.1bn in benefits to New Zealand by 2025.[62] As we have already noted, such figures are specious, particularly as they make no accounting for costs. A review of the Peterson Institute modelling carried out for the Sustainability Council of New Zealand, which tried to assess both the benefits *and* the costs of the TPP for New Zealand, estimated the net economic benefits to be less than a quarter of those claimed.[63]

Government Approval of a TPP Agreement

The legal position in New Zealand for the making of treaties has been set out by lawyer Jane Kelsey.[64] Contrary to the beliefs of many politicians, lobbyists and commentators, Parliament does not have the power to make treaties, which resides with the Executive, that is, the Cabinet. As the Cabinet Manual makes clear, Cabinet approval of the signing of an agreed agreement text by the responsible Minister is the definitive step that binds the government to act in good faith towards its negotiating partners and constitutes a 'good faith obligation' under international law. If Parliament were to be invited to vote on a TPP agreement, this would be merely a symbolic gesture. As Kelsey notes, successive governments have blocked changes to parliamentary standing orders and legislation proposed by minor parties that would have given Parliament a stronger role in approving treaties. In the case of a TPP agreement, implementation in New Zealand may require changes to New Zealand law, but because of the constraints imposed by international law there will be no parliamentary opportunity to modify the agreement itself.

Given the manner in which the concerns of the TPP pervade many aspects of individual, community and national life, the legal situation in relation to the ratification of the TPP can be viewed as an unwarranted limitation of democratic process. In this respect it is relevant to note that in the US the power to make treaties also rests with the Executive, in this case the President, but he or she can only exercise this power with the support of a two-thirds vote in the Senate. In the UK, treaty ratification is a Royal Prerogative, but the treaty must be placed before Parliament 21 days prior to ratification. In Japan, treaty ratification requires the approval of both Houses of Parliament (although things get more complicated if the Upper House rejects a treaty approved by the Lower House).[65]

TPP: an Overview

All the participants in the TPP negotiations are members of the WTO, and thus their trade relations are already highly liberalised in relation to merchandise trade, trade in services and foreign investment. Furthermore, the participants are already associated in a web of bilateral and pluri-lateral trade agreements including the CER, ASEAN, AUSFTA, NAFTA and others. In order to be meaningful, each trade agreement needs to go further than its predecessors. In existing trade agreements New Zealand has yielded up many rights and privileges for the projected benefits of increased trade. What remains to be given up in trade negotiations will now be cutting to the quick of those things that New Zealanders value dearly. As this chapter has suggested, this may include loss of control in situations of economic crisis, loss of control of decision making in relation to resources and environment, the exposure of taxpayers to unlimited litigation from overseas investors, higher costs for social services and in particular for medicines and medical care, and a narrowing of public interest access to copyrighted and patented materials.[66]

What started out as a modest trade pact among a number of small Pacific nations has become a mega pact involving two of the world's largest economies and global powers, Japan and the US. It is shaping up not as a 'free trade' agreement, but as an 'investor rights' agreement. On past experience it will be the potential gains and losses for these largest countries (perhaps with Canada in addition) which will determine the shape and content of the final draft pact document. It is without doubt the entry of Japan and Canada into the negotiations that precipitated the reversal of policy of the US agricultural lobby towards the content of the TPP, but with no diminution of their intransigence towards the organisation of the New Zealand dairy industry. With the entry into the negotiations of these two economic powers New Zealand's proper interests are likely to be further marginalised.

New Zealand, while coming to terms with the realities of relative power, does not have to have its trading fate determined wholly by others. Moreover, it is possible for smaller countries to negotiate trade deals with countries, particularly regional countries, of roughly equal power. This is a move becoming increasingly adopted, particularly among developing and middle-income countries as they seek to avoid unreasonable impositions by the wealthy and the powerful (and of the international trade and financial organisations). Nor should New Zealand subscribe to what might be called the lemming theory of trade negotiation – that if other small countries kowtow to the powerful then New Zealand must do the same. Not all countries have, or should have, the same aspirations. To decline one set of opportunities is to be open to others. When in 1984 New Zealand's Prime Minister David Lange barred nuclear-powered and nuclear-armed ships from using New Zealand ports or entering New Zealand waters, the sky did not fall, nor the world end.

The unalloyed virtues of the TPP have been loudly and persistently proclaimed by New Zealand neoliberals and supporters of laissez-faire trade. We have taken a more sceptical view, arguing in favour of reasoned limits to the idea of 'free trade'. The laissez-faire view is undiscriminating, short-sighted, and does not respond to the real complexities of trade issues or to New Zealand's best interests. Furthermore the curse that is laid upon open discussion of the TPP by a secrecy that permits citizens no access to its terms until after it is signed diminishes us all.

At the end of Chapter 4 we quoted from an interview with economist Joseph Stiglitz in which he said that free trade agreements were really just managed agreements for the benefit of the United States, which has most of the negotiating power. In that same interview he went on to say: 'So one can't think that New Zealand would ever get anything that it cares about', adding the warning: 'You'll lose'.[67]

Part III

THE FUTURE

6

Public Goods and the Common Good

The Issue

The economies of the world face major and novel challenges in the years and decades ahead. These relate in particular to natural resources availability and the degradation of the environment, climate change, and the surging increase of population globally and of population ageing in developed countries. Responding adequately to these challenges will require substantial changes in economic policies, social organisation, and individual conduct.

An important characteristic of these twenty-first-century challenges is that they are of substantial scale: geographically they can extend across the world, temporally they can involve extended and even inter-generational time scales, and they can involve uncertainties well beyond the abilities of science to measure or reduce. Furthermore the matters at issue do not involve private goods that are commonly traded in markets, but 'public goods', for which there are, in general, no natural markets. They fit poorly within a free market paradigm of economics based on private ownership, full information, competition and change at the margin. As philosopher, business magnate and philanthropist George Soros observed: 'Markets are designed to allow individuals to look after their private needs and to pursue profit. It's really a great invention and I wouldn't under-estimate the value of that, but they're not designed to take care of social needs'[1], that is, to take care of public goods and the common good. In this chapter we step through the issues raised by market failure in the face of social needs and the manner in which they need to be dealt with in the twenty-first century. The dominant theme that emerges is the importance to be attached to cooperation rather than competition.

Public Goods and Externalities

Orthodox economics makes a distinction between public goods and private goods. Private goods are the commerce of market exchange between producers and consumers, and include the weekly groceries, a pair of shoes, whitegoods, petrol and oil for the car, a new house. In such cases the property rights are well defined, even if the house buyer takes out a mortgage. As economists describe them, private goods have the properties of being 'rivalrous' and 'excludable' in consumption. A good is rivalrous in consumption if one person's consumption of it precludes another's, and is excludable in consumption if it is possible to prevent other individuals or groups from consuming it. If I buy a steak pie, it is my property and not yours (it is excludable), and if I eat it for lunch you cannot have it for dinner (it is rivalrous). Pure public goods, on the other hand, are both non-rivalrous and non-excludable.[2] National defence is the archetypal example of a pure public good. Once it is provided, I cannot be excluded from its services (it is non-excludable), and your consumption of its services does not change my own (it is non-rivalrous). Other examples of pure public goods include law enforcement, air pollution control, disease control, quarantine control, flood control, street lighting, building and development control. Education and health, while being mainly private goods, also have public goods characteristics, as improvements in either contribute to the overall well-being and quality of society. In all these cases private property rights are either undefinable, or if defined are partial and incomplete, and the simple idea of market transaction and exchange is vitiated.

In a purely market system public goods will always be undersupplied by private entrepreneurs. This is because the property of non-excludability prevents entrepreneurs from receiving due payment for the good or service from those who use it. Consider the private provision of street lighting. Although a private entrepreneur may have been engaged by the residents of the area to provide lighting, non-residents who use the area at night also benefit but avoid payment, to such a degree that the lighting system installed may be inferior or not provided at all, even if demand for the system among residents is extensive and strong. Nor is it easy to determine the real willingness of non-residents to pay for the street lighting – and hence enable the optimal level of street lighting to be provided – as they may understate their true willingness to pay. 'Free riding' is the term applied to individuals who pay less than their fair share of the cost of providing a public good, or consume more than their fair share of a public good when it is provided. And just as there are public goods, there are also 'public bads', such as crime, pollution discharges and epidemic diseases, which in a purely market system will be over-provided, for the same reason that public goods are underprovided, namely that those responsible are not called upon to pay the full social cost of their activities.

Closely related to the idea of a public good is that referred to by economists as an 'external effect', or 'externality'. An external effect exists where the activities of a producer or consumer affect the production of other producers or the utilities of other consumers, but the effect is not valued in the market or otherwise compensated for. External effects can be positive as in the street lighting example, where the non-residents benefit but do not pay, or where R&D knowledge transfers from one company to another that did not pay for the research. Beekeeping, busking and gardens provide positive externalities. Many externalities are negative and involve the environment – for example road congestion, polluting discharges to the air, water and land, and loud rock music in residential neighbourhoods.

The mixed economy approach to dealing with a negative external effect is to try to internalise the cost to the person responsible for it, in order to bring the private cost into line with the full social cost. This is the substance of the 'Polluter Pays Principle' endorsed by the OECD back in 1975. Let us consider for argument's sake the case of a fertiliser factory emitting waste chemicals into the atmosphere and which affect the health of people in communities downwind from the factory. With no pollution abatement, market equilibrium is established at a level of output and a level of pollution that is higher than would be socially optimal. The 'traditional' mixed economy approach requires the government to impose a tax on the pollution emitted by the factory. This would increase the unit cost of production, raise the price of the fertiliser, lessen the amount of fertiliser bought and to that extent curtail the atmospheric pollution. The basics can be shown in a simple diagram (Figure 1). The horizontal axis shows the amount of pollution put into the atmosphere (increasing to the right), the vertical axis shows marginal cost[3] in dollars. MAC represents the marginal abatement cost faced by the factory owner assumed to rise to higher values the greater the level of abatement; MDC is the marginal damage cost faced by the community, assumed to fall to lower values as greater levels of abatement are achieved. From an economic efficiency point of view, the optimal level of abatement is achieved at E, where the marginal cost of abatement is equal to the marginal cost of damage (with emissions of OA); or as we may say, the social marginal cost of abatement is equal to the social marginal benefit of the damage alleviated. This defines what economists refer to as the 'optimal level of abatement'. (The 'optimal' nature of E can be seen from the graph: to the right of A there are gains to be made from further abatement as the marginal damage is greater than the cost of alleviating it, that is, MDC is above MAC; and to the left of A the marginal cost of abatement is higher than the benefit achieved from it, that is, MAC is above MDC.) To achieve this optimum in practice the government needs to impose a tax per unit of emissions on the factory owner equal to OT. This internalises the cost of the externality to the person responsible for it – in this case the factory owner – and with all relevant costs now accounted, a socially optimal output of fertiliser is achieved.

Figure 1. The economics of pollution control

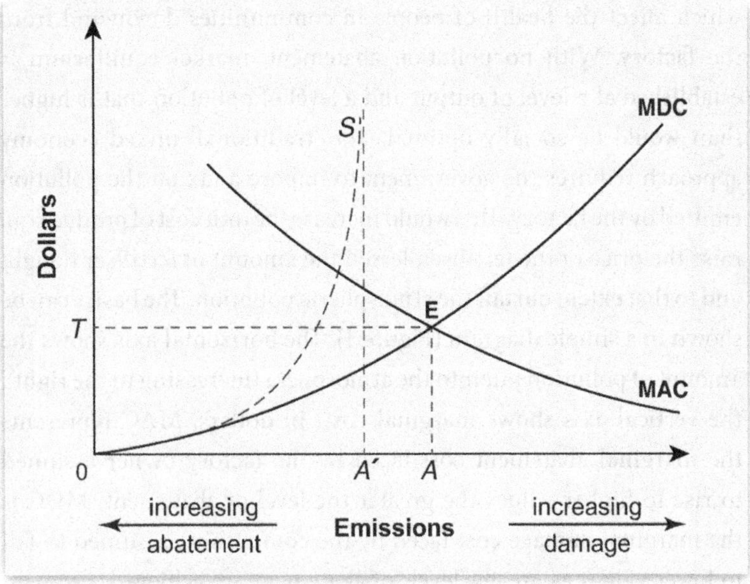

There are of course difficulties in arriving at such an outcome practically, not the least of which is the accurate estimation of the damage costs required to set the appropriate level of tax, but that is what the method tries to do. There are however some important benefits of imposing a tax in this way. For a start it provides a permanent incentive to the factory owner to reduce pollution (through technological improvements), and it tries to minimise total abatement costs, something that direct regulation does not do.

An alternative open to government is to directly regulate the factory. This could be done by banning pollution discharges above a specified amount with fines for transgression, or requiring the installation of specific pollution abatement technology. This is a common method used by governments in some situations on account of its simplicity and directness, but is generally frowned upon by economists on account of its 'inefficiency' characteristics. It is a method that can be effectively used in situations of deficient knowledge where avoidance of damage is paramount. For example in our case of the fertiliser factory, if the health effects of the pollution were poorly understood but possibly life-threatening, the government might decide to adopt a precautionary approach which sets an acceptable minimal level of abatement at A′ rather than A (Figure 1), in order to avoid the risk of damage to people's health. Such regulation is commonly used in restricting the use of agricultural pesticides, limiting the concentrations of food additives and environmental contaminants in human and animal foods, and in engineering structural design, for example.

The pure laissez-faire approach to the pollution problem is rather different. Its intent is to require that private legal rights exist covering all the economic elements of the situation, and then to allow the market – or at least bargaining between private parties – to determine the outcome. Consider the simplest case of a factory putting polluting discharges into a lake which has one other function, that of providing water to a water supply utility which provides drinking water for a nearby town. The lake is not owned by either the factory or the utility. If the property right in the lake is assigned to the utility such that the factory must compensate the utility for its expense in treating the lake water, and if (as in Figure 1) MDC is the marginal damage cost to the utility from the factory's pollution and MAC is the marginal abatement cost confronted by the factory, then it can be shown by an argument similar to that given above that the two parties will negotiate to the point of economic efficiency at E with emissions of OA. On the other hand, if the property right is with the factory, then the utility will need to offer payment to the factory to reduce its discharges, and once again the two parties will negotiate to the point E with emissions of OA. This is the substance of the celebrated – some would say notorious – theorem due to Ronald Coase, which demonstrates that irrespective of the way the property rights are assigned, the same economically efficient solution will, in theory, result through bargaining and without government intervention.[4] While it may be true that with regard to economic efficiency the allocation of rights makes no difference, the distributional consequences of the allocations are diametrically opposed, for in the case where the right is with the factory, it is the victim who has to bribe the perpetrator to desist from his or her polluting activities.

Setting this ethical issue to one side, practical problems arise in many cases for this approach. Let us return to the case of the fertiliser factory. In this case it is likely to be difficult to identify precisely who the parties are that have been affected by the pollution and should be involved in the bargaining; their large numbers and geographical dispersion are likely to make information dissemination, organisation, and bargaining problematic; and information itself may be limited. These factors can raise the cost of bargaining to the point of impracticality.

One potentially fruitful method that has emerged in recent decades based on the rationale of the maximal use of markets has been that involving tradable permits (the so-called 'cap-and-trade' system). Consider the case where there are many fertiliser factories (this is an agricultural country). Here, the government would determine the maximum amount of pollutant permissible for discharge into the atmosphere (in say tonnes per year), and auction divisible units of this total to fertiliser factory owners as rights to pollute up to the amount of units held. These issued rights, privately held, can be bought and sold in a market, so that if a factory holds more rights than it needs it can sell its excess to other factories that require them. The government, or a government-responsible agency, will be required to monitor factories' compliance. Many economists support this approach as a way of reducing, at least in theory, overall compliance costs. It is opposed by many environmentalists on the ethical ground that public goods such are the air quality should not become private property but rather should be counted as part of an inalienable common good.

All these methods attempt to correct the divergence between private costs and benefits and the more inclusive social costs and benefits. What might be the 'best' means of proceeding in any specific case in the real world will depend on many things, including the costs of assembling the necessary information, the costs of monitoring, how widespread or concentrated are the communities involved, how deleterious the pollution might be, and whether or not its effects are likely to be irreversible. We can say two things however: first, that individual methods have moral consequences and that economic efficiency is not the sole criterion of merit; and second, that all responses require government intervention of some sort.

Common Property Resources

There is a further important set of economic issues involving 'publicness', relating to what are called common-pool resources, or common property resources (CPRs). These are resources that can be considered as 'partially' public goods, as they are non-excludable in usage but are rivalrous in consumption. Like public goods, CPRs involve what are referred to as 'social dilemmas': situations in which the rational actions of self-interested individuals does not produce a socially optimal outcome. Private interest is at odds with collective interest. Fisheries, forests, oil fields, water resources, grazing lands and biodiversity all have properties of CPRs. All environmental public goods are likely to become CPR problems when natural limits of usage are exceeded and rivality ensues in relation to access.

The archetypal model of a CPR problem is the so-called 'tragedy of the commons', proposed originally by biologist Garrett Hardin.[5] Consider a community in which herdsmen graze their cattle on the common pastures. Each animal provides a profit for its owner, so that it advantages each herdsman, as a rational actor, to add an additional animal to the commons. And the same is true for every member of the community. The consequence of each acting in his own self-interest is that the commons becomes over-stocked, the resource over-utilised and finally destroyed. Eventually all lose in the situation of an unregulated commons. Hardin may have overstated his case originally by assuming that personal self-interest was the only motivating factor in the herdsmen's behaviour and that the common was unmanaged. This does not undermine the significance of the issues he raised, and the directions in which solutions to the problem lie. It was Hardin's initial view that the only adequate response to the impending 'tragedy' was direct intervention ('mutual coercion mutually agreed upon'), although in later years he conceded the possibility of solutions from free market to socialist, depending on the details of the case. What remains in no doubt, is Hardin's claim that 'Individualism is cherished because it produces freedom, but the gift is conditional: the more the population exceeds the carrying capacity of the environment, the more freedoms must be given up.'

Recent research work in behavioural economics has explored the problem of the management of the commons more fully, and broadened our perspective on where useful policy responses might lie. But let us return briefly to public goods. Behavioural economic research has demonstrated conclusively that although free riding does occur in situations involving public goods, it is by no means universal behaviour. On the contrary, research using what are called 'public goods games' has shown that individuals are prepared voluntarily to contribute a substantial portion of their resources towards the provision of a public good, while at the same time reserving a meaningful fraction of their resources to themselves.[6]

Such results also indicate that in any community there is likely to be a spread of individuals, from those less inclined to free ride to those who are more inclined to do so.

Research using similar games aimed at modelling the management of CPRs has shown similar results. The key requirements for 'solving' the social dilemma over time are the ability of participants to communicate among themselves, the ability to sanction (and so inhibit free riding), and the ability to modify the rules of their association in the use of the common resource. And these laboratory results have been confirmed by widespread field studies of groups facing community action problems. From communal mountain grazing in Switzerland, to groundwater extraction and irrigation in California, to inshore Sri Lankan fisheries, it has been shown that those CPRs which have been managed successfully over generations share these characteristics. And it is clear that communication among participants is of critical importance as it involves not only the exchange of information, but the building of mutual commitment, the development of group identity, the creation and reinforcement of norms, and the increase of trust. These threads are drawn together by reciprocity: when others act cooperatively, individuals are by and large prepared to do so too. And this does not depend on material inducements, but rather on the appeal to group cohesion and cultural norms, and especially to norms of fairness.[7]

What this points to is the importance of cooperative rather than competitive action in solving CPR problems. Matters of equity, accountability, conformity to social norms, and adaptability to changing circumstances or new knowledge, must all enter as criteria alongside economic efficiency – and not be considered as inferior to it – if the world is to succeed in meeting this century's challenges.

Risk, Uncertainty, Ignorance

It is a characteristic of many public goods that their properties are not well understood scientifically, difficult to quantify, and often impossible to adequately associate with a monetary value. How then should decision making proceed in such cases?

The limits of science. When investigators study a scientific phenomenon and develop some hypotheses about it which are subsequently confirmed by experiment, there is a tendency to believe that the phenomenon has been 'understood'. There is also a tendency to believe that by undertaking more research and using more technological expertise, this is always possible. This belief is false. Scientific knowledge is limited in several ways. Science itself discriminates among 'risk' situations – those that involve a situation with a known set of possible outcomes to each of which a statistical probability can be assigned; 'uncertain' situations – those for which the range of outcomes may itself be indeterminate and/or to which outcome probabilities cannot be assigned; and beyond that, situations involving 'indeterminacy' or 'ignorance', not just ignorance in the sense that it might be reduced by subsequent scientific or social inquiry, but ignorance that is irreducible.[8]

Consider the genetic mutations in microorganisms. Their genetic material can undergo mutation from any one of several causes such as naturally occurring errors in their biochemical processes, or exposure to ionising radiation, mutagenic chemicals or viruses. It cannot be known in advance what mutations will occur, whether the organism carrying the mutation will be favoured or disfavoured in the environment in which it finds itself, or whether it will prove pathogenic to some other species, including humans. Take the case of the influenza A virus which causes influenza in birds, some animal species and humans. The H1N1 strain was responsible for the Spanish flu pandemic of 1918–19 in which up to 50 million people died; in 1968–69 a strain dubbed H3N2 was responsible for a pandemic in Hong Kong in which 750,000 people died; in 1997 a highly pathogenic mutant strain H5N1 endemic in birds in South-East Asia was responsible for the deaths and cull of many millions of domestic poultry and wild birds, and when transmitted to humans death ensues in 60 per cent of cases. Most recently an H7N9 strain found in China in March 2013 was responsible for 72 deaths in the first two months of 2014. It could not be known in advance when each of these threats would emerge or how virulent they would be once they did. Nor did anyone predict the emergence of the AIDS, SARS, or have awareness of the Ebola virus before its deadly impact, or of the virus responsible for Middle East respiratory syndrome (MERS).

Or consider events that are extremely rare, such as serious nuclear reactor incidents. Probabilities of such events are sometimes calculated but they have little merit, first because the numerical estimates are so minute as to be beyond useful interpretation, and second because there can be no proof that all possible modes of reactor failure have been identified. And there is no practical possibility of determining the failure rate directly because of the need to build and operate thousands of reactors and operate them for thousands of years to obtain the necessary data. For similar reasons it is impossible to predict the occurrence of large-scale earthquakes or tsunami, volcanic eruptions, meteor impacts, or the outbreak of solar flares large enough to knock out the world's communications systems.

Then again, consider natural ecosystems. When a stable ecological system in nature is subject to external assault or change (say a wildfire, or the loss of a species), it may be sufficiently resilient to recover its original equilibrium, or one very close to it. However if the assault is such as to exceed the resilience of the ecosystem, then it becomes unable to recover its original state and can flip into a completely different mode and evolve in a totally unpredictable way. Here again scientific knowledge of the resilience of ecosystems is rudimentary and limited in principle.[9] Herein lies the danger from potential climate change effects of immense consequence such as the collapse of the Greenland ice sheet, the shutdown of the oceanic thermohaline circulation in the North Atlantic, and the desertification of the world's grain belts.

Precaution. The situations just mentioned are examples of what is referred to as 'phenomenological ignorance' – ignorance irreducible on account of the nature of the phenomenon under consideration. And as is evident some of these situations are of profound importance to humankind. Faced with such situations, and if we value the future, we would be wise to adopt a cautious approach to ecological and economic management. This is no more than common sense. Ecologist Buzz Holling expressed it in evolutionary terms when he noted that for any species, far better than maximising efficiency or reward (as a predator species might wish to do with regard to catching prey, or as herdsmen might wish to do with regard to their cows on the common), is to maintain sufficient flexibility of response to stay in the game.[10]

The Precautionary Principle (PP) has become an internationally recognised guiding principle for a prudential response to scientific uncertainty and indeterminacy. It encapsulates the idea that decision makers need to take a precautionary approach to policies which may damage life support systems, especially where the damage may be serious and/or irreversible. The idea has been adopted widely in international declarations, including in the Preamble to the Montreal Protocol to the Vienna Convention for the Protection of the Ozone Layer (1987), in the Ministerial Declaration of the Third International Conference on the Protection of the North Sea (1990), the OECD Council Recommendation on Integrated Pollution Prevention and Control (1991), the Convention on Biological Diversity (1992), and the UN Framework Convention on Climate Change (1992). The most commonly quoted statement of the Principle is the one that emerged from the 1992 UN Conference on Environment and Development that states in part that: 'Where there are threats of serious or irreversible damage, lack of full scientific certainty shall not be used as a reason for postponing cost-effective measures to prevent environmental degradation.'[11]

Stated in this way the PP is a formal principle that provides a rationale for action, while the nature of the action to be taken will depend on the specifics of the circumstances involved. As the statement makes clear, the decision to invoke the PP is to be based on two key considerations: the threat of serious or irreversible damage, and the lack of scientific knowledge. Both of these involve normative political issues. With regard to the former it will be a matter of judgement as to the seriousness of the threat and consequently the level of response that is appropriate. And the latter requirement precludes invoking the PP based on imagination or prejudice lacking scientific basis, or in those situations involving risk in which knowledge of cause and effect and probabilities are relatively well known. Beyond its advocacy by international and regional organisations, the PP has also been adopted in a number of national jurisdictions, including Australia, Canada and India, and has been applied in a range of economic, environmental and public health areas. On the other hand, as far as is known, a TPP agreement will not recognise the legitimacy of the PP.

The formal assessment of risk as practised in the mid-twentieth century was essentially a technical procedure for determining the magnitude of the damage and the probability of its occurrence. With more recent experience of broad-scale systemic risks associated with issues such as DDT dispersal, nuclear waste disposal, avian influenza, genetically modified organisms and climate change, it has become increasingly apparent to experts themselves that such techniques were limited, and that they retained substantial subjective components both in problem definition (What do we take as the boundary to this problem?) and in interpretation (What risk is 'acceptable'? What does 'irreversible' mean?). In these circumstances there can be no 'best' answer in a scientific sense. What was seen to be lacking was an explicit consideration of the conflicting value judgements and legitimately divergent interests that underlay the risk-evaluation process itself.[12] A 1996 report of the US National Research Council Committee on Risk Characterization emphasised the characterisation of risk as being the outcome of an analytic *and* deliberative process, which depends critically not only on the systematic scientific analysis appropriate to the problem, but on deliberation in formulating the decision problem, guiding the analysis, seeking its meanings, and improving the abilities of the affected parties to participate in the process.[13] In 1999 the International Futures Programme of the OECD set out on a three-year study of emerging twenty-first-century systemic risks. In its final report it reasserted the importance of this dual approach of analysis and deliberation as adopted by the US body, emphasising the idea of 'citizens as partners', and the importance of precaution.[14] Particularly in relation to systemic risks, democratic process is now acknowledged as an integral part of risk assessment and regulation.

We take these developments as strong evidence in favour of the proposition that, in relation to the suite of environmental and resource use problems that will characterise the twenty-first century, rationality, risk aversion, and indeed common sense, require that they be considered for decision within an augmented democratic frame.

The Tyranny of Small Decisions

There is another category of social dilemmas which although less discussed, can be important in some circumstances. Political economist Alfred Kahn, who gave this dilemma its name, was reflecting on his experience on a privately operated commuter train service from Ithaca in upstate New York.[15] Each day individual commuters would make the decision whether to travel to work by the train or by alternative means, car, bus or aeroplane. However revenue derived by the train operator was not enough to keep the train in service and it ceased operating, despite the fact that commuters would have been prepared to pay additionally to keep the service going. Citizens in making rational decisions day by day were led to an outcome which was suboptimal for all. As Kahn noted: 'Each selection of x over y constitutes also a vote for eliminating the possibility thereafter of choosing y; if enough people vote for x, each time necessarily on the assumption that y will continue, y may in fact disappear.' But the opportunity to express a choice on the future of the railway at the level at which its continuation was determined, was never offered. The Ithaca commuters were the victims of the 'tyranny of small decisions' (TSD).

A situation involving TSD has some of the characteristics of one involving a public good, as being provided for one it is provided for all, and for as long as it is provided it would – according to economic calculation – pay a rational individual to understate (at least to the railroad) the value of the service, that is, to free-ride. TSD situations also have some of the characteristics of a 'tragedy of the commons' because it is the cumulative effect of individual decisions over time which lead to the demise of the service. However it is a distinct issue because here the market never in fact offered the citizen a choice at the relevant level to influence the outcome. 'Market failure' occurs because the market presupposes that the cumulative effect of the small decisions of individuals at the margin will lead to a social optimum, whereas here the appropriate operational decision is non-marginal, and citizens are not provided the opportunity to express their choice at that level.

The influence of TSD situations is particularly significant in environmental matters, such as in the incremental encroachment of urban development onto tracts of land of high agricultural value. The insistent nature of the problem was highlighted by the degradation of the Florida Everglades throughout the twentieth century.[16] As ecologist William E Odum described it, this occurred not from any decision consciously made, but from the accumulation of a multitude of small independent choices to add one more drainage canal, one more roadway, one more retirement village, one more well to provide Miami with drinking water. No choice was ever made to reduce the annual flow of water into the Everglades National Park, or to intensify the effects of droughts, or to encourage unnaturally hot, destructive wildfires, yet all these things happened. And it is not clear how –

or at what cost – they can now effectively be reversed. These things happened because the choice was not offered at the appropriate 'higher' and more general public decision-making level. Sensible small-scale decisions do not necessarily accumulate to sensible large-scale decisions. And this small-scale decision making is what laissez-faire economics promotes.

The Common Good

Phrases such as 'the public interest', 'the public good', 'the common good', 'the general welfare', 'public value' all make reference to similar ideas, namely a thing or things shared in society, and which are in some sense widely beneficial. The fact that the idea is so commonly expressed suggests that it is a meaningful and valuable one. Here we will use the expression 'the common good', by which we mean, as John Rawls expressed it, 'certain general conditions that are … equally to everyone's advantage', or as theologian and sociologist Oswald von Nell-Breuning described it: 'the value to be realised by means of cooperation'. By preferring the phrase 'the common good' we have tried to avoid confusion with the idea of a 'public good', or 'public goods' which – as discussed above – have come to signal specific things in economic parlance. The choice of phrase 'the common good' is not intended to suggest that everyone necessarily agrees on what is in the common interest, but it does intend that the common good is not the same as – indeed it is more extensive than – the collection of public goods measured in economics, for reasons we will now describe.

Laissez-faire economics does not recognise the idea of the common good – apart perhaps from the 'good' constituted by the rules under which the free market is set up institutionally and the assumption that the efficient use of resources constitutes a common good. This is the meaning of the quotation from Prime Minister Margaret Thatcher given in the Preface, of Hayek's scorn for the idea of social justice, and of philosopher Nozick's focus on the self; and it is the meaning implicit in the free market (Coasean) solution to the fertiliser factory pollution problem in which it does not matter whether the polluter has to pay for his pollution discharges or the community has to bribe him to reduce them.[17]

When laissez-faire economists approach the issue of public goods in theory, what they attempt to do is to shoehorn them into a framework of private property rights that can then be exchanged in markets, thus avoiding identifying anything as a holding in common. This can indeed be done with some public goods – for example a private education system can run in parallel with a public one. In other circumstances it can be mimicked – for example on toll roads or for cable television excludability and therefore the ability to charge can be enforced. And in other circumstances it might be attempted – for example in charging admission to national parks and areas of natural beauty. But note one thing that has happened already: by setting these things to market criteria, there is a denial of any cooperative or social value attached to the good or service. The assumption is of selfish holding, not sharing; inclusiveness is devoid of value. In the case of private education for example it denies value to social intermingling and the sharing of culture(s); in the case of admission to national parks it denies that they are part of a common heritage that should be equally accessible to all. (We have of course already met this situation in Chapter 3 with the New Zealand government's requirement that SOEs of all provenances be required to compete commercially.)

The mixed economy approach on the other hand does recognise the common good: it is inherent in Bentham's greatest happiness principle. And in practice it underpins the economic technique of cost benefit analysis (CBA) used in public decision making. Suppose there is a proposal that government undertake a major infrastructure project (a dam, or research institute, or suburban development) or implement a new policy (on housing, or education, or health or agriculture). Should it proceed? The approach of CBA is to identify all the benefits of the scheme (positive and negative) and all the costs, and determine whether the money sum of all the benefits across the community (perhaps weighted in favour of disadvantaged groups) is greater or lesser than the sum for all the costs. The technique is widely used. Nonetheless it is not free of difficulties of measurement and interpretation.

Estimating costs – for example for building materials, or bulldozers – is often relatively straightforward, as these goods are commonly traded in markets. Benefits on the other hand (both positive and negative) are often much more difficult to estimate. There may be a lack of scientific information about the thing being considered: for example about the level of fish stocks in an ocean fishery, or the effects of a chemical on the environment. And with issues of very large scale such as climate change, it is not just market prices that are in doubt but the course of the future economy itself. Then there may be difficulties in translating scientific information into monetary terms: it may be possible to list the merits of a public safety measure, but how should they be valued? What is the value to be placed on safe food, or on a life saved? And the further we move away from market exchange, the more problematic does CBA become. How does one put an economic value on, for example, unique objects: the historic treaty site at Waitangi, say, or Mt Aspiring? Or on abstract qualities (which often involve unique things of cultural significance) such as social norms – of queuing, truth telling, helping someone in need, blood donation – or on Anzac Day commemorations, or on fair trials, an impartial public service, or the ability to trust politicians?

The point here is not to denigrate CBA as a technique for the economic consideration of public projects, but rather to point to its limitations. We can try the exercise of making a list of issues which economics might wish to value monetarily – from the 'easy' to the 'hard' and further to the 'guess at' and the 'impossible in principle'. There will be a point somewhere along this list beyond which items will be declared to be more appropriately the preserve of disciplines other than economics, such as politics or sociology or philosophy, and this is where we may say that what the orthodox economist can measure as 'public goods' comes to an end. But what of those items that lie beyond that point? Even as they are not included in economic method, they remain part of the extended concept of what we have chosen to call the common good. (A few economists may wish to claim that such an exclusionary point is never reached. Examination of the global archives of cost benefit analyses will show that claim is false.)

The points we wish to make are three. The first relates to the reason for separating 'the common good' from 'public goods'. When one commits to the use of an economic technique, there is a strong tendency to discount or ignore those elements of the problem that do not fit the technique. The economic idea of a public good invites us to treat its 'publicness' as an aberration from the idea of a private good, and one that can be tweaked, estimated in money value, and accommodated into the framework of efficiency economics, or alternatively ignored. We claim on the contrary that it is important to retain the truth that economics does not cover all matters, and one way of doing this is in our choice of words. The second point of note is that CBA is a method that emerges from the idea of a mixed economy: laissez-faire economic theory provides no warrant for CBA. Thus in demonstrating the limitations of CBA in relation to the common good – as we have just attempted to do – we have demonstrated a fortiori the failure of laissez-faire economics to accommodate this concept.

The third point is more substantive, and relates to the moral positions that stand behind the contrasting views of individual behaviour and decision making in the realms of the family, the market, and the common good. It has been set out most clearly by British academic and politician David Marquand.[18] The private realm of family life is consistent with individual moral conduct which is – within broad limits – of no one's concern outside the family.

The market realm is characterised by a moral code of self-centred behaviour, competition, and one dollar one value. The realm of the common good on the other hand, associated as it is with the idea of the civil society, is characterised by cooperation, sharing, and one person one value. These three realms are different, despite the fact that the boundaries between them may at times be indistinct. This is why favouritism and nepotism, quite acceptable in the private realm, are unacceptable in the realm of the common good, and why the buying and selling of votes or government policies or justice are considered crimes. Three consequences follow. First, in a capitalist democracy all three moral realms are important. Second, to apply the moral criteria of one realm to another is merely to corrupt it. Third, there is a profound contradiction involved in a free market policy approach to issues which in their essence involve the common good, particularly such issues of large scale such as climate change and natural resource use. It is a contradiction that can only be resolved by rejecting that approach.

Deliberative Democracy

This leaves us with an important question for real world policy formulation and decision making: How should we proceed in areas in which the 'common good' is important? We may still assemble data, derive statistics, and make forecasts, but these technical acts do not approach the core issue, that of valuation. We have however had some intimations as to where an appropriate answer to this question might lie: recall the importance that attaches to communication and mutual commitment in solving CPR problems; the discussion of risk management and the emergence of the idea of 'citizens as partners' in the co-determination of response to uncertainty; and in the case of very major or once-for-all decisions, the possibilities inherent in Rawls' maximin criterion.

'Deliberative democracy' refers to a cluster of proposals around the idea that genuine democracy consists not merely of voting at elections but involving in addition augmented public discussion and deliberation by citizens on matter of moment.[19] What is envisaged is the idea of an ideal forum for communication and debate in which both citizens and officials justify their public policy positions by giving reasons that can be accepted by those who are, or will be, bound by it. To fulfil this purpose is to require that communication and debate be based on the principle of reciprocity: that engagement with others will be on the basis of moral equality and mutual respect. And the principle of reciprocity is supported by two further principles, namely: publicity – requiring that reasons given be available for the consideration of all; and accountability – requiring that in the forum each is accountable to all.

The claim is that as a result of public deliberation citizens are more likely to accept decisions which are based on the merits of the case rather than imposed on the basis of wealth or power; and that at the very least deliberation allows for citizens to clarify issues, sift self-interest from public-interest claims, and determine the relative merits of various public-interest claims. In deliberating, individuals are not just expressing personal preferences as they do in market transactions, but rather that they are engaged in making judgements (as, for example, a juror is called upon to do).[20] The claim is not that deliberation will resolve all disagreements, but rather that in a context of moral equality and mutual respect reside the best opportunities for doing so. Furthermore deliberation contains within it the means of its own improvement, as in the processes of debate citizens can learn from each other, identify their own errors, and develop new means of deliberation which are more widely justifiable. Put simply, deliberation is proposed as an enriched political process supporting civil society and the democratic ideal.

In practice, the various means by which officials and citizens might interact covers a wide spectrum: from the provision of information and social surveys by government at one end, to citizen-initiated referenda at the other. But if discourse and deliberation are to be central, then it is processes such as those that involve advisory bodies and citizen panels, consensus conferencing and deliberative polling, that need to take centre stage. In this context an important practical issue relates to the decision-making power that is to be vested in the deliberating group: commonly seen as a complement to representative democracy. Deliberative democratic techniques have already been applied practically in a wide range of situations, from the local to the international, from determinations on such issues as health budgeting priorities and surrogate consent for medical research, to those involved with the maintenance of biodiversity, and the raising of venture capital in response to climate change.[21] Its value in bridging the gap between technical specialists and citizens in public matters involving high uncertainty has already been referred to.

We commenced this chapter with a quotation from George Soros and we will end it with another: 'In today's global economy the production of private goods has taken precedence over the provision of public goods. Correcting this imbalance is a major policy challenge …'[22] In the following chapters we will explore the nature of this challenge for New Zealand, particularly in the areas of climate change and natural resources use.

7

The Twenty-first Century – Climate Change

Global Warming and Climate Change

The science. The sun provides radiant energy to the earth. On the surface of the earth this energy is absorbed and re-emitted as longer-wavelength infra-red radiation. Some of this re-emitted radiation escapes the atmosphere but the majority is absorbed by molecules of atmospheric gases (particularly carbon dioxide and water vapour) and is re-radiated back towards the earth, warming the surface. These processes, collectively known as the 'greenhouse effect', are all parts of the natural cycle which maintains the steady state of the global ecosystem. This steady state allows plants to grow and life to thrive. If the infra-red radiation from the earth were not trapped in the atmosphere in this way, the average surface temperature of the earth would not be around +15°C but 30°C lower at –15°C: a very chilly prospect.

In the years following World War II, concern began to mount among scientists that the burning of fossil fuels might be contributing carbon dioxide to the atmosphere in sufficient quantities to affect the earth's temperature. In observations now regarded as classic, advanced air-monitoring instruments atop the Mauna Loa volcano in Hawaii demonstrated that atmospheric carbon dioxide concentrations were indeed increasing over time; and the sampling of carbon dioxide trapped in air bubbles in drill cores from below Antarctic ice sheets showed that rises and falls in the atmospheric concentration of carbon dioxide were synchronous with warm and cold eras in the earth's history. Forty years on and it is almost universally recognised that the warming of the atmosphere due to human activity since the industrial revolution is a real phenomenon, and one that holds serious consequences for humankind.[1, 2]

It is now known that there are a number of so-called 'greenhouse gases' (GHGs) involved in atmospheric warming:

- Carbon dioxide (CO_2): by far the most abundant gas involved, has increased in concentration by over 30 per cent since pre-industrial times due particularly to increased combustion of fossil fuels (coal, oil, natural gas) and to deforestation (loss of CO_2 absorptive capacity);
- Methane (CH_4): atmospheric concentrations have increased due to expanded rice cultivation, cattle, sheep and other ruminant rearing, biomass burning and coal and petroleum mining;
- Nitrous oxide (N_2O): originates from microbial processes in soils and water – its concentration in the atmosphere has been rising since the beginnings of the industrial revolution as a consequence of the use of nitrogenous fertilisers and intensive animal farming;
- HFCs, PFCs, SF_6: these are purely synthetic, industrially manufactured, products. HFCs are used as refrigerants, PFCs in semiconductor manufacture, and SF_6 is used as an insulator in high-voltage electrical equipment.

In terms of their warming effect, the concentration of a chemical in the atmosphere is one important variable, but two other factors are of critical importance: the efficiency with which the chemical molecules absorb infra-red radiation, and the average lifetime of the molecules in the atmosphere (before they are dissolved out or transformed in subsequent chemical reactions). Reflecting these factors, the 'global warming potential' (GWP) of a gas measures its ability to trap heat in the atmosphere relative to carbon dioxide (see Table 2). One of the worst offenders in this regard is tetrafluoromethane (a PFC), with an atmospheric lifetime of some 50,000 years and a more than 5,000 times greater efficiency in absorbing infra-red radiation than CO_2. In the right-hand column of the table, the GWP of each gas is combined with its estimated year-2000 emissions and converted to 'carbon dioxide equivalents' (CO_2e) – the amount of carbon dioxide that would produce the same global warming as the estimated emissions of the specified gas – and expressed as a percentage of total emissions.

Table 2: Characteristics of Major Greenhouse Gases (GHGs)

Gas	Lifetime in the atmosphere (years)	100-year global potential warming (GWP)	Percentage of year 2000 emissions (CO_2e)
Gases subject to the Kyoto Protocol			
carbon dioxide (CO_2)	5–200	1	77
methane (CH_4)	12	21	14
nitrous oxide (N_2O)	114	310	8
hydrofluorocarbons (HFCs)	1.4–270	140–11,700	0.5
perfluorocarbons (PFCs)	740–50,000	>5,000	0.2
sulphur hexafluoride (SF_6)	3,200	23,900	1

Sources: IPCC, *Climate Change: The Physical Science Basis*, 2007, pp. 212–13; N.H. Stern, *The Economics of Climate Change*, 2007, p. 224.

The IPCC. The first international body to express concern that the continuing expansion of human activities and their associated warming of the atmosphere might cause significant regional and even global changes in climate was the World Meteorological Office (WMO), which hosted the first World Climate Conference in 1979. Decisions taken at that conference led on to the Vienna Convention for the Protection of the Ozone Layer, and to its subsequent protocol (the 'Montreal Protocol') which entered into force in 1989 as an international treaty directed at phasing out the production and use of chemicals responsible for ozone depletion in the stratosphere.

In 1988 the WMO together with the United Nations Environment Program (UNEP) established the Intergovernmental Panel on Climate Change (IPCC), the role of which would be to assess the scientific, technical and socio-economic information in relation to human-induced climate change, its impacts, and options for response in either mitigating or adapting to its effects. The first assessment report of the IPCC issued in 1990 provided a major scientific basis for negotiations which led to the United Nations Framework Convention on Climate Change (UNFCCC), completed at the United Nations Conference on Environment and Development in Rio de Janeiro in 1992. The Framework Convention came into force on 21 March 1994, and enjoys almost universal acceptance among governments, having been ratified by 191 countries. Its ultimate objective is expressed as the '… stabilization of greenhouse gas concentrations in the atmosphere at a level that would prevent dangerous anthropogenic interference with the climate system' (Article 2). Principles underpinning actions to achieve this objective include specifically a precautionary approach (Article 3.3), and the recognition of the demands of equity and of responsibility to future generations (Article 3.1). A key practical advance was made at the third annual Conference of the Parties to the UNFCCC held in Kyoto, Japan in 1997. In a Protocol attached to the UNFCCC – universally known as the Kyoto Protocol – most industrialised nations, together with some transitional economies of central Europe, agreed to legally binding reductions in emissions of six prominent greenhouse gases.

The IPCC issued its second assessment report in 1995, its third (dubbed TAR) in 2001, its fourth (A4R) in 2007. The assessment of the scientific evidence in A4R is that global atmospheric concentrations of carbon dioxide have risen from a pre-industrial level of about 280 parts per million (ppm) to a 2005 level of 379 ppm, an atmospheric concentration that exceeds by far the range of concentrations experienced over the last 650,000 years (180–300 ppm) as determined from ice core sampling. The evidence of the warming of the climate system is deemed 'unequivocal', and that this is due mainly to the effect of human activities since 1750 can be held with 'very high confidence'.[3]

The A4R has spelled out future projections of the effects of climate change on different regions of the world in the event of no remedial actions being taken. In South Asia it emphasises increased rainfall variability, declining crop yields, increased incidence of climate-induced diseases, and serious effects of sea level rise in the low-lying coastal areas of Pakistan, India, Bangladesh and Burma where 56 million people may be at risk from flooding. For North America the report points to: increases in weather-related extremes – hurricanes, storms, droughts, heatwaves and wildfires; an extended growing season but with increased fire risk; the vulnerability of coastal cities and communities to storm-surge flooding, coastal erosion, and sea level rise; and a maladapted urban form and building stock. In Australia, already the driest continent in the world, average temperature rises have been experienced since 1950, with future changes in rainfall distribution, increases in heatwaves and bushfires, droughts and floods 'virtually certain'; there will be a critical impact on water security in the Murray-Darling Basin which includes 70 per cent of Australia's irrigated crops and pastures; and ecologically rich sites such as the Great Barrier Reef will be particularly at risk from loss of biodiversity and the increasing acidity of sea water.

Analysis of the impacts and vulnerabilities of New Zealand to future climate change indicates, according to the A4R medium-emissions scenario: a mean temperature rise of 0.1–1.4°C by the 2030s and of 0.2–4.0°C by the 2080s; a 60 per cent increase in mean westerly component of wind speed giving more rain in western areas (particularly in the South Island) and less in the east (Canterbury, Gisborne); sea level rises of about 70 mm (the predicted global average); increases in variability of weather patterns producing droughts and fires in those places already prone, increased floods, landslides, and increasing storm surges in coastal areas. These changes will result in substantial infrastructure threats particularly in coastal cities and communities, and on the floodplains of major rivers. They will also induce changes in agricultural possibilities, including declining water security for intensive dairying in Canterbury, and rising temperatures making kiwifruit less viable in Northland. There will be threats to biodiversity as species find it hard to adapt, and increases in risks to human health as temperature rises in the North Island provide more receptive conditions for the mosquito vector of dengue fever. However not all effects will be bad, at least in the short to medium term. Increased precipitation in the Southern Alps will provide increased opportunities for hydro power; in western and southern areas pastoral farming may gain from longer growing seasons; apples, red wine grapes and kiwifruit will be viable in more southerly latitudes; and plantation forestry will benefit from elevated CO_2 levels. Winter heating bills will go down, and the tourism industry may benefit.[4,5]

These are among the most predictable of effects of climate change in these regions, given present knowledge. Standing behind these are the possibilities of much more major effects – effects that have the potential to overwhelm the resilience of the earth's ecosystem. Rising temperatures could result in the weakening of natural carbon sinks both on land and under the oceans and the release of methane locked in wetlands and permafrost (particularly in the Russian Arctic), both adding substantially to the atmospheric burden of GHGs. The melting of the Greenland ice sheet and the collapse of the West Antarctic ice sheet, if they occur, could raise global sea levels by 5–12 metres over a timescale of centuries.

The IPCC's fifth series of assessment reports (AR5) are being published across 2014. The IPCC estimates that since the appearance of A4R, research on the effects of climate change has doubled in volume. The AR5 reports reinforce earlier findings, and in particular: that each of the last three decades has been successively warmer than any preceding decade since 1850; that over the last two decades the Greenland and Antarctic ice sheets have been losing mass, and glaciers have continued to shrink almost worldwide; and that the rate of sea level rise since the mid-nineteenth century has been larger than the mean rate during the previous two millennia. Research observations over recent decades have shown that climate change has caused impacts on natural and human systems on all continents and across the oceans. Changing precipitation or melting snow and ice are altering hydrological systems and affecting the quality and quantity of water resources; many terrestrial, freshwater, and marine species are shifting their geographical ranges, migration patterns and abundances; there have been overall negative impacts on crop yields, raising significant issues in relation to future food security; and impacts from recent climate-related extremes, such as heat waves, droughts, floods, cyclones, and wildfires, reveal significant vulnerabilities and exposure of ecological and human systems to climate variability.[6] These impacts it must be emphasised, are not some hypotheses about the future, but are with us now. As Rajendra Pachauri, chairperson of the IPCC has observed: 'Nobody on this planet is going to be untouched by the impacts of climate change'.

Neoliberal Opposition to Climate Science

In April 2001 the IPCC issued its third assessment report (TAR). Compiled as a consensus document and endorsed by the vast majority of the world's leading scientific organisations, the report confirmed the existence of human-induced global warming and predicted a rise in mean global temperature of between 1.5°C and 5.8°C by the end of the century unless action was taken to reduce greenhouse gas emissions. The newly elected and neoliberal US President George W. Bush took prompt action. He assured Republican senators that he would not regulate CO_2 emissions on account of the 'incomplete state of scientific knowledge' and that he would not sign the Kyoto Protocol as it would harm the economy and hurt American workers.[7] Bush's National Security Advisor Condoleezza Rice told a luncheon with ambassadors from the EU who wished to engage with the new President on the subject of climate change, that 'Kyoto is not acceptable to the Administration or Congress'.[8] In response, the US Union of Concerned Scientists wrote that both the reasons given were 'without merit'. Bush turned for advice to the nation's pre-eminent scientific body, the US National Academy of Sciences, an expert panel of which confirmed the reality of climate change and endorsed the work of the IPCC. Bush made no change to his policies. In January 2007 the US House of Representatives Committee on Oversight and Government Reform heard sworn testimony from US scientists alleging pressure to tailor their writings on global warming to fit with the Bush administration's scepticism. A survey conducted by the Union of Concerned Scientists reported that 150 federal climate scientists had personally experienced at least one incident of political interference in the previous five years, for a total of at least 435 such incidents.[9]

In the UK the contributions from the premier libertarian think tank the Institute of Economic Affairs over the years have included titles such as 'Global Warming: Apocalypse or Hot Air' (1994), 'Climate Change Reconsidered' (2004) and 'Global Warming False Alarms' (2007). Nigel Lawson, Chancellor of the Exchequer in Margaret Thatcher's government, referred to the Stern Review of climate change economics (see below) as 'scaremongering' and 'no basis for policy decisions'. The climate change agenda was, he believed, in the grip of a new religion, the most profound danger of which was that our societies 'abandon our own traditions of reason and tolerance, and to embrace instead the irrationality and intolerance of eco-fundamentalism.'[10] In Australia, former Australian Liberal Party member and speech writer Guy Pearse, writing in 2007, accused Liberal Prime Minister John Howard of 'wilful blindness' on the matter of global warming and climate change, and that the Prime Minister and several key ministers had been 'captured by a group of industries and their lobbyists'.[11] More recently Tony Abbott, as leader of the Australian Liberal Party in opposition, declared in 2009 that 'We can't conclusively say whether man-made carbon dioxide emissions are contributing to climate change', and later the same year expressed his sentiments more expansively at a political party meeting in rural Victoria: 'The argument is absolute crap. However the politics of this are tough for us.'[12] Since his election as Australian Prime Minister in September 2013 Abbott has abolished the Australian Climate Change Commission, plans to abolish the Clean Energy Finance Corporation and repeal the carbon tax on large-scale polluting companies introduced by his immediate predecessor. It appears that such politicians either have not understood the science, or have been prepared to bow to moneyed interests, and/or put ideological belief before scientific evidence and indeed before the future well-being of their nation's citizens.

There have moreover been more sinister forces at work. The *Guardian* newspaper revealed that US billionaires have been secretly routing funds through two libertarian trust funds in order 'to redefine climate change from neutral scientific fact to a highly polarised "wedge issue" for hard core conservatives'.[13] This 'dark money' grew from $900,000 in 2002 to almost $30m in 2010, and went variously to libertarian think tanks such as the American Enterprise Institute and the Heartland Institute (subject to its own climate change funding scandal in 2012[14]), to contrarian scientists at Harvard and other institutions, as well as to obscure local forums.[15] The tactics used by corporate-sponsored climate change deniers to distort the science of climate change and to sully the reputations of the scientists involved have been recorded in a number of recent books.[16] In 2013, US resource economist Robert Repetto could still write that 'Denial of climate change is nearly a litmus test of Republican right-wing conservatism'.[17]

It is now over 30 years since the first international conference on global climate change and 25 years since the establishment of the IPCC. It is a regrettable accident of history that this period of rising concern over such a critical issue has corresponded with the rise of neoliberalism, one of the main contributions of which has been to deny the reality of climate change and to retard the exploration of its consequences and of options for dealing with them.

The Economics of Climate Change

Economics and the Stern Review. From the point of view of economics, the existence of a stable climate is a public good and climate change is a negative externality: those responsible for emitting GHGs into the atmosphere and disturbing its stability are not paying the full social cost of their activities. Climate change has in fact been described as 'market failure on the greatest scale the world has seen.'[18] Furthermore, climate change is a very particular type of externality. The first and most evident particularity is that it is global in its reach and is therefore a problem for all countries irrespective of their relative contribution to the atmospheric GHG burden. The second relates to the time the GHGs stay in the atmosphere. The problem here is that it is not just a matter of stopping the current *flow* of emissions to make the problem go away, but it is the cumulative effect of the *stock* of previous emissions, which will remain in the atmosphere for many years to come whatever remedial actions are taken now to limit additions to that stock, that lies at the heart of the problem. Allied with this is the fact that the earth's system of atmosphere, oceans and land surface is very slow to adjust to change. These characteristics ensure that the effects of global warming will persist and will develop over a long period of time. Third, the effects of temperature rise are non-linear: that is to say that the effects of a global rise in average temperature of 2.0°C will be more than four times as damaging as a rise of 0.5°C. Moreover the quoting of average values – as must often be done in summary analyses – disguises the increase in the numbers of extreme weather events that will be associated with global warming.

In 2005 the then Chancellor of the Exchequer in the United Kingdom, Gordon Brown, concerned about climate change, commissioned a review of the economics of responding to climate change by moving to a 'low-carbon' economy. The review was carried out by a team led by economist Nicholas (now Lord) Stern. The 'Stern Review' has since become a benchmark for more recent considerations of the subject.[19] Stern based his study on the physical science of global warming that had been revealed by the studies of the IPCC. He went on to estimate the economic impacts of climate change itself and to examine the policy challenges in managing the transition to a low-carbon economy. Stern noted that the atmospheric concentration of GHGs prior to the Industrial Revolution was about 280 ppm CO_2e and that this had risen by the end of the twentieth century to about 430 ppm CO_2e, indicative of an average temperature rise of 0.5°C over the period. According to Stern's analysis, in order to avoid the worst effects of climate change it would be necessary to restrict temperature rise to less than 2.0°C, requiring that the concentration of GHGs not exceed about 550 ppm CO_2e (440–500 ppm CO_2 only). To accomplish this, emissions would need to peak in the next 10–20 years and then gradually fall by 1–3 per cent per year. By 2050 global emissions would need to be about 25 per cent lower than current levels. (Even so, stabilisation at 550 ppm CO_2e was a very modest target: climate modelling suggested that at this concentration there was still a better than even chance of exceeding a 2°C increase from pre-industrial levels.)[20] Consistent with the proposed path to GHG stabilisation, Stern estimated that the cost of achieving the emissions reductions would be about 1 per cent of global GDP in 2050. On the other hand a 'business as usual' scenario would entail a cost of between 5 and 20 per cent of GDP.

Stern's central conclusion was that climate change is a very serious threat to humankind and one that demands an urgent global response, particularly in relation to the reduced use of fossil fuels. If prompt and decisive action is taken now, it would be possible to avoid the worst aspects of climate change. On the other hand, if this action is not promptly taken, then there is a risk of disruption to economic and social activity on a scale similar to those associated with the great wars and the economic depression of the first half of the twentieth century.[21] When the International Energy Agency issued its *World Energy Outlook* in 2011 it observed that there were few signs that the urgently needed change in direction in global energy trends was under way, and that the door was already closing on limiting global average temperature rise to 2°C.[22]

In July 2013 the WMO released a major report on the global climatic conditions over the first decade of this century. It noted that the world had experienced unprecedented high-impact climate extremes over the preceding decade, which was the warmest since the start of modern measurements in 1850.[23] Stern himself, interviewed in 2013, reflected: 'Looking back, I underestimated the risks ... Some effects are coming through more quickly than we thought'. Had he known this 'I would have been much more strong about the risks of a four- or five-degree rise.'[24] Observational results published in March 2014 show that the northeast Greenland ice sheet, previously considered cold and relatively stable, is now melting at an unexpectedly high rate. Completely melted it has the capacity to raise global sea level by more than seven metres.[25]

Policy instruments. Global energy production from burning fossil fuels used in the power, transportation, building and industry sectors is responsible for about 57 per cent of anthropogenic GHG emissions, while agriculture and changes in land use (especially deforestation) and wastes account for about 41 per cent. Almost all of the gas from energy production consists of CO_2; in agriculture and land use, deforestation produces CO_2, and agriculture and wastes produce CH_4 and N_2O. To mitigate the effects of global warming there is a range of possible responses available to governments. These include increasing efficiency in energy use (through improved insulation, more efficient domestic appliances), changing to low-carbon technologies (including wind, solar, wave, and hydrogen as power sources, and carbon capture and storage), and encouraging reductions in energy use. The reduction of non-fossil-fuel-related emissions through afforestation and reforestation provide signal opportunities, as do improved land management practices. Evidently a range of approaches will be required to combat climate change effectively and at low cost.

There are a number of economic instruments that can be brought to bear in pursuit of such a policy goal. These include direct regulation, taxes and charges, tradable permits, voluntary agreements, subsidies, research and development, and the provision of information. Evidently these vary widely in environmental effectiveness, cost-effectiveness, distributional consequences and institutional feasibility.[26] Here we will pursue only the high-profile debate over the relative merits of a tax or a cap-and-trade system for the direct reduction of GHG emissions. In the case of a tax, it could be applied on major energy users on the basis of the amount of CO_2e emitted. However it is clear that the level of tax would need to be adjusted over time as experience revealed what change in emissions had been induced by the level of tax applied. In the case of cap-and-trade, producers as well as importers of fossil fuels would be required to hold annual permits issued by the government covering their emissions for the year. The total number of permits – and thereby the number of tonnes of CO_2e permitted to be emitted – would reduce by, say, 3 per cent each year. There are similarities in the approaches: both are designed to correct market failure by restricting the emissions of carbon – the source of the problem – and to use market processes to find the same efficient outcome. Both in practice would focus on the limited number of firms responsible for the majority of emissions, and for efficiency both require monitoring, reporting and verification.

There are however differences. The tax directly affects the price of emissions, and relies on market forces to bring about the reduction in fossil fuel use and thereby emissions; cap-and-trade directly reduces fossil fuel use and relies on the market to set the price. Reaching an emissions target therefore appears more assured, at least in theory, under cap-and-trade than under a tax. Under a tax the consequences of fluctuations in economic conditions are borne by industry, whereas under cap-and-trade they are borne by the government. A tax generates revenue for the government. This revenue might then be used to offset other taxes, promote low-carbon technologies, or compensate those sectors of the economy hardest hit by the tax itself, such as lower income households whose use of energy relative to income is higher than others, and for whom alternative means of adjustment are fewer. In the case of cap-and-trade, if the permits are auctioned by the government this also provides revenue that can be used in the same way. If the permits are *given* to industrial polluters (a process known as 'grandfathering'), then no revenue accrues to the government, and the giving of permits to industry represents a free gift which can be disposed of howsoever industry may wish.

The question of which approach is better has been the subject of heated debate among economists, politicians and citizen groups. For policy at a national level the tax has much to recommend it: it represents a direct imposition on those industries responsible for the emissions, is easy to understand, provides funds to the government which can recompense those most affected or used in other ways, and is relatively transparent in its workings. It recommends itself as appropriate for a small country such as New Zealand in trying to curb its own emissions. Sweden, Denmark, Norway, Finland and the Netherlands have all had carbon taxes since the early 1990s, and states and provinces in several large countries also have such taxes. However current economic judgement – combined without doubt with intense lobbying from vested interests – appears to favour a cap-and-trade approach with international trade in permits permitted (see Kyoto Protocol below).[27] (Interestingly, in none of the published arguments on the relative merits of the two approaches does it appear that consideration has been given to which might be the more open to abuse.)

Recently there appears to have been something of a resurgence of advocacy in favour of a carbon tax, particularly in the wake of the collapse of the international carbon trading market. CEO of ExxonMobil Rex Tillerson favours a tax as 'more direct, more transparent and more effective' whereas cap-and-trade 'inevitably introduces unnecessary cost and complexity'.[28] Concern has also been expressed that cap-and-trade merely perpetuates a business-as-usual approach, when what is required is a much more radical approach that will drive the transformation of society and technology that climate change requires.[29] On 11 April 2014 leaders of the IMF and World Bank called on finance ministers to use fiscal policies, such as carbon taxes, to combat climate change. IMF Managing Director Christine Lagarde stated that carbon taxes and removing fossil fuel subsidies were 'intelligent' means to reallocate resources to benefit the environment.[30] All things considered, for a small country like New Zealand conscious of and anxious to preserve its environmental quality, a carbon tax is probably the mechanism to be preferred.

The Kyoto Protocol

The Kyoto Protocol to the UNFCCC is an international treaty that allows countries to enter into legally binding obligations to reduce their emissions of greenhouse gases. The text of the Protocol was agreed among UNFCCC countries at their meeting in Kyoto in 1997, and came into force in February 2005. The binding obligations under the Protocol to reduce emissions were specified as referring to two commitment periods, the first from 2008 to 2012, and the second from 2013 to 2020, measured against a baseline year (1990 being that most commonly adopted by individual countries).

Parties to the UNFCCC fall into a number of categories. Those listed in Annex I to the Convention are the industrialised countries and some economies in the stage of transition. Annex B parties are those Annex I parties to the Convention, listed in Annex B to the Kyoto Protocol, which have undertaken either first or second period commitments. Among Annex B parties, of which there are currently 24 countries plus the EU, the strongest commitments for the first period were made by Denmark and Germany, which undertook to reduce their annual emissions to 79 per cent of their 1990 emissions levels. At the other end of the spectrum, Spain undertook to restrain its emissions to 115 per cent of 1990 emissions. New Zealand, like several other countries, undertook to keep emissions at 100 per cent of their 1990 value. The US chose not to be bound by the Protocol and did not ratify it. Australia under Prime Minister John Howard also chose not to ratify the Protocol, but did so under Prime Minister Kevin Rudd in 2007. Non-Annex I parties to the UNFCCC, comprising mainly developing countries, while committed to the goals of the Convention but not have binding commitments, could participate in the Protocol in a number of alternative ways.

The intention of the Protocol was that individual countries should primarily reduce emissions within their own borders and by national-level measures. However a number of more flexible mechanisms were also to be permitted. The first involved international emissions trading. To each Annex I country undertaking a binding commitment in relation to emissions, the Kyoto secretariat would issue carbon credits (technically called 'assigned amount units' or AAUs, each representing 1 tonne CO_2e) to cover their agreed cumulative emissions over 2008–12. These AAUs could be bought and sold in a special market, similar to a share market, and this would establish an international price for carbon. At the end of the commitment period each Annex I country would have to hand back to the Kyoto secretariat sufficient AAUs to cover their actual emissions over the period. Countries with surplus AAUs could sell them in the market, while those with a deficit would have to purchase more. The main international market for AAUs is currently the EU Emission Trading Scheme (EU ETS) launched in 2005. Some countries (for example South Korea) and some states (for example California, some Chinese provinces) have set up their own markets to enable individual companies to trade carbon credits in a complementary manner. Other flexible options for Annex I countries to meet their commitments include the Clean Development Mechanism, in which they can invest in emissions-reducing projects in Non-Annex I countries; and Joint Implementation, by which means Annex I countries can invest in emissions-reducing projects in another Annex I country.

This elaborate plan permitting international transfers of carbon credits has fallen on problematic times. The carbon price for trades in the EU ETS market collapsed from €15–20 in 2010 to below €5 in 2012, where it currently sits. The reasons for this collapse were a combination of the global financial crisis which reduced economic activity and the need for credits, and the issuing of excessive numbers of credits by the EU itself in the first place. The reorganisation of the market among the 27 member countries is likely to be a protracted affair.[31]

Using data provided by individual countries, the UNFCCC has calculated that aggregate emissions from all Annex I countries over the period 1990–2008 – excluding emissions from land use, land-use change and forestry, commonly referred to as LULUCF – declined by 6.0 per cent, while aggregate emissions including LULUCF declined by 10.7 per cent.[32] In all individual Annex I countries the growth of emissions was slower than the rate of growth of GDP. Several countries succeeded in keeping total emissions in 2008 without LULUCF at or below their 1990 levels despite recording strong economic growth: Belgium, Denmark, Finland, France, Germany, Luxembourg, Monaco, Netherlands, Sweden and the United Kingdom.[33] Despite these successes, it is clear that much greater commitments are going to be needed in the future if the world is to stabilise GHG concentrations in the atmosphere. The IPCC A4R report of 2007 indicates that to keep GHG concentration at less than 550 ppm, Kyoto Annex I countries will need to reduce their emissions to 10–40 per cent below 1990 levels by year 2020, and to 40–95 per cent below by year 2050, even if developing countries make their own substantial reductions.[34] The only Annex I country to have made and maintained a voluntary pledge in line with this requirement is Norway.

New Zealand, Emissions Trading, and the Kyoto Protocol

According to New Zealand's official climate change information website, the government's principal policy response to climate change is the New Zealand Emissions Trading Scheme (NZ ETS).[35] We will therefore examine the NZ ETS, particularly in relation to the New Zealand's commitment to the Kyoto Protocol.[36]

New Zealand was one of the Annex I countries that undertook binding commitments for the first commitment period of the Protocol. It negotiated one of the most lenient of commitments, to reduce emissions to 100 per cent of their 1990 value, on average, over 2008–12. In its 2011 report the UNFCCC recorded that for New Zealand, total aggregate emissions over the period 1990–2008 had grown by 22.7 per cent excluding LULUCF (the ninth worst performance by any Annex I country), and by 62.4 per cent including LULUCF (the worst performance of all Annex I countries barring Turkey).[37] In December 2012 signatories to the UNFCCC held a meeting in Doha to decide on what commitments parties would make for the Protocol's second commitment period, 2013–20. In the event, a number of Annex I countries committed to reducing GHG emissions by at least 18 per cent below 1990 levels in this eight-year period. Preceding the conference on 3 December 2012, Minister for Climate Change Tim Groser announced that New Zealand was on track to exceed its first-period Kyoto commitment to 2012, and that New Zealand would not be undertaking a binding commitment for the second period. New Zealand would however make a non-binding 'pledge' for the second period. New Zealand was, Minister Groser said, 'ahead of the curve', and it was time to move on.[38] In what follows we outline the New Zealand ETS and examine the merit of the Minister's claim.

Politics and the NZ ETS. In recognition of the growing importance of the climate change issue, in 1991 the then Minister for the Environment in the National Government, Simon Upton, stated his government's commitment to an interim target of a 20 per cent reduction in CO_2 emissions by 2000; and in 1994 he foreshadowed the introduction of a modest NZ$10/tonne carbon tax. This was opposed by the Natural Resource Users Group, a coalition of industry and mining interests. In 1996 this group together with the Major Energy Users Group, the Manufacturers' Federation and other industrial interests opposed to a carbon tax, came together to form an umbrella group called the Greenhouse Policy Coalition, which campaigned actively against the carbon tax proposal.[39] No more was heard from the National Government on carbon taxes. The revised policy would be to negotiate voluntary agreements for carbon reductions with individual companies.

With a new Labour government elected in December 1999, Parliament in 2002 passed the Climate Change Response Act 2002, which established the legal framework to allow New Zealand to ratify the Kyoto Protocol and so address its obligations under the UNFCCC. New Zealand ratified the Kyoto Protocol on 19 December 2002. Not surprisingly the issue of a possible carbon tax or emissions trading scheme resurfaced. In 2005 the government announced a proposed carbon tax of NZ$15/tonne carbon on the use of fossil fuels to come into effect on 1 April 2007. This set off renewed howls of protest from the Greenhouse Policy Coalition, as well as the Business Roundtable and Business New Zealand.[40] The main reasons put forward by these groups against a carbon tax were – as they had been a decade before – that it would work against New Zealand's international competitiveness especially in relation to those countries not bound by Kyoto commitments, and in the longer run cause companies to relocate overseas to non-Kyoto countries; that it would not have much impact on emissions anyway because most New Zealand GHG emissions were from agriculture and transportation, sectors for which there were no quick fixes; and that it would be contrary to the principles of a good tax system because of its selectivity. The first argument has some merit in a long-run context, but ignores the economic and other opportunities that an early shift to other forms of energy and new technologies would provide; the second argument is in the overall scheme of things trivial as a start needs to be made somewhere and options are often less limited than they may appear at the time; and the third argument is nonsense because the tax would have attempted to correct the externality arising from global warming that already existed. The Greenhouse Policy Coalition considered that 'positive incentives' would be better than a carbon tax.[41] The notion that there was a genuine real-world problem out there demanding an urgent solution does not appear to have been top of mind. New Zealand energy companies on the other hand appeared generally to have favoured the tax proposal.

In the face of this lobbying, and of the opposition to the tax from the New Zealand First Party (Labour's coalition partner at the time), Minister David Parker announced in December 2005 that the government would not be proceeding with the proposed carbon tax, and that other ways of managing New Zealand's greenhouse gas emissions would be considered. In September 2007 Minister

Parker announced details of a proposed Emissions Trading Scheme involving substantial concessions to major emitters, and in 2008 introduced the Climate Change Response (Emissions Trading) Amendment Bill to give substance to the framework foreshadowed in the 2002 Climate Change Response Act. The Bill passed into law in September 2008. In December of that year the National Party returned to power and promptly set up a committee to review the ETS legislation. In consequence, further amendments to the Act were made in November 2009 and again in November 2012. These changes weakened the government's response to climate change even further. And at this point it is salutary to remind ourselves why this whole exercise was supposedly put in train: namely the recognition that globally material is being added to the atmosphere that has a social cost currently estimated to be somewhere between US$12 and US$50 per tonne of carbon added, that this cost is increasing over time, and that an effective scheme is needed to reduce this damage.

The NZ ETS as set out in and developed from the legislation involves the government's creation of carbon credits in the form of units – NZUs – each representing one tonne of CO_2e.[42] These units are provided by the government to selected companies in the stationary energy, industrial process, and liquid fossil fuel sectors. Once in circulation the units can be traded without restriction. At the end of the annual accounting period carbon emitters are required to provide the government with sufficient units to cover their emissions in the previous year. Those companies not having sufficient NZUs to cover their emissions, or that had not been allocated NZUs, could purchase units on the market from surplus companies, or physically reduce their emissions by changing their use of technology.

The NZ ETS now in place has some interesting characteristics:

- The credits are to be *given* by the government to the industries affected. These credits have monetary value in the hands of the recipients, either if they are sold or if they permit the recipient to continue adding GHGs to the atmosphere. This gift represents a substantial transfer to wealth to emitting companies from taxpayers, who have no control on how these funds are spent;

- The scheme has no defined cap on total emissions. Thus to refer to the scheme as a 'cap-and-trade' system, as the government does, is mischievous. Furthermore the number of credits given to each company is determined not by their emissions at some historical date (and are therefore limited), but given in accordance with present production levels. This provides no incentive for companies to limit increases in production as they can simply obtain more permits as emissions increase; and those companies that reduce pollution receive fewer credits. In an even more extreme move, companies required to respond to government under the scheme need only return one credit for each 2 tonnes of emissions, with this additional subsidy to industry to remain in place indefinitely;
- The gifting of credits to emitting companies has no justification in economic theory. The economically appropriate means of allocation is to auction the credits, a process which is less distortive of the economy, provides a direct incentive for company innovation, and provides funds to the government. Furthermore, auctioning is a transparent process and not subject to covert lobbying designed to secure allocative favours. Ross Garnaut, Australian economist internationally known for his work on climate change, has stressed that in relation to emissions trading 'there are no identifiable circumstances that would justify the free allocation of permits'[43];
- The phasing down of the annual allocation of credits over time will be at the rate of 1.3 per cent per year, starting from 2016. This means that on present plans New Zealand taxpayers will be providing subsidies to emitting industries until well into the latter part of the century;
- The entry into the Scheme of the agricultural sector,

responsible for half of New Zealand's total emissions, is deferred indefinitely.

In addition, the scheme permits (with some exceptions) New Zealand companies to buy credits in international carbon credit markets for surrender to the New Zealand government in lieu of NZUs. With the collapse of prices in the EU ETS and the collateral fall in the value of New Zealand credits, New Zealand companies can make up any shortfall in NZUs at little cost and without change of behaviour.

Criticisms of the New Zealand ETS legislation along similar lines to those above were made at the time the amendments to the legislation in 2009 were being formulated and passed through the House.[44] On the other hand the executive director of the Greenhouse Policy Coalition at that time described the changes as 'a welcome move in the right direction', and the chief executive of Business New Zealand described the changes as providing for a 'more measured transition into a full trading scheme'. Editorially the *New Zealand Herald* called the Bill 'backward legislation' and 'a miserable offering to the international effort'. Speaking in parliament to the third reading of the Bill, Labour Party climate change spokesperson Charles Chauvel described the ETS as 'fundamentally flawed on multiple levels. It is economically irrational, socially inequitable, environmentally counter-productive and fiscally unsustainable'.[45] That would seem to be an eminently reasonable assessment.

Making the Kyoto numbers match. How is it that if New Zealand has one of the worst performances in the world in relation to the growth of emissions in recent years, it is on course to fulfil its Kyoto commitments as Minister Groser claims? It is necessary to look at the numbers. In 1990 in the brave new world of carbon accounting in New Zealand, the government stated its aim of bringing CO_2 emissions down to 20 per cent below their 1990 level by 2005. In 1997 when New Zealand adopted the Kyoto Protocol, this aim had been lowered to reducing emissions to 100 per cent of their 1990 levels over the Kyoto first commitment period 2008-12: it being understood internationally that this obligation would be met without counting credits arising from local plantation forestry. In 2002 when New Zealand ratified the Protocol it was clear that forest credits would not be excluded from the accounting. In 2006, in government discussion documents examining measures to reduce greenhouse gas emissions post-2012, no explicit targets at all received mention, only broad principles. Proposals underlying the NZ ETS merely stated the goal of 'reducing New Zealand's net emissions below business-as-usual levels'.[46]

The agreed estimate for New Zealand's gross emissions in 1990 is 61.92 million tonnes of CO_2e. Thus under the Kyoto Protocol the country's first period commitment would involve emissions of 61.92 x 5 = 309.6 Mt CO_2e (with some accounting adjustments the projected figure is 315.9 Mt). According to the Ministry for the Environment's 2013 calculations, New Zealand's cumulative emissions over the period 2008–12 from the energy, industrial processes and solvents, agriculture and waste sectors was 363.5 Mt CO_2e. To this must be added the contribution of the forestry sector. As growing trees absorb CO_2 from the atmosphere, the planting and growing of trees will count as a credit. Conversely the cutting down of trees or change of scrubland to pastoral activities will increase emissions and count as a debit. And according to the Kyoto rules forestry changes occurring since 1990 can be used to meet emissions targets. The Ministry for the Environment estimates that forestry will cause 14.3 Mt of emissions due to deforestation but will sequester 91.5 Mt due to forest and tree growth. Thus projected emissions for the first commitment period in net terms are 286.3 Mt. Consequently New Zealand's projected net position is +29.6 Mt, by which calculation New Zealand will readily meet its Kyoto first-period commitment.[47] As Minister Groser proclaimed.

Note that the key figure in achieving this result is the 91.5 Mt due to forest growth. However these forests are scheduled to be harvested later this decade and in the 2020s, and when they are they will count as a debit and provide an immense hole in New Zealand's greenhouse gas accounts. What this accounting amounts to is that the inaction by government pushes the responsibility for greenhouse response onto those who will be living in the decades to come. The government's claim that New Zealand is meeting its responsibilities under Kyoto in particular and responding actively to global warming, are conjuring tricks. Is this what is meant by being ahead of the curve?

So where are we now? When Minister Groser made his 'ahead of the curve' announcement, he gave the following reasons for New Zealand's withdrawal from any second period Kyoto commitment: 'You cannot seriously argue you are dealing with climate change unless you start to tackle the 85 per cent of emissions that are outside [Kyoto]', referring to the fact that India, China and the US as well, were not party to the Kyoto binding commitment arrangements (India and China as developing countries, the US as not having ratified the Protocol). Although the statement has superficial appeal, the implied argument is at least glib and debatably false, for the following reasons. First, it was never the intention of the Kyoto arrangements that they would be a once-for-all-time static document unresponsive to the needs and wishes of its participants. A commitment for the second period in no way interferes with the development of alternative future mechanisms for carbon reduction, which indeed the UNFCCC are already exploring and which are aimed at drawing in developing countries. Second, it takes no cognisance of the economic opportunities open to early adopters of new technologies forced by the discipline of reducing CO_2 emissions. Third, it takes no recognition of the fact that Annex I countries, including New Zealand, have historically been responsible for the majority of the world's carbon emissions since industrialisation, and need to take some responsibility for that fact. Fourth, it ignores both moral and international political aspects of the decision. On the moral side New Zealand must choose how it wants to be seen by the world, and on the political side it fails to recognise that smaller countries have little more than moral suasion with which to influence the conduct of the large and powerful. The New Zealand government's withdrawal from Kyoto would appear to have much to do with its lack of commitment to dealing with climate change, born of ideology and the privileging of short-term commercial interests.

As a fig leaf to cover New Zealand's withdrawal from a second-period Kyoto commitment, Minister Groser on 16 August 2013 announced that New Zealand would commit to a self-defined and non-binding 'conditional responsibility target' to reduce GHG emissions to 5 per cent below 1990 levels by 2020, not under the Kyoto Protocol but under UNFCCC mitigation targets.[48] Flimsy as this proposal is, we may doubt its reality given the record of government backtracking on previous commitments. Nonetheless the New Zealand government has undertaken other more positive initiatives in the international arena. It has been instrumental in setting to the Global Research Alliance on Agricultural Greenhouse Gas Emissions, and has joined the international Climate Change and Clean Air Coalition which focuses on the reduction of short-lived climate pollutants including soot, methane and HFCs.[49] These are both valuable long-term initiatives, but are no substitute for the urgent short-term measures required to combat global warming.

Government actions on the domestic front to reduce carbon emissions and use cleaner fuels present a very mixed picture. In 2007 the Labour government introduced into Parliament a Biofuels Bill requiring petrol and diesel sold in New Zealand to contain a percentage of biofuels, with this percentage to increase over time. Partly on the recommendation of the Commissioner for the Environment, the Bill did not proceed. In 2009 the National government introduced a three-year biodiesel grants scheme aimed at kick-starting a biodiesel production industry, but this was unsuccessful as it provided no long-term certainty to investors or to fuel purchasers. In 2006 a solar water heating programme provided grants for the installation of solar water heaters, but this was discontinued on the basis of cost benefit calculations. A limited home insulation programme, Heat Smart, was introduced in 2009 with a 2013 completion date, when it was replaced with a Healthy Homes programme (involving $100m over three years) directed to low-income households.

In 2007 New Zealand was generating about 70 per cent of its electricity from renewable sources (mainly hydro and geothermal), and in September of that year Prime Minister Helen Clark announced a national target of 90 per cent electricity generation from renewables to be achieved by 2025, with wind power to make up the majority of this percentage increase. This national target has also been taken up by the Key government, which in 2011 published a National Policy Statement for Renewable Electricity Generation. This is a planning document that directs councils in their decisions in relation to renewable energy generation. It is policy as wand waving. New Zealand remains one of few high-income countries to have no policies specifically encouraging generation of electricity from renewable sources.[50] It remains quite unclear how the 90 per cent target will be achieved on schedule, particularly given the continually rising trend of total electricity generation against which the percentage of renewables generation has been following a *falling* trend since before 1980.[51]

In the 12 years since the original Climate Change Response Act little has been achieved in reducing carbon emissions in New Zealand, which continue to rise. Large polluters continue to pollute, and the burden of adjustment has been pushed out for taxpayers and the younger generations to contend with in the future. Current New Zealand government policy towards climate change appears as little more than smoke and mirrors.

Paradigm Failure (Again)

There are no doubt several reasons underlying the government's window-dressing on global warming and climate change: electoral advantage, mistrust of the citizenry, and the intentional favouring of some sectors of society likely among them. Whatever those details might be, it is clear that we have a failure of the paradigm to accommodate the scale of the issue at hand.

We have the attempt of a free market economic paradigm to respond to the world's largest externality problem. The externality is not a marginal consideration on the borders of the market, it is central to the problem: it is *the* problem and needs to be addressed directly as such. Given its outstanding importance this should involve transparency on the part of government and the broad-based engagement of citizens. The laissez-faire approach to climate change by the New Zealand government in setting up an anaemic market-based response, with minimal regulation, and by preferencing emitting industries at the direct expense of taxpayers, should not be considered acceptable. Furthermore it is clear that the effects of climate change will be wrought across society in accidental fashion, without reference to desert or merit or income. In these circumstances the laissez-faire approach which rejects the idea of support for those that will be most affected and in need – such as farmers – pitches interest against interest and engenders opposition to essential change, rather than cooperation in the quest for a better future. This should not be considered acceptable either.

In August 2013, former Prime Minister and currently Administrator of the UNDP Helen Clark, interviewed by the political editor of the *New Zealand Herald*, attested that the reputation that New Zealand has built up over many years for being a good player and honouring its international commitments is a very precious one and needs safeguarding.[52] Despite all the difficulties inherent in responding to climate change, New Zealanders must choose how they wish to be and to act in the world. And that is not merely a matter of marketised costs and benefits, but involves our moral relationship with the rest of the world. And that moral choice is inescapable: not to act against the threat of climate change is as much an expression of morality as it is to act against it.

On 16 February 2014 John Kerry, US Secretary of State in the Obama administration, gave a talk in Jakarta on climate change, and its significance for the future of Indonesia and the world.[53] Here are some excerpts from what he had to say:

> 'When 97 per cent of scientists agree on anything, we need to listen, and we need to respond. Well, 97 per cent of climate scientists have confirmed that climate change is happening and that human activity is responsible … And they agree that, if we continue to go down the same path that we are going down today, the world as we know it will change – and it will change dramatically for the worse …'
>
> '… we need to move on this, and we need to move together now. We just don't have time to let a few loud interest groups hijack the climate conversation … I'm talking about big companies that like it the way it is that don't want to change, and spend a lot of money to keep you and me and everybody from doing what we know we need to do. First and foremost, we should not allow a tiny minority of shoddy scientists and science and extreme ideologues to compete with scientific fact. Nor should we allow any room for those who think that the costs associated with doing the right thing outweigh the benefits … We certainly should not allow more time to be wasted by those who want to sit around debating whose responsibility it is to deal with this threat, while we come closer and closer to the point of no return.'
>
> 'I am very well aware that these are not easy choices for a country to make … But I urge governments to measure the full cost to that coal and that oil … You have to factor in the long-term cost of carbon pollution. And they have to factor in the cost of survival. And if they do, then governments will find that the cost of pursuing clean energy now is far

cheaper than paying for the consequences of climate change later.'

'... None of this is beyond our capacity.'

8

The Twenty-first Century – Natural Resources

Population, Natural Resources, Food, Globally

It is generally agreed that the species *Homo sapiens* appeared on the surface of the earth about 200,000 years ago. Not until about the middle of the seventeenth century of our era did the growth in human numbers start to accelerate, at which time the total world population stood at a little over 500 million. Even so it was not until about the year 1800 that the world's population reached one billion people. It took only another 130 years to add a second billion, another 30 years to add a third billion, another 15 years to add a fourth billion, another 12 years to add a fifth billion; and reached 6.8bn in 2009. Although the rate of population increase has moderated somewhat since the 1970s, the UN Population Division's revised estimates for 2010 project that the world's population will increase by 2.5bn to reach 9.3bn by 2050.[1] (See Figure 2) This is equivalent to adding a city of over one million people per week for the next 40 years. This rise will occur mainly in high-fertility regions (principally Africa, Asia and Latin America), the population of which is projected to rise from 5.7bn in 2010 to 8.0bn in 2050. Population of more developed regions is likely to rise slightly from 1.24bn to 1.31bn.

Figure 2. World population 1000–2100 CE

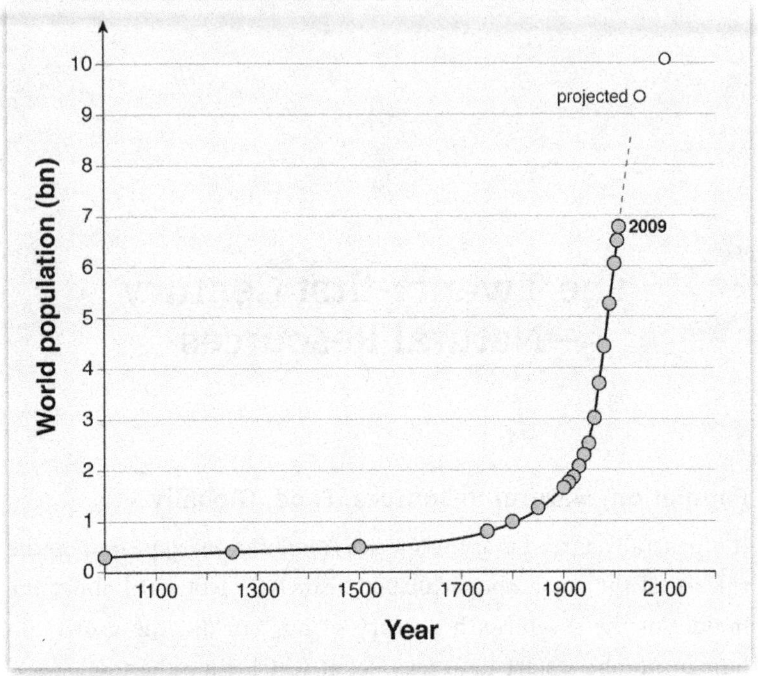

Source: UN Population Division, *World Population Prospects: The 2010 Revision*, 2011, and various.

Of the world's current population, the World Health Organization (WHO) estimates that about one third are well fed, one third are underfed, and one third are starving. According to World Bank estimates, in 2005 21 per cent of all humanity (1.4bn persons) fell below the international poverty line income of $1.25 a day, and almost 50 per cent were living on less than $2.50 a day.[2] A study conducted by the WHO concluded that of the world's 6.9 billion, 1.1bn (16 per cent) lack access to safe drinking water, 2.6bn (38 per cent) lack basic sanitation, and over 3.5 million die annually as a result of inadequate water, sanitation and hygiene.[3] If the expanding world population is to be fed and the poverty of the poorest alleviated, an increase in world food production of 50 per cent over the period to 2050 is likely to be required.[4] This appears to be an unrealistic expectation given that world cereal grain yields have been falling over the last 50 years, and that grain production (which makes up 80 per cent of the world's food supply) has not risen on a per capita basis since the 1980s.[5]

The huge increase in world population over the last 200 years is unique in the history of the earth. Nowadays the single species *Homo sapiens* co-opts for its own use about 40 per cent of total net primary production of terrestrial ecosystems (both natural and those developed by humans).[6] One measure of this impact of humans on the environment is the human 'ecological footprint', defined as the amount of biologically productive land and water area required to produce the resources an individual consumes, and to absorb all the wastes he or she produces, using prevailing technology and resource management practices. Although difficult to quantify, estimates indicate that all of humanity requires about 1.5 earths to support its consumption, or otherwise put, the earth required about 18 months to regenerate the resources used in a year.[7] Such a situation cannot persist.

The state of the world's natural resource base is being degraded at an alarming rate. Consider the following:

Soils. Topsoil provides the growth substrate for all the world's crops and grasses. It is a diaphanously thin layer, measurable in centimetres rather than metres, which covers much of the world's earthly surface. When removed by erosion, the subsoil becomes part of the tillage layer and productivity falls. Scientists have estimated that topsoil losses exceed 'tolerable soil loss' limits on 40 per cent of US croplands, and that soil should not be considered a renewable resource from a perspective of less than 100–200 years for some soils, and up to 1,000–10,000 years for others.[8] A study by the World Resources Institute and United Nations agencies indicates that nearly 40 per cent of the world's agricultural land is severely degraded, a circumstance that is likely to undermine the long-term productivity of these soils.[9] The world's agricultural lands are losing up to 75bn tonnes of fertile topsoil per annum due to water and wind erosion, representing a serious productivity loss.[10] All up, the current loss of arable land is estimated at 30–35 times its historical rate. Desertification is increasing worldwide, and up to 50 million people may be displaced by its effects in the next decade.[11]

Water. Water too is becoming a scarce resource in many parts of the world. About one third of the world's crop production is irrigated. Overuse of irrigation water has resulted in 20 per cent of this land suffering from waterlogging and salinity, lowering productivity. In many areas of the world, from China to India to the US, irrigation water supplies are only sustained by mining groundwater aquifers, with ever-lowering water tables, higher costs, and threat of resource exhaustion. Furthermore agricultural water supplies are subject to increasing claims from alternative uses for cities and towns, and for in-stream environmental uses. In many regions of the world water scarcity has resulted in limitations on agricultural and industrial production, in ecological degradation, and in threats to human health.[12]

Fisheries. A recent international study of the world's fisheries concluded that 90 per cent of all large fishes have disappeared from the world's oceans in the last half century, devastated by the effects of industrial fishing. As one of the study's authors expressed it: 'the point is that there is nowhere left in the ocean not overfished'.[13] The collapse of the Californian sardine fishery (1950s), the Peruvian anchovy fishery (1970s), and the Newfoundland cod fishery (1990s) are merely examples of a worldwide trend.

Biodiversity. Biological diversity, or biodiversity, refers to the web of ecological interactions among species and their ecological niches. It provides critical benefits to humankind in the form of services arising from the interactions of species in the environment itself, such as erosion control and water purification by plants and soil micro-organisms, soil fertility, pest control, and pollination and seed dispersal by insects, birds and animals. Each individual species also represents a storehouse of genetic information of potentially great value to the health and welfare of humankind, as in for example providing sources for drugs and medicines. However the number of species whose existence has been listed as 'critically endangered', or as 'endangered', or as 'vulnerable', is increasing in all major groups of species, some very substantially.[14] The Secretariat of the UN Convention on Biological Diversity attests that 'biodiversity is in decline at all levels and geographical scales'.[15]

Food. The provision of food globally is being squeezed between the increasing demand from a growing population and growing affluence (however ill-distributed) on the one hand, and the declining ability of the resource base, due to land degradation, erosion, and water scarcity, to provide for it. Over the last decade, world food reserves have fallen by one third and at times have touched dangerously low levels. The FAO World Food Price Index, although at historically low levels, has more than doubled since 2000. Other forces acting to drive up world grain prices in the longer term include the substantial increase in the use of grain for the production of fuel ethanol for automobiles: in 2011 the US harvested almost 400 million tons of grain, 32 per cent of which went to ethanol distilleries. (One estimate suggests that the grain required to fill a 25-gallon fuel tank of an SUV with ethanol just once would feed one person for a year.[16]) For those in poorer countries who expend a great proportion of their income on food, food price rises could spell disaster if they continue into the future.

Rising prices and increasing food scarcity have led to leading exporting countries, concerned by these phenomena in their own countries, to temporarily curb exports: as was done in the food price crisis of 2008 by Russia and Argentina in relation to wheat, and Vietnam in relation to rice. Another response has been for potential food deficit countries to buy or lease land in other countries on which to grow food for themselves. This movement is led by China, Saudi Arabia and South Korea, and has so far been directed mainly at land in Africa. A 2011 World Bank estimate is that the amount of land already involved in these transactions (at least 140 million acres) exceeds the cropland devoted to corn and wheat in the US.[17]

Energy. Oil accounts for about one third of the world's primary energy supply and more than 95 per cent of its transport energy use. Whether 'peak oil' has been reached already or will be at some time in the immediate or foreseeable future, it is true now that world discoveries of conventional oilfields peaked in the 1960s, discoveries fell below annual production in the 1980s, and conventional sources of oil are becoming more difficult to access and more costly to develop. Unconventional sources of oil such as oil sands, oil shales, heavy crude oil and deep water oil are subject to high production costs, and high environmental risks. World prices for oil and natural gas have trebled since 1999. Despite the large quantities of oil available from unconventional sources they are not capable of replacing crude oil from conventional sources, particularly so in the face of increasing demand.[18] There is a 'growing consensus that the era of cheap oil has passed and that we are entering a new and very different phase.'[19] In the past this readily available, flexible and low-cost energy source has not only fuelled agricultural, manufacturing and transport activities directly, but it has also underwritten the immense increase in industrial production of fertilisers and pesticides required to maintain the agricultural 'green revolution' in less developed countries. Its declining availability is likely to lead over time to higher costs for food, shortages in countries least able to sustain such changes, and social unrest.

Overview. The Millennium Ecosystem Assessment carried out between 2001 and 2005 has pointed to the strong probability of continuing degradation of the global ecosystem, impeding its ability to meet the growing demands upon it for food, fresh water, fibre and energy, and increasing the risk of poverty for some groups. The study concluded that: 'The challenge of reversing the degradation of ecosystems while meeting increasing demands for their services can be partially met under some scenarios ... but these involve significant changes in policies, institutions and practices which are not currently under way'.[20] A more recent report from UNEP confirms the depth of the crisis, pointing out that by some estimates the projected loss of ecosystem services could lead to a 25 per cent loss of the world's food production by 2050.[21]

Finally, it needs to be stressed that the degradation of the environment and loss of agricultural capacity described above has been going on gradually over historical time. In the future, as these effects become coupled with those due to climate change, their consequences will be magnified, perhaps to ruinous extent. This is the big picture: worries about the stability of financial markets, while perhaps of some immediate concern, pale into insignificance by comparison. The twenty-first-century world is one fraught with many dangers. It is a world that neoliberal economics does not comprehend.

The Idea of Sustainability

In the 1970s and amid rising concerns for the state of the world's population, environment and natural resources, the idea of 'sustainability' emerged as a key unifying principle. In its modern sense, the notion of sustainability emerged from ecology: that branch of biology that studies the relations of organisms to one another and to their physical surroundings. In this science an ecological system, or ecosystem, is understood as the community of living organisms (plants and animals and microbes) together with the non-living components of the environment (air, water, inorganic soil) interacting as a system. Thus an ecosystem of interest might be as small as a Walden pond, or as large as the world itself, or as diverse as a grassland, a desert, an ocean or a tropical rainforest. Sustainability refers to the ability of the ecosystem to endure over time in many of its important properties while at the same time continuing to evolve. The ability of an ecosystem to retain its overall stability in the face of disturbance is referred to as its 'resilience', a concept we have met with already in Chapter 6.

Humans are likewise part of global, regional and local ecosystems. From a human perspective, the core idea of sustainability requires that we act so as to create and maintain 'the conditions under which humans and nature can exist in productive harmony, that permit fulfilling the social, economic and other requirements of present and future generations.'[22] In 1987 the World Commission on Environment and Development defined 'sustainable development' as 'development that meets the needs of the present without compromising the ability of future generations to meet their own needs'. Sustainability, it is clearly recognised, has economic, environmental, and social/cultural dimensions.

One point in particular needs emphasis here. Proponents of sustainability take the view that life on earth is worth preserving: that the well-being of this generation's children and their descendants and of the natural environment that supports them, matter. This is an ethical stance, and it is an ethical stance supported in this book. And if sustainability is a virtue, then it is inevitably part of the common good.

Let us look more closely at what sustainability implies for the economy. When we think about the human impact on the environment, we can think of it as a consequence of three things: population, the level of affluence and consumption, and the technology in use. If population increases, then other things being equal the demands placed on the environment increase, and the same occurs with rising affluence; whereas at any given level of population and affluence, technology can have an environmental impact to a greater or lesser degree dependent on the type of technology chosen. These observations are often expressed in the 'IPAT identity': if P stands for population, A is an index of per capita affluence (consumption of resources), and T is an index of environmental disruptiveness of the technology in use, then the overall environmental impact I can be written as $I \equiv P.A.T.$[23] As this relationship suggests, these variables can be traded off against each other. For example the impact on the environment of a rise in affluence can be offset by either a decrease in population or the use of less disruptive technology (or both). Given the current unsustainable nature of the world economy, it should be a major goal of economic policy to reduce environmental impact I. From what has already been said it is evident that in several important respects the global economy has overreached the capacity of the environment to support it: that is the world economy has reached a position of unsustainability. The virtues of technological change, so often promoted by laissez-faire economists as the means to resolve all such problems, have evidently failed to protect the world from the situation it now finds itself in.

From a sustainability perspective the scale of the economy becomes a key strategic variable. Technology under a sustainability regime needs to emphasise not the throughput of resources (such as currently measured by GDP) but the productivity derivable per unit of resource used, and products and processes themselves need to emphasise recycling both in the economy and in natural ecosystems (that is, biodegradability). In terms of resource management, sustainability points towards the management of a renewable resource in such a manner that the rate of harvest does not exceed the rate of natural productivity (that is, its regenerative capacity), and the rate of emission of a waste does not exceed the assimilative capacity of the environment to receive it (that is, its ability to cleanse itself without deleterious effect). The concept of maximising net present value as employed in orthodox economics needs to give place to the concept of maximising sustainable yield as the outer bound of renewable resource use. Non-renewable resources on the other hand, such as minerals (including fossil fuels) are only exploitable at the cost of their depletion. In the case of non-energy minerals this can be overcome to some degree by recycling. One proposal for using non-renewable resources 'quasi-sustainably' would involve the investment in exploiting a non-renewable resource being paired with an investment in a renewable resource in such a way that at the end of the life of the non-renewable resource, the renewable one would be providing an annual sustainable yield equal to the income component derived from the non-renewable one.

It is the idea of sustainability that lies at the heart of the new discipline of 'ecological economics'. What this ecological approach to economics emphasises is the importance of maintaining our stock of 'natural capital'. Economists generally make a clear distinction between capital – as an asset or a stock of assets – and income – the flow of goods and services over time yielded by capital. In orthodox economics capital has commonly been taken to mean capital produced by economic process, for example buildings, machines, education and so on. From a sustainability perspective this is incomplete. Here the capacity of the environment to provide the things we need must also be taken into account as 'natural capital', part of the store of things that we can call upon to provide for our well-being. And at the centre of concern for natural capital must be the maintenance of those elements which provide the services essential for the support of life itself, clean air, clean water and basic food: all of which are essentially irreplaceable by manufactured capital, or only so at extravagantly high cost. (see Appendix 2)

If we are to manage the economy adequately, then it is fundamental that account be taken of changes in natural capital and their influence on income. In terms of national accounting, it needs to be noted that the System of National Accounts (SNA), the internationally standardised method by which governments around the world estimate economic quantities such as GDP, is a relatively recent invention, having received its first publication by the United Nations in 1953. While it is a valuable tool for systematising consideration of these economic quantities, its limitations have always been acknowledged. GDP was never considered to provide a complete representation of a country's welfare, although it has come to be employed by some economists and media commentators as if it does. Although the computed figure for GDP accumulates all the marketed things that go to form the national product (national income), there are a lot of things it leaves out. For example it does not include household work, which contributes to well-being, nor the costs of unemployment, which subtract from it. If a car accident occurs, GDP goes up because of the additional employment of tow-truck and insurance operators, but nowhere is the loss of well-being to those involved in the accident accounted.

If a stand of native forest is cut down, GDP rises because of the additional employment and sale of the timber, but nowhere is the loss of the forest, or of the services it provided in erosion control, biodiversity retention, or in the absorption of carbon dioxide and the respiration of oxygen, brought to account. Nowhere is it acknowledged that one form of capital asset (building materials) has been created at the cost of the loss of another (the forest). As resource economist Robert Repetto observed: 'A country could exhaust its mineral resources, cut down its forests, erode its soils, pollute its aquifers, and hunt its wildlife and fisheries to extinction, but measured income would rise steadily as these assets disappeared.'[24] Clearly, the anomalous treatment of natural capital in the SNA can dangerously overestimate the performance of economies, and send erroneous signals to policy makers. The UN has responded to this situation in recent years by developing an expanded national accounting framework in which accounts for individual natural resources can be juxtaposed to SNA accounts, although few countries have as yet adopted this expanded frame. Other research has moved more definitively to encompass both environmental and social concerns within a national accounting framework: a matter to which we return in the next chapter.

The disjunction between the laissez-faire view of the economy and one that recognises sustainability is demonstrated sharply by their differing approaches to the passage of time. In market economics and in the commerce of our day-to-day lives, it is certainly true that a dollar tomorrow is worth less than a dollar today. The relationship between the monetary value a person attaches to an event in the future relative to the event in the present, is expressed in his or her personal rate of time preference. (The cumulation of individual time preference rates over the economy as a whole is evidently related to the market rate of interest.) The significance of the time preference rate – and the market interest rate – can be seen from the fact that a rate of 0.10 ('10 per cent') discounts the value of an event in 20 years' time to a fraction of 0.15 of its value now, and an event in 50 years' time to a fraction of 0.01 of its value now; and at a rate of 0.05 ('5 per cent') the discounted values for 20 and 50 years in the future are 0.38 and 0.09 respectively. Higher interest rates give relatively more weight to the present, lower interest rates more weight to the future.

The Stern Review of the economics of climate change exemplifies clearly the two differing views in relation to sustainability – in this case in relation to intergenerational valuation. Based on sound economic analysis Stern argued that the appropriate interest rate in his analysis would be the sum of two terms: the first being the 'pure rate of time preference', that is to say the time preference between two points in time assuming no change in the level of consumption; and the second an adjustment that takes account of a likely rise in per capita consumption over the period. On the first point Stern took the view that it was morally indefensible to discriminate between individuals as a consequence of their birth dates. That is, the moral weight to be given to the life of a person in 50 or 100 years' time was not different from that to be given to a person now living. Therefore the only appropriate pure time preference rate in this case was zero.[25] And in allowing for the possibility of increasing consumption over time, Stern arrived at a long-term interest rate of 1.4 per cent, which he then used in his base-case analysis.

The choice of such a low interest rate, uncommonly low by market standards (except in the wake of the GFC) created much controversy among economists, particularly those of free market disposition. Yale University's distinguished climate change economist William Nordhaus, among others, complained that Stern's call for immediate action on climate change was illegitimate because it did not employ the market interest rate and therefore overvalued the future. On the other hand, support for the Review's interest rate came from other distinguished economists including Robert Solow, James Mirrlees, Amarta Sen and Joseph Stiglitz, all Nobel Laureates. Fundamentally the choice of interest rate in this analysis (the 'social rate of time preference') comes down to a choice between one that reflects merely the personal choices of individuals now living, and one that recognises that this generation has some responsibility in terms of stewardship of the planet, for generations yet to be born.

New Zealand, Resources and Environment

How does New Zealand measure up in terms of resource use and sustainability? Modification of the environment is the price of human settlement. And indeed human settlement in New Zealand has wrought a substantial transformation of these islands. In the earliest days this was mainly through the use of fire in forest clearance, but gained pace and variety with Pakeha settlement and as the economy expanded and diversified. Exotic plants and animals were introduced and the over-exploitation of resources became more common. Only about 1 per cent of the original mature kauri forest survived nineteenth- and twentieth-century logging. While there is little point in trying to document environmental changes in the historic past, it is very relevant to try to achieve some estimate of environmental change over the last half century – the period covering both the rise of the neoliberal economy in New Zealand and global rise in awareness of environmental problems (dating, say, from the first UN

Conference on the Human Environment in Stockholm in 1972). Even so this task confronts difficulties. Often the things we would like to know are hard to measure scientifically, so we have to make do with indicators that we can measure; often in environmental measurement there are problems of the location and number of sampling points to be used (and the dangers of the unreflective use of averages); and the financial burden of adequate monitoring programmes can be high. In New Zealand the initiation of such programmes is relatively recent and in some cases programmes are only in their developmental phase. Nonetheless the importance of the issue demands that we try to understand the state of the New Zealand environment and trends over time.

Population. In late 2013 New Zealand's population reached 4.5 million, doubling since the late 1950s: that is, within the lifetime of New Zealanders over the age of 55 years. Population density is around 16.6 persons per square kilometre, low by international standards.

Soils. Landcare Research has highlighted the facts that whereas 25 per cent of New Zealand's GDP is derived from soil-dependent industries, and whereas that topsoil may take centuries to replace once lost, nevertheless New Zealand loses some 400 million tonnes of soil each year due to slumping and erosion, and half of this ends up in waterways and in the ocean – a rate of soil loss 10 times the world average.[26] There is in New Zealand an estimated 1.14 million hectares of hill country pasture (4.25 per cent of land area) classed as erosion prone, with 70 per cent of the vulnerable area in the North Island, most significantly in the Manawatu and Gisborne areas. Erosion from hill country areas is estimated to cost New Zealand between NZ$100m and NZ$150m each year through the loss of soil and nutrients, loss of production, damage to houses, fences, roads, phone and power lines, and damage to waterways and aquatic habitats.[27] On the other hand satellite imaging suggests that during the 1990s hill country erosion eased in some regions, due both to conversion of pasture to exotic forestry and the retirement of farming lands and their reversion to scrub.

Water. Water quality in New Zealand's major rivers declined between 1998 and 2007 according to a National Institute of Water and Atmospheric Research (NIWA) report.[28] Nitrogen and phosphorus loadings have increased greatly at many sampled sites due in particular to fertiliser use, and expansion of the dairy industry which has increased from 2.7m head of stock in the early 1990s to over 4.6m in 2012. Nitrate leaching into waterways in Canterbury has more than doubled over the period, and concentrations in well water have reached levels that put infant health at risk. Some New Zealand rivers now run dry in summer because of the over-allocation of water extraction rights. Ministry for the Environment data for recreational water quality compiled over five consecutive summers to 2011–12 shows that for 210 freshwater beaches sampled, 46 per cent are graded either 'very poor' or 'poor' (based on potential faecal contamination), and of 248 coastal beaches sampled 16 per cent 'very poor' or 'poor'. In a recent report by the Parliamentary Commissioner for the Environment on water quality and nutrient pollution it was found that without significantly increased intervention it was almost inevitable that there would be continuing deterioration in water quality in many catchments across the country, particularly in Canterbury and Southland.[29] The recent introduction and spread of the parasite giardia and of 'rock snot' (*Didymosphenia geminata*) throughout New Zealand rivers and waterways only serve to emphasise the ongoing nature of the contamination problem.

Fisheries. In a recent international assessment of the management of marine ecosystems, New Zealand ranked first among 53 maritime countries. Even so the assessors noted that New Zealand 'does not approach the high standards set either by international conventions or by consensus among scientists and managers.'[30] With regard to fish catch and its sustainability, considerable confidence has been expressed in New Zealand's quota management system, recognised as being one of the best worldwide. This is very good for New

Zealand. Nonetheless a note of caution does need to be added: in the 1980s and 1990s the Canadian Federal Department of Fisheries and Oceans considered their fishery science to be the best in the world right up to the date of the disastrous collapse of the Newfoundland cod fishery in 1992.[31] This is not to criticise either agency so much as to point to the limited knowledge of the ecosystems involved in ocean fisheries. One failing of New Zealand's quota management system may be found in the power and influence of bottom-trawling quota holder associations in minimising or blocking conservation management initiatives.[32]

Biodiversity. New Zealand has one of the worst records for biodiversity conservation of any country in the world. The early introduction of rats, dogs, pigs and goats has been followed by fire, land clearance, over-exploitation of resources and the further introduction of exotic plants and animals that have had a cumulative and deleterious effect on natural biodiversity.[33] More recently, cats, stoats and possums have taken their toll on indigenous fauna, particularly birds, not evolutionarily accustomed to such predation. The International Union for Conservation of Nature (IUCN) rates 37 per cent of New Zealand's 215 native bird species as threatened with extinction, 34 per cent of 797 plants under some level of threat, 68 per cent of freshwater fish as threatened, and the freshwater crayfish and mussel also in danger.[34] Unmanaged brown kiwi populations in the North Island are declining at a rate of 3 per cent per year, and there are continuing range declines of most forest and alpine birds. On the other hand there has been stabilisation of some iconic threatened species on isolated islands, and there have also been advances in mammalian predator management. One general observation that can be made is that it is not necessary to have a large human population or high population density to cause serious environmental damage.

Food. As a country with much fertile land and relatively low population, national food security is high. For New Zealand the main resource issues are the environmental terms on which food is produced, and the country's ability to export agricultural products to feed others.

Energy. New Zealand is singularly blessed by the fact that it can currently produce some 70–75 per cent of its electrical energy needs from renewable sources (of which hydro represents about 75 per cent, geothermal 18 per cent, and wind 5 per cent), with the remaining 25–30 per cent being provided by thermal generation from gas and coal (of which 84 per cent and 15 per cent respectively).[35] However New Zealand is not well placed in relation to liquid fuels that serve transportation needs. About one third of transport fuel needs are provided by local production, the remainder being imported. Given the risk of rising global energy costs there is considerable potential for measures to improve liquid fuel use efficiency, and to augment the use of public transport and electric vehicles.

Overview. In consideration of New Zealand's environmental performance over the 20 years since the first Earth Summit, the consensus of New Zealand scientific opinion would be that there have been losses in important areas, with limited evidence of positive progress on the ground.[36] While New Zealand's real GDP may have increased over these years, it has done so at the cost of the environment degradation. Given the attitude of recent governments there is little evidence that this will not continue into the future. Two further matters of overriding importance need to be stated. First, it is the physical, biophysical and ecological characteristics of the New Zealand environment that determine the immutable outer bound within which the economy and society must operate. No environment, no economy, no life. Second is that the pressures on natural resources will be exacerbated in the future as the effects of climate change and increasing population become increasingly manifest. New Zealand's greatest future challenge is likely to be to achieve the desired balance between these contending forces within a context of sustainability.

The New Zealand Resource Management Act

Process and outcome. In the years following World War II, laws relating to the use and management of the country's natural resources – in New Zealand as in many other countries – came into being in an ad hoc manner, in response to the many different issues as they arose: gold mining, soil erosion, urban development, air pollution. This produced a disparate and uncoordinated collection of laws, which were often difficult for parties to negotiate. With the ascendance of the fourth Labour government in 1984 and the spirit of reform then dominant, the opportunity arose for a thorough-going reform and unification of these laws.

The Resource Management Act (RMA), which passed into law in 1991, was a remarkable piece of legislation. The motivating force behind the RMA was Geoffrey (now Sir Geoffrey) Palmer, Minister for the Environment in the Labour government (1987–1990). He was faced with the very substantial task of reconstructing major pieces of legislation including the Town and Country Planning Act, the Water and Soil Conservation Act, the Soil Conservation and Rivers Control Act, and the Minerals Act (which finally ended up elsewhere[37]).[38] Day-to-day management of the process was given to a core group of officials which reported to a specially convened Cabinet Committee. A key element was to be the engagement of the public with the ongoing work of the technical experts. Throughout this time the Ministry for the Environment published a newsletter *Viewfinder*, providing information and discussion of the reform process, and in the early days a freephone was made available for feedback from the public. In August 1988 an initial discussion paper was published, which was followed by a period of extensive public consultation; in December 1988 the government's proposals for the framework for the new law were published and public submissions called for (of which there were 1256); in December 1989 the drafted legislation was introduced into Parliament and referred to a select committee which received over 1400 submissions, many of them heard in person; in August

1990 the select committee reported back to Parliament. However the resultant Bill reached only its second reading stage before Parliament was prorogued for the impending general election.

The conceptual foundation of the legislation that lay before Parliament was provided by the principles developed in the widely regarded 1987 report of the World Commission on Environment and Development entitled *Our Common Future* (the 'Brundtland report'). Central importance was given to the concept of sustainability. The core of the proposed Act was set out in Part II: Purpose and Principles, which stated in four brief sections the underlying philosophy of sustainable management, the matters of national importance and other matters to which recognition must be given by those exercising functions and powers under the Act, and the role of the Treaty of Waitangi. This Purpose and these Principles were to be applied in all areas covered by the Act, including land, coastal marine, rivers and lake beds, water, discharges, noise, adverse effects, and in the recognition of customary activities.

In the October 1990 election the Labour government was defeated at the polls. The Minister for the Environment in the incoming National government, Simon Upton, while a supporter of the general thrust of the resource management review project, established a small group to review the Bill and to make recommendations. The group's recommendations narrowed the scope of the legislation in relation to social concerns and focused more precisely on promoting the sustainable management of natural and physical resources. In May 1991 the Minister introduced to Parliament the new government's proposed amendments to the Bill, and after consideration by a select committee and final debate, the Resource Management Act was passed by the House in July 1991 and commenced on 1 October 1991. The wording of Part II of the Act as passed is given in Appendix 3. The content of this Part, representing as it does the core understandings of the Act, has been at the centre of debate and controversy in subsequent years.

In interpreting the intention of the Act, Upton was later to assert in relation to part II:

> ... In reality, the outcomes required by these paragraphs [section 5(2)] will be progressively given specific content as rules or standards are promulgated under the Act. ... The key point is that they cannot be traded off as a means of enabling the community to pursue its wellbeing. ... The balancing of costs and benefits, to the extent that it occurs, will be about the effects that will be permissible consistent with the thrust of paragraphs (a), (b) and (c). In other words, effects which do not erode the core prerequisites of sustainability.[39]

Thus in Upton's view, the core elements of New Zealand's natural capital were to be maintained and not reduced, not to be subject to the tyranny of small decisions, and not to be manipulated in cost benefit trade-offs.

New Zealand's RMA was remarkable for a number of reasons. First, the Act represented world-leading legislation in its focus on sustainability as the core requirement for a vital economic and social life into the future. Second, the Act was established after widespread and thorough discussions over several years, and consequently it was bipartisan – in broad measure both major political parties committed to it. Third, and most remarkably, the thrust of the legislation was in opposition to the free market advocacy that was at the heart of both Labour and National parties' policies during this epoch. As strange as it may seem, it was as if the front and back legs of the policy horse were galloping off in opposite directions.

The debate over philosophy. The successful passage of this legislation, even after the change of government, was not achieved without extensive behind-the-scenes contestation. Early governmental discussion as to the purpose and principles of the legislation, as later recounted by Upton, focused on the general purpose clause and whether the ideal of sustainable development should be accorded overriding status. The non-Treasury view wished to emphasise the idea of good environmental management and the importance of achieving the necessary outcome. On the other hand the Treasury's laissez-faire view emphasised process rather than outcome, contending that 'the overall goal of this Act is to ensure that resources (or rights to resources) are allocated to wherever they are most highly valued to society'. As Upton recounts it, this Treasury view was promoted on the basis of three arguments:

> First, it [Treasury] objected to the word 'good' as injecting normative value. The objection appeared to be founded on the premise that statements of value, other than by individuals expressing preferences, have no place in public policy. Secondly, it believed that the Act was about resolving conflict between resource users, not environmental management. Thirdly, it objected to the elevation of good environmental management at the expense of efficiency and fairness.[40]

These claims that public decisions involving common property resources and the common good do not involve value judgements, and that society should accept efficiency outcomes as necessarily 'fair', are breath-taking in their presumption. It has been a major task of this book to expose the factual and moral inadequacies of these propositions. Fortunately for New Zealand it was the non-Treasury view that prevailed. New Zealanders who value their future well-being owe both Sir Geoffrey Palmer and Simon Upton a profound debt of gratitude for their work and perseverance in achieving this Act.

Threats to the integrity of the Act. In the years subsequent to its passage into law the RMA has had to endure sustained attacks on its content, with the purpose of whittling away its provisions and favouring free market opportunism. In February 2009 the newly returned-to-power National-led government announced a programme designed to 'simplify and streamline' the RMA in two phases. Initial changes were made in the Resource Management Amendment Act of 2009.

In February 2013 Environment Minister Amy Adams released a discussion document outlining the second stage of proposed reforms.[41] Although many changes in the Act were envisaged, those that raised particular concerns included the increased weight to be given to economic considerations relative to environmental ones, constraints on public participation in the examination of planning proposals, decreased protection for urban trees, and the Minister's expanded ability to amend national policy statements without consultation. The most contentious proposals were those aimed at amending Part II (Purposes and Principles) of the Act. Sir Geoffrey Palmer, in a memorandum on the changes proposed for Part II, expressed the view that they would 'significantly and seriously undermine environmental protection under the RMA.'[42] The Parliamentary Commissioner for the Environment Dr Jan Wright concurred with that judgement, pointing out that the proposed changes to sections 6 and 7 were 'far more radical than any previous amendments to the RMA'. She continued by insisting that 'The RMA is not, and should not become, an economic development act'.[43] Dr Wright also drew attention to the unseemly haste with which the changes were being progressed: 'The month provided for public response to this discussion document is in stark contrast with the four years of consultation that preceded the establishment of the RMA.'[44] New Zealand's premier business group, The New Zealand Initiative, made no public submission on the proposed legislative changes, as far as is known. Interestingly the government's February discussion document contains within it neither the word 'precaution' nor the word 'inter-generational'. To maintain as Environment Minister Amy Adams did that despite the proposed changes 'core environmental protections have been maintained in the RMA'[45] is to misunderstand the meaning of words.[46]

In the event the February discussion document received over

13,000 public written submissions, and over 2,000 people attended more than 50 public meetings, hui and council meetings to discuss it. Analysis of those written submissions that addressed the proposed changes to Part II of the Act (particularly sections 6 and 7) showed that: of 89 submissions by business groups, 31 per cent expressed unreserved support and 50 per cent partial or conditional support; of 66 by local governments, 58 per cent gave partial or conditional support while 20 per cent were opposed or expressed serious concern; of 40 by iwi, hapu and Maori organisations, 59 per cent were opposed or seriously concerned, while 17 per cent indicated partial support; of 86 by NGOs, environmental and community groups, over 70 per cent indicated opposition or serious concern. By far the greatest number of submissions were received from individuals, the vast majority of whom opposed or had serious reservations about the proposed changes.[47]

In August 2013 the Minister released the government's summary of the reform proposals.[48] Legislation covering amendments to the RMA (excluding those proposed in relation to Part II) were considered in the House and formally passed into law as the Resource Management Amendment Act 2013. It is proposed that a second amendment bill covering Part II of the RMA will be introduced at a later date. As of April 2014 this had not been done.

There have however been more indirect forces in play over the years which undermine the true responsibilities and intentions set out in the RMA. The idea of a 'whole of government' approach to the functioning of the public service (otherwise known as 'horizontal management' or 'joined up government') has been assiduously promoted as part of the neoliberal reform programme in New Zealand, as elsewhere. This is the idea that public service agencies by working across portfolio boundaries can achieve efficiencies in the delivery of public services.[49] In principle there is much to recommend such an approach. But it is not always relevant, and needs to be used selectively.[50] The question here arises as to what it is exactly that is to be shared: is it simply a matter of information, or of resources and work, or does it extend to matters of mandate and authority? While the compatibility of inter-agency objectives may be almost complete in some cases – for example with agencies involved in biosecurity – the domination of the New Zealand government's environmental portfolios by the government's free market agenda provides counterexamples.

Changes introduced in the Crown Minerals Amendment Act 2013 have made it easier to mine on stewardship land[51] and harder to upgrade this land to reserve status: instead of the Minister of Conservation approving new reserves as previously, this power has now been appropriated by Cabinet. The Ministry for the Environment on its website page 'About the Ministry' declares its mission to be not 'environmental stewardship' but 'environmental stewardship for a prosperous New Zealand', and in explaining its role it declares in its initial statement 'The environment supports New Zealand's economy through our use of natural resources.' The Minister's foreword to the Ministry's 'Statement of Intent 2013-2016' opens: 'New Zealand's environment plays a unique role as both a contributor to our economic performance, as well as …'[52]. Instead of providing a forthright statement in support of the New Zealand's environmental quality, the Ministry chooses to point to the environment as being a business input. The definition of 'sustainability' provided on the Ministry's website makes reference to business, explains why sustainability makes for sound business practice, but makes no reference to citizens, or even consumers.[53] Not only does this approach have the effect of burying environmental issues beneath economic efficiency criteria, but it means that in government decision making, environmental advocacy by the responsible department is not part of public discussion but is shrouded in covert inter-agency debate. The recent failure of the Department of Conservation (DOC) to present to the hearings over coal mining on conservation land on the Denniston Plateau on the West Coast[54], and the controversy over the

Department's submission to the Board of Inquiry on the Ruataniwha Dam in Hawke's Bay, are visible examples of this concern. The quiet crisis at DOC has been much discussed.[55]

The Ownership of Land

A matter involving natural resources that raises different issues is that of ownership. Ownership gives power to determine the use to which a natural resource is put. It is an issue raised in acute form by foreign ownership of New Zealand resources. It is an issue particularly relevant for New Zealand on account of the country's small economic size. Here we consider the matter of overseas ownership of privately held New Zealand land – or to be more precise of 'land plus any improvements on it' – with an emphasis on agricultural and rural land. Issues of ownership in relation to foreign debt and investment have been explored in Chapter 3.

It is probable that there is no group of people on earth who do not in part define themselves in relation to place. Place provides hearth, sustenance, environment and social context for the physical and imaginative growth of the group's members. It imbues each of its members with a sense of familiarity, of belonging, of relationship, of values: in a word, of identity, which provides a compass for adult life and a basis on which other experiences in other environments can be lived and perhaps embraced. And it often provides a place of homecoming too. It gives meaning – psychological, social and cultural – to the lives that we lead and might wish our descendants to lead. It is not to be expressed in money value but is more readily affirmed in the creative arts: be it the cartoons of Murray Ball, the pottery of Barry Brickell, the carvings of Paki Harrison, the paintings of Colin McCahon, the novels of Maurice Gee, the short stories of Patricia Grace or the poetry of Sarah Broom. It endures in a way that our own lives do not. It is part of New Zealand's common good. And with the idea of identity in relation to place goes inevitably some idea of – some wish for – sovereignty: the ability to exercise the necessary authority to maintain, organise and renew one's own society and one's own place. To both these ideas of identity and sovereignty the idea of ownership is key. It is the owner and not the tenant who determines what will happen on the land. Dispossession is not a state to be desired.

New Zealand is, on the other hand, part of the world at large. For New Zealand, autarky – complete political and economic self-sufficiency – is not and has never been an option. New Zealand has always been an outward-looking nation, with trade and the flux of peoples having been at the heart of its experience and its prosperity. And these influences and pressures have been augmented by globalisation, air travel, the emergence of the internet, and international opportunities more generally. However foreign investors in New Zealand resources do so for their own motives, which may or may not be supportive of the aspirations which New Zealanders have for their own country. At base, the foreign investor's motive is the generation of profit and its removal elsewhere. Asset stripping, tax avoidance, dishonesty, and environmental degradation have all occurred in the past. If New Zealand is to be valued by its citizens as a social and cultural entity and not just a location on the map, a careful and monitored approach to land ownership is warranted.

The neoliberal view in favour of the internationalisation of the world economy and the ascendancy of markets, while in favour of private ownership, takes no view on who those owners might be. Quite the opposite: provided private property rights are respected, whatever is most efficient is what should obtain.[56] The New Zealand government recognised the importance of regulating foreign investment in 1973 with the passage of the Overseas Investment Act 1973 and the setting up of the Overseas Investment Commission (OIC) within the Reserve Bank. Its role was however limited to considering only very high value investments (in 2005: NZ$50m+), investments in sensitive land and in fishing quotas. The Overseas Investment Act 2005 replaced the OIC with the Overseas Investment

Office (OIO) as part of Land Information New Zealand, and with a reorientation towards asset and land sales as a means of encouraging overseas investment in New Zealand. As expressed in the 2005 Act, its purpose is purportedly to control the ownership overseas persons can have of 'sensitive New Zealand assets'. What is meant by 'sensitive land' is set out in the Schedule to the Act, which defines several different types of land, each with an area threshold above which concern is to be triggered. An overseas investor in sensitive land must satisfy a number of criteria and also needs to show that the overseas investment will, or is likely to, be of benefit to New Zealand. However even if the proposed overseas investment or the overseas investor does not meet the requirements, the Minister can still grant the application (section 20). As commercial law firm Bell Gully advised its clients, and as is clearly set out in the Act: 'The degree of Ministerial discretion which has been built into New Zealand's overseas investment regime provides the government of the day with flexibility to effectively alter the application of the legislation by altering its overseas investment policy without the need to change the legislation.'[57]

The OIO and the OIC before it appear to have acted with a very light hand. Over the 11 years 1994–2004 the OIC approved 2107 applications and refused 57 (2.6 per cent); the OIO over the years 2006–12 approved 983 applications and refused 19 (1.9 per cent).[58] Very little monitoring appears to be undertaken by the OIO to ensure that overseas investors are fulfilling the required criteria under the legislation. Only three prosecutions for delinquency have been completed in the first five years of its existence. The 'good character' criterion for applicants can be fulfilled merely by the provision of a statutory declaration from a lawyer: a procedure that has clearly failed in a number of cases. The Office has been variously accused of being a rubber stamp, more a doorman than a bouncer, and by New Zealand First leader Winston Peters as a betrayer of New Zealand's interests.[59]

The fact that laissez-faire economics takes such a cavalier attitude to the matter of the ownership of New Zealand land is brought out by the fact that the OIO neither systematically collects nor publishes useful statistics that might be used for planning and review, as distinct from administration. Organisations such as Federated Farmers have had to make requests to the OIO under the Official Information Act in order to assemble useful statistics.[60] It has in large measure been left to others, including the citizen group Campaign Against Foreign Control of Aotearoa (CAFCA), to try to estimate useful statistics that the government appears reluctant to provide. Despite the pertinence of the matter, in 2012 Prime Minister Key could only give his 'understanding' that less than 1 per cent of New Zealand farmland is foreign owned, a figure that could not be confirmed by OIO and which appears many times less than that suggested by independent estimates.[61]

In 2011 the National Business Review estimated that 36 per cent of the New Zealand share market was in foreign ownership. Foreign ownership is dominant in the sectors of banking, insurance, petroleum energy and in supermarkets. On a volume of production basis about 70 per cent of the wine industry, including several of New Zealand's signature brands, are foreign owned. In 1999, according to the United Nations' Food and Agriculture Organization, 72 per cent of pine forests were foreign owned, and the figure appears to have increased since that time. Analysis of OIO data since August 2005 by Terralink International indicates that over the subsequent seven years to 2012 some 312,600 ha of land had been consented for foreign ownership, with rural land accounting for 279,400 ha (1.5 per cent of the total rural land in New Zealand). Of the rural land consents, 165,200 ha were in the pastoral category, 92,000 ha in forestry, 14,900 ha in dairy, and 4,300 ha in horticulture.[62] Given the huge surge in FDI into New Zealand that occurred in the decade of the 1990s, a conservative estimate of total transfers of land to foreign ownership over the 28 years since 1984 might be four or five times the figure of 1.5 per cent, or 6.0–7.5 per cent overall. Other estimates suggest 8.7 per cent in foreign ownership in 2012.[63] (There are many difficulties in estimating this figure: Statistics New Zealand classifies foreign ownership data at a 10 per cent threshold while OIO uses a 25 per cent threshold; not all OIO consents translate into purchases; estimates of land usage can be different depending on whether they are done by aerial and satellite imagery or from land transfer records; and OIO data themselves contain many complications.)

In recognition of the existence of the common good, New Zealanders have every right to challenge the narrow neoliberal belief in the irrelevance of land ownership. Indeed the great majority of New Zealanders appear to oppose foreign land sales: in a poll carried out for TVNZ in 2012, 87 per cent of those interviewed said they were opposed to the sale of the Crafar farms to an overseas company, and 70 per cent said that that was irrespective of the nationality of the purchasing company.[64] The quality of public debate on the issue has not been adequate, with groups on either side appearing mainly to talk past each other. Those in favour of land-ownership restriction present arguments against foreign ownership of land; free-marketers on the other hand commonly argue for foreign investment in general without confronting the specifics in relation to land. Meanwhile the government proceeds by declaration as if discussion and debate were irrelevant: and indeed if free market ideology provides the answer, then debate is pointless.

As a final matter let us consider how societies in other jurisdictions to which New Zealand might wish to compare itself deal with foreign ownership of their land. In the province of Alberta, for land outside cities and towns and not involved with mines and minerals – land classified as 'agricultural and recreational' – non-Canadian citizens are restricted to owning 20 acres or less, although this might be overcome through a shareholding in a Canadian-controlled company. A provision does exist for the granting of exemptions by the provincial Governor. In EU-member Denmark, non-EU citizens are not permitted to buy or own real estate unless they are already living in the country or have previously resided there for a period of five years. There are additional restrictions on non-EU citizens purchasing property in and around popular coastal areas. A further restriction applies to agricultural land, which places an obligation on the owner (or tenant with substantive powers) to reside on the land. In Norway, the government in a national statement has stated its preference that agricultural land be in private ownership, with the private owner living on and operating the farm. Local municipalities can give concessions for company ownership of agricultural land, but the residence qualification is not waived and the practice not encouraged.

With regard to New Zealand's approach to the matter of land ownership, it is fair question to ask whether residence should precede ownership. In 2012 Greens co-leader Russel Norman introduced a Member's Bill into the Parliament designed to amend the Overseas Investment Act 2005 to prevent overseas persons from purchasing sensitive New Zealand land. The Bill was negatived on its first reading, with 59 votes from opposition parties in favour of the Bill proceeding, and 61 votes against the Bill proceeding from the government and its supporting parties.[65]

In one of his reflections on American country life, farmer and man of letters Wendell Berry made the distinction between 'a country' and 'a beloved country'. He reflected that when one adopts the latter perspective then 'the question of what a beloved country is to be used for quickly becomes inseparable from the questions of who will use it or who is to prescribe its uses, and what will be the ways of using it.'[66] Perhaps what New Zealand needs is more people who see it as a beloved country?

9

New Zealand: Retrospect and Prospect

Looking Back

New Zealand's economic and social experience of the last three decades has been dominated by a neoliberal paradigm that has emphasised: the vigorous promotion of unfettered markets both domestically and internationally; the privatisation of public assets; the favouring of business interests; the reduction of taxes, particularly on the wealthy; the withdrawal of government from economic management; and the withdrawal or limitation of social services.

This paradigm has not served New Zealand well. In the more than two decades leading up to the global financial crisis of 2007–08 it has, in economic terms:

- failed in its avowed intent to enhance economic growth;
- failed to solve the problem of New Zealand's low productivity;
- failed to reduce New Zealand's overall debt burden;
- yielded up strategic control of the New Zealand economy to others for little tangible benefit; and

- failed to adequately engage with the major twenty-first-century issues of climate change and sustainability.

With its single-minded focus on economic efficiency, and the short term, , the paradigm has thoroughly failed New Zealand society at large, having:

- emphasised self-seeking behaviour to excess and to the detriment of social values;
- increased inequality in society not only of income but also and consequently of opportunity;
- taken little concern for New Zealand's environmental quality, which continues to decline; and
- contributed to the muting of public debate and the undermining of democratic processes.

The idea that whatever the economic problem is the default response is the free market, is fundamentally absurd. Maximising efficiency may be a useful short-term economic strategy, but it is undeniably inferior to one that ensures long-term survival. What is lacking in free market economics is a perspective that pays respectful attention to the resilience and stability of the ecosystem in which the economy operates and of which human society is a part. Free market economics fails to recognise the existence of limits: physical limits imposed by nature and described by the laws of science, limits in human technological capability, and the intellectual limits of economic theory itself. Economics is not the source of all values: it provides a method for achieving things on the basis of values determined elsewhere. In a twenty-first-century world, globalisation on free market terms can produce economic benefit in the short term for a small country like New Zealand, but such gains are likely to be made at the cost of exploitation and loss of sovereignty in the longer term. If New Zealanders wish to have a sustainable society, or a reasonably equitable society, or one that values full employment, or one in which there is adequate sovereignty, then they need to look elsewhere.

Where We Are Now

The present reality for New Zealand is that the economy is not sustainable, and is not moving towards becoming so. If New Zealand is to control its own destiny, this cannot continue. The story set out in this book emphasises the need for a new and radically different paradigm, one which will better respond to the needs of the twenty-first century. In practice, there is no doubt that change in the years ahead will be substantial: the primary question is whether it will be planned and orderly, or chaotic. Our story so far leads to the following reflections:

- There are likely to be few simple answers. There will be need for choices and trade-offs, not all of which will be at the margin. In making these choices we will need to bear in mind the observation of Garrett Hardin about the conditionality of freedom: the more the carrying capacity of the environment is exceeded, the more freedoms must be given up;
- As individuals and as a nation we will face serious ethical challenges, relating particularly to ideas of justice and fairness and the importance we give to them;
- If economic growth is to be a relevant consideration in the future, it must be defined within the context of a sustainable society;
- In welcoming interchange with the rest of the world we must beware of not being drawn into bargains which are disempowering and from which there is no release;
- Government must have an expanded role as participant in managing the economy and as the repository of our shared social values. The most crippling legacy of decades of neoliberalism may prove to be the degradation of the role government under its regime, and the difficulty of reestablishing the government's ability to fulfil its proper functions;
- Democratic processes must play a greater part in society in advising government and ensuring its transparency and probity, particularly so on account of the scale and uncertainty surrounding major twenty-first-century issues.[1]

In constructing a view of the future and moving to action, we can identify at least three areas which are of signal importance. The first and pre-eminent one concerns the conduct of civic and political life, not only because of its foundational importance for democracy, but also because it sets out the terms upon which the other issues are to be addressed. A second area of importance is that of achieving a sustainable economy and society in the face of declining resource and environmental quality, and of climate change. And a third area is the identification and measurement of genuine well-being: after all, that would seem to be the purpose of it all. In what follows we will consider these three areas of justice, sustainability and well-being, and give some indications as to policy approaches that might enhance them. Parenthetically we might add that the problem of international debt, despite its immediacy is, we believe, one of lesser order. For every monetary debt in the world there is somewhere else a credit: that is to say that the debt problem is in principle soluble. This is not the case for issues of sustainability: beyond what is sustainable there are no credits, only debits. Furthermore, we consider the monetary debt issue to be one that should find its proper resolution within the context defined by the three issues we have just identified.

Looking Ahead: Democracy, Rights and the New Zealand Constitution

New Zealand is a liberal democracy with a parliamentary system of government, set formally within the context of a constitutional monarchy. Sir Kenneth Keith in a contribution to the New Zealand Cabinet Manual has set out clearly what a constitution involves, and the main features of the New Zealand constitution:

> A constitution is about public power, the power of the state. It describes and establishes the major institutions of government, states their principal powers, and regulates the exercise of those powers in a broad way. While all constitutions have these general characteristics, each

> constitution is affected by the national character of the state it services. …
>
> The New Zealand constitution is to be found in formal legal documents, in decisions of the courts, and in practices (some of which are described as conventions). It reflects and establishes that New Zealand is a monarchy, that it has a parliamentary system of government, and that it is a democracy. It increasingly reflects the fact that the Treaty of Waitangi is regarded as a founding document of government in New Zealand. The constitution must also be seen in its international context, because New Zealand governmental institutions must increasingly have regard to international obligations and standards.[2]

Although the content of the constitution is spread around in a number of places, its main expression has now become lodged in the Constitution Act 1986, which sets out the main elements of New Zealand democracy in terms of the powers given variously to the sovereign, executive, legislature and judiciary. These include the powers to pass, to assent to and to implement laws, particularly in relation to matters of public finance. The constitution also sets out, implicitly if not explicitly, a set of core values that the society upholds (including those expressed in 'conventions' based on social norms if not legal recognition). Thus the constitution expresses by inclusion or exclusion beliefs about individual freedoms, about equality, and about what is to be considered fair and just. Among these core values the idea of democracy is pre-eminent. In this regard the constitution sets out the requirement that for a bill before Parliament to be passed into law it requires a simple majority of votes in favour (provided a quorum is present). Rare exceptions to this requirement include those decisions which require either a vote in favour by a majority of 75 per cent of all members of the House, or alternatively that the vote be carried by a simple majority of valid votes cast at a poll of electors.[3]

The New Zealand Bill of Rights Act 1990 is part of the suite of

Acts that put New Zealand's commitment to the 1977 International Covenant on Civil and Political Rights into New Zealand law. However this Act is neither 'entrenched law' (that is, it is not one of the laws requiring the exceptional circumstances for change just mentioned), nor is it 'supreme law' (that is, one that has supremacy over other laws, such that if another law were in contradiction of it, then that other law would be discounted). The same is true of large parts of the constitution itself, which can in principle be changed by a simple majority in Parliament, although there are some conventions that might put a brake on that action in some circumstances. These facts bear out the New Zealand tradition that holds Parliament to be the supreme body in matters concerning the principles of government, rather than the courts. As to economic, social and cultural rights, the New Zealand constitution contains no direct reference to them. However some recognition of these rights is indicated in places in New Zealand legislation: on education (1877), old age pensions (1898), social security (1938), and medical benefits (1941).[4] The expression of these rights, such as they are, is now complemented by New Zealand's obligations under the International Covenant on Economic, Social and Cultural Rights, ratified by New Zealand in 1978.[5]

In looking to New Zealand's future and from the perspective of sustainability, two questions arise: What is to be considered as fair and just for individuals in an era of climate change and resource scarcity? To what extent should the answer to that question be reflected in New Zealand's constitution?

In the years following World War II when the International Covenant on Economic, Social and Cultural Rights was being developed and negotiated, the environment was not a topic of particular interest. This is not surprising, as at that time the environment was taken to be without limit in terms of possible human demands upon it. No threat, no need for environmental protection under the rubric of human rights. It is now known that the assumption was false and the consequence therefore moot.

High-profile environmental problems such as those associated with global DDT dispersion, and the disasters of Minamata, the Love Canal, Bhopal and Chernobyl, raised international awareness that environmental pollution can threaten health, welfare and even life, and led to a growing recognition of a genuine relationship between environmental quality and human rights. In a case heard before the International Court of Justice – the principal legal organ of the United Nations – Judge Christopher Weeramantry stated in a separate opinion that: 'The protection of the environment is likewise a vital part of contemporary human rights doctrine, for it is a *sine qua non* for numerous human rights such as the right to health and the right to life itself. It is scarcely necessary to elaborate on this, as damage to the environment can impair and undermine all the human rights spoken of in the Universal Declaration and other human rights instruments.'[6] There is also a growing body of argument that the distinction between economic, social and cultural rights, and civil and political rights, cannot be sustained.[7]

At a national level too, an evolution has taken place in the identification and highlighting of environmental rights. In 2005 the NGO Earthjustice could report that: 'Of the approximately 193 countries of the world, there are now 117 whose national constitutions mention the protection of the environment or natural resources. One hundred and nine of them recognize the right to a clean and healthy environment and/or the state's obligation to prevent environmental harm. Of these, 56 constitutions explicitly recognize the right to a clean and healthy environment, and 97 constitutions make it the duty of the national government to prevent harm to the environment ...'[8]. Of all countries that have included human rights to environment in modern constitutions, it is India that has been the most prominent. In the Constitution of India, adopted in 1949 following India's independence from Great Britain in 1947, Article 48A requires as a directive principle of state policy that 'The State shall endeavour to protect and improve the environment and to safeguard the forests and wild life of the country'; and Article 51A(g) places on every Indian citizen the duty 'to protect and improve the natural environment including forests, lakes, rivers and wild life, and to have compassion for living creatures.'[9] In the years since, India has accumulated substantial jurisprudence on these matters and provides an example of what can be accomplished in a democratic state, given a modern constitution and a motivated judiciary and polity.

Given the importance at many levels of the environment to New Zealand, positive mention of environmental rights in the constitution is appropriate. The purpose of doing so would be to express both an ongoing national commitment to environmental quality, and the rights and duties of citizens and government in relation to environmental care. One major practical value of this might well be the guidance that it would provide to the judiciary in their determinations of the complex issues relating to environmental common goods, and to which the mathematical computation of economic costs and benefits must fail to do justice.

If it is so as we have argued, that participation in civil society has been declining in recent years and that democracy needs strengthening and reaffirming for the future, then it is imperative that practical steps be taken to augment the understanding of the privileges and responsibilities of citizenship. At one level this could be done through expanded civics education in schools. This suggests in addition the value of philosophy and ethics as subjects of secondary study. Such an augmented civics education might also include a study of the dangers of political advertising and manipulation. In society at large many opportunities exist for the enhancement of democratic understanding and democratic outcomes. One set of opportunities exists in the greater use of panels advisory to government along the lines of the successful Land and Water Forum. Citizen conferences and publicly held national issues conventions involving randomly chosen citizens offer further sets of opportunities. With regard to elections specifically, a start might be made with a revamped Electoral Finance

Act that would adequately ensure transparency and accountability from all those involved in elections and ensure that money and wealth have no undue influence on electoral outcomes. Campaign discourse might be improved through such means as signed voluntary codes of campaign ethics, and the provision of voter guides. At a much more expansive level political scientist James Fishkin has proposed the holding of a nationally dedicated 'Deliberation Day' in the lead-up to major elections. In this proposal, registered voters would be drawn together in local and regional meetings – of say 15 to 500 people – to discuss the issues central to the campaign, and for which day's work of citizenship participants would be paid on condition that they voted at the polls.[10]

A further possibility recalls New Zealand's own history. In the early nineteenth century a movement emerged in Scotland and then in England, of educational establishments designed to provide library and learning facilities for the working classes in society and to assist the incorporation of scientific knowledge into the industrial practices of the day. Their success brought imitation overseas in countries including Canada, Australia, New Zealand and the US. With the passage of time a few of these establishments evolved into universities in their own right, while others became libraries, museums, or adult education or recreational centres. In nineteenth-century New Zealand, Mechanics' Institutes (as they were called) existed in all the major centres and many smaller towns. It might well be argued that New Zealand in particular and the world in general, now stand on the threshold of change just as momentous as the industrial revolution, and that as citizens we are in need of similar community-based institutions of knowledge and debate to guide our understanding of the major forces shaping the future and our inevitable choices in relation to them.

What the brief description of the New Zealand constitution given above also shows is the manner in which values are expressed in a well-ordered democratic state. At its head are the foundational, if not quite immutable, matters of principle that are expressed in the constitution; below that are the recurrent products of legislation and regulation that are the more mutable outcomes of mechanisms involving parliament and civil society; and below that are the transactions of individuals involving their personal choices in markets. Perhaps nothing can express more clearly the legitimate place of the market and market transactions in a nation's life.

Before leaving the matter of citizenship consideration should also be given to the particular roles of those involved in the professions. As discussed in Chapter 6, it is important to distinguish three distinct realms of moral conduct, relating to the family, the market, and the common good. For those in the professions their roles cross over the boundary between the arenas of the market and of civil society, and between the ethics of the market and the ethics of the common good. The most prominent profession in this regard is no doubt that of medical doctors. While they commonly operate within a market context, their ethical codes recall the Hippocratic Oath of ancient Greece and a much broader responsibility to society. The New Zealand Medical Association Code of Ethics states that: 'The medical profession has a social contract with its community. In return for the trust patients and the community place in doctors, ethical codes are produced to guide the profession and protect patients. ... Standard treatises on medical ethics cite four moral principles: autonomy, beneficence, non-maleficence, and justice.'[11] Other professions – among them lawyers and those involved in the administration of justice, engineers, teachers, public servants, and academics – also have (or should have) their own social contracts with the society of which they are part, and which to a greater or lesser degree recognise similar ethical principles. In return for the trust that society puts in these professionals, the community grants them certain rights to the certification their own qualifications, the control of professional admissions, and of accountability to their fellow professionals. (The dislocation of the compact between members of the academy and society – or at least between academics and the New Zealand government – as a result of neoliberal policies, has already been noted in Chapter 3.) As trust is at the foundation of civil society, professional organisations and governments have a particular responsibility in the future to uphold the moral principles inherent in these social contracts, market principles notwithstanding.

Looking Ahead: Well-being as a Policy Variable

Well-being. Two thousand years ago the Greek philosopher Aristotle reflected that 'The life of making money is a life people are, as it were, forced into, as wealth is clearly not the good we are seeking, since it is merely useful, for getting something else.'[12] On this matter little has changed since those days. Today it is well recognised that GDP is an inadequate measure of national well-being, and not just for reasons related to natural resource use as discussed in the previous chapter. Surveys in the US have shown that despite a doubling in real income per capita during the half-century between 1950 and 2000, self-estimates of happiness have not increased. A similar story can be told of the United Kingdom, where estimates of happiness have been static since the mid-1970s, and of Japan. In continental Europe the position has been mixed over this period, with some countries recording slight upward trends in happiness and others registering falls: but even for those countries recording improvements they have been small in comparison to the substantial increases in real income over the same period.[13]

In recent years there has been an upwelling of interest from a policy perspective, in the study and analysis of happiness and well-being. Partly this can be seen as a natural and expanded interest in economic development. Based on the work of Amartya Sen on human capabilities (referred to in Chapter 2), the UNDP developed the Human Development Index (HDI), which combines indices of life expectancy, educational training, and standard of living, to produce a rudimentary overall index of human well-being. This is now the subject of annual calculation in a wide range of countries. In the US in the latter years of last century, environmental economist Herman Daly and philosopher John Cobb developed an Index of Sustainable Economic Welfare (ISEW), which has been further developed as the Genuine Progress Indicator (GPI).[14] The GPI identifies a range of issues not included in calculations of GDP for which monetary values are estimated and added to give a more genuine reflection of well-being than GDP. (A list of issues included in the GPI is given in Appendix 4.) There is currently no international standard for this index, but GPIs have been estimated for a number of countries and regions, and some of these estimates are made on a regular basis. Countries involved include the US, Australia, Austria, Canada, Chile, France, Finland, Italy, the Netherlands, Scotland and UK; regions include the states of California and Maryland in the US, and the provinces of Alberta and Nova Scotia in Canada. In New Zealand, GPIs have been calculated for Auckland, Waikato, Wellington and Canterbury regions, and foundational work was carried out for a GPI at a national level over the years 2006–09. The results of analysing GPIs over time have been to show that whereas GPD may have grown, GPI has increased much more modestly, if at all. In the US, calculated GPI appears to have been static or to have fallen since the 1970s.[15]

In 2008, President Nicolas Sarkozy of France established a high-level international commission to advise him on how best to measure economic performance and social progress. The commission, chaired by economists Joseph Stiglitz and Amartya Sen and coordinated by economist Jean-Paul Fitoussi, provided their report in 2009. The commission declared that 'the time is ripe for our measurement system to *shift emphasis from measuring economic production to measuring people's well-being*. And measures of well-being should be put in a context of sustainability' (authors' italics)[16]. It was the authors' considered judgement that well-being is a multi-dimensional concept that includes: material living standards (income, consumption and wealth); health; education; personal activities including work;

political voice and governance; social connections and relationships; environment (present and future conditions); and insecurity, of an economic as well as a physical nature. The issue of adding up the different measures to produce a single overall index they considered one that could be set aside for the present as subordinate to establishing a broad statistical system that captured as many of the relevant dimensions as possible.

Reflective of this new orientation, there have been parallel developments elsewhere. Based on its work on social indicators over many years, the OECD has initiated a project to calculate a Better Life Index based on 10 objective measures and one subjective measure of personal well-being.[17] The United Nations General Assembly in 2011 adopted a resolution on happiness, and called for a holistic approach to development.[18] Allied with this has been the promotion of a project to measure trends in national happiness globally. This UN project is based on the Gallup World Poll and employs indices of GDP per capita, social support, healthy life expectancy, freedom to make life choices, generosity, and perceptions of corruption. The 2010–12 report on these indices headlines the observation that the happier countries tend to be the richer countries, but more important for happiness than income are social factors like strength of social support, the absence of corruption, and the degree of personal freedom. It is observed once again that while living standards have generally risen over time, happiness has increased in some countries but not in others.[19]

Of particular interest in this area has been the approach of the Himalayan Kingdom of Bhutan which, since 1972, and based on Buddhist spiritual values, has developed an Index of Gross National Happiness for national policy purposes. This is a combined index based on 33 individual indicators spread across nine domains (psychological well-being, health, education, cultural diversity and resilience, time use, good governance, community vitality, ecological diversity and resilience, and living standard).[20] In New Zealand, Statistics NZ's General Social Survey, is designed to provide information on a similar, if less diverse, set of indicators. Although the use of well-being measures in policy settings is in its infancy, there is evidence emerging that the application of well-being-based policies at national and sub-national levels do lead to better policies and better policy processes.[21]

Well-being, GNP and sustainability. The precise relationship between a country's well-being and GNP (or GDP) has been a matter of debate for some years. The emergent consensus is that well-being and GNP are correlated, but not in a straightforward linear manner. Using results compiled over many years by the World Values Survey, political scientist Ronald Inglehart and co-workers have graphed an index of subjective well-being (SWB) against GNP per capita for a wide range of countries. Their results confirm that more prosperous countries do tend to have higher levels of well-being, with overall results scattered over a curved area shaped rather like a boomerang. Countries with higher incomes and higher SWB index values – including New Zealand and other OECD Member countries – tend to cluster along the right arm of the curve, while under-developed countries and the former Communist countries of Eastern Europe tend to cluster along the left arm (Figure 3(a)).[22] The explanation offered for this is that for under-developed countries, small increases in GNP per capita – implying as they do higher caloric intake, better clothes and shelter, and increases in basic medical care – are important in increasing physical and economic security and satisfaction with life, and thus constitute a region on the graph where 'economic gains' are of particular importance. However as countries reach a certain threshold of economic development and the most accessible gains in life expectancy and physical well-being have been assured, then the non-economic aspects of life – 'lifestyle' attributes that emphasise values, freedom of expression, social participation and lack of corruption – become more important. In these studies too it was found that happiness correlates with democracy, as a reliable source of individual free choice.[23]

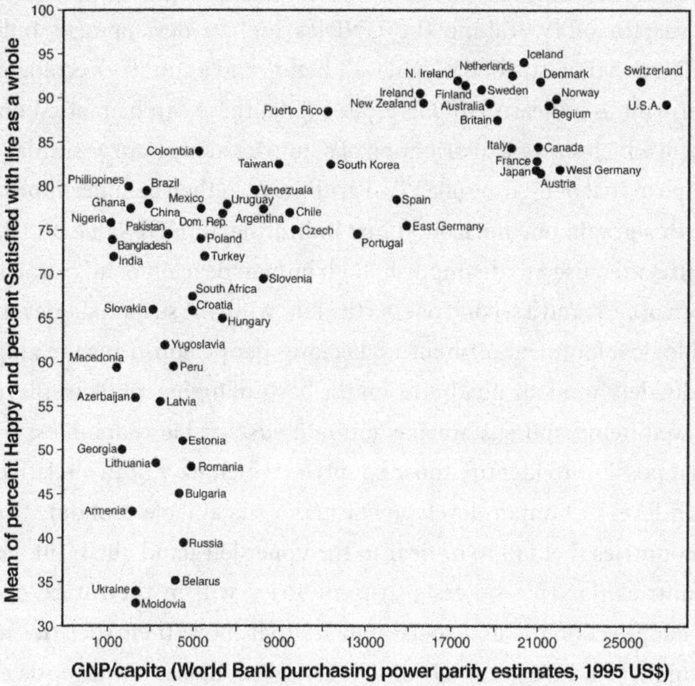

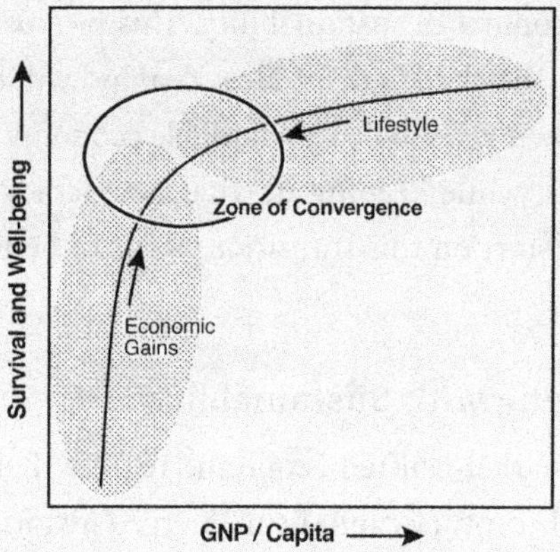

Figure 3. Level of economic development and subjective well-being.

3(a)(above) Survey results for 65 countries.

3(b)(left). The sustainability overlay and shift in survival strategies.

Sources: See note 22 this chapter.

This analysis can be carried further by adding the requirement of sustainability. Taking the UNDP's human development index (HDI) as a measure of national well-being, and a country's ecological footprint as a measure of GNP per capita, these can be plotted on a graph which shows a distribution of countries along a curve similar in shape to that of Figure 3(a).[24] Two gridlines can then be superimposed on this graph: one horizontal line indicating an HDI value of 0.8, a figure often used to distinguish 'high human development' countries from others; and a second one vertical showing the sustainable level of ecological footprint of about 1.8 hectares per person. Thus the graph is divided into four quadrants on the basis of higher and lower levels of well-being and sustainable and non-sustainable economies. It is then possible to identify those countries which have both a relatively high level of human development and a sustainable economy: that is countries that fall in or near to the upper left-hand quadrant. Few countries do. This suggests that countries will in the future need to adopt economic and social policies that move their societies not to higher and higher levels of a 'lifestyle' economy, but towards the 'zone of convergence', which balances economic gains and lifestyle criteria within an overall context of sustainability. This proposition is displayed in Figure 3(b). The challenge for New Zealand will be to make the transition to its own version of a sustainable economy over time, with its own policies, while keeping its vital democracy and level of well-being high. A start on this transition needs to be made now.

Looking Ahead: Engaging with Sustainability

Actions and Actors. The market-centred economic regime that has characterised late-twentieth-century capitalism emerged historically as a product of the Industrial Revolution of the eighteenth century, a time when humans were much less numerous and natural resources superabundant. Man-made capital was the limiting factor in economic development. In this circumstance one need have few concerns for the goods and services provided by the environment, or perhaps even for the concentration of wealth in the hands of the few that provided the means for increasing man-made capital and economic growth. Just how omnipresent this presumption in favour of economic growth became in the course of time can be gauged from the fact that nowadays a 'recession' is officially defined in the UK and the EU as two consecutive three-month periods of negative economic growth, as measured by real GDP! Meanwhile the world has changed. Since the eighteenth century world population has increased more than seven-fold, man-made capital increased beyond measure, and now it is natural capital that has become more and more the limiting economic factor. Fish catch is not limited by the number of fishing boats, but by the number of fish in the sea.[25] The logic of science attests to the fact that it is impossible to have continuing economic growth, as currently experienced, in a finite world.

In recent years there has been something of a convergence in the thought of leaders in the physical and ecological sciences, and in the commercial and civil spheres, towards recognising the necessity of change and determining the means by which it might best be effected. An increasing number of world leaders in government ranks are also being convinced of these needs. From the scientific perspective a systemic and integrated approach is deemed essential, one based on core principles: of precaution, of responsible access to common pool resources, of adaptive management, of comprehensive stakeholder awareness and participation, of scale-matching (decisions being taken at the most appropriate level), and of full cost allocation in markets.[26] Aspects of these principles have been discussed in earlier chapters. All require for their implementation the action of government, either in an initiatory role or in support of initiatives taken by others.

One of the ideas promoted initially by business is for 'triple bottom line' reporting by companies and non-profit organisations.[29] The idea – otherwise known as TBL, 'people, planet, profits', 'sustainability reporting', or 'social accounting' – is that a company's accounts should include not merely statements of financial profits and losses, but also accounts of changes for which the company has been responsible in the areas of environment and society and which relate to sustainability (issues of energy use, pollution reduction, employee education, and fair trade in relation to production processes carried out in less developed countries, spring to mind). While the measurement and reporting of such changes are included in the basic version of TBL accounting, this is also seen by some as encompassing the company's values, strategies and internal processes. At the present time there exist few agreed standards for TBL reporting, and the performance of New Zealand companies – even those few which currently accept the notion – is not high.[30] The issue of corporate social responsibility is likely to remain a challenging one for companies for some time, particularly as they emerge from the fevered epoch of neoliberalism. On the other hand it might well be claimed that in this emergence, capitalist firms need only rediscover an abandoned pre-neoliberal business ethic, namely that of civic responsibility and a concern for the welfare of company employees as individuals.[31]

The World Business Council for Sustainable Development (WBCSD) was founded in 1992 in the wake of the Rio+20 United Nations Conference on Sustainable Development, and is a global association of some 200 international companies dealing exclusively with the issue of sustainable development. In recent years 29 of its member companies engaged in a project, *Vision 2050*, to develop a vision and a path to the achievement of sustainability by 2050.[27] Introducing their report the co-chairs summarised their vision as 'a planet of 9 billion people all living well – with enough food, clean water, sanitation, shelter, mobility, education and health to make for wellness – within the limits of what this small, fragile planet can supply and renew, every day.' The New Zealand Business Council for Sustainable Development, the New Zealand affiliate of the WBCSD, is the peak industry body for sustainable development in New Zealand. It has developed a *Vision 2050* report for New Zealand, and has initiated other programmes on this theme.[28]

A more recent global non-profit initiative is The B Team, co-founded by Sir Richard Branson and Jochen Zeitz, and launched in 2012 with CEO the New Zealand entrepreneur Derek Handley. This initiative will consist of international CEOs and business leaders with the mission 'To catalyse a better way of doing business for the wellbeing of people and the planet'. The intended focus will be on action in response to a series of specific challenges, accelerating and augmenting the actions of others 'where our collective voice can make a difference'[32]. The impact of this initiative on New Zealand's economic and social life remains for the future to reveal.

From New Zealand civil society, a wide span of active organisations, included among them such groups as the Environmental Defence Society, the Child Poverty Action Group, Generation Zero and educational, medical and religious groupings, will have much to contribute in the transition to a sustainable economy. An increasing number of charitable foundations are committed to supporting efforts towards this goal. And on the government agency side, Statistics New Zealand has taken an initiative towards monitoring the country's progress towards a sustainable state in publishing measurements of a series of indicators relating to concepts of efficiency, fairness, the meeting of needs, and the preservation of resources.[33]

Sustainability and security. A sustainable society is one that recognises the physical limits of planetary resources and is prepared to live within those bounds: life within bounds defined by system resilience. Sustainability is not a point to be attained but a territory to be explored. It can provide individuals with wide vistas of choice and opportunities for a rewarding life. (One might observe that in the longer run it is the only territory that provides such advantages.) In making these choices we should not assume that life at the boundary is preferable to life in the hinterland: precaution is a much better survival strategy than maximising short-term economic benefit. Some conditions are essential to a sustainable society – most particularly the availability of clean air, clean water, and adequate food – whereas other conditions, while important, are less critical. Together these conditions might be referred to as 'security conditions'. It is important that New Zealand define the stake it intends to have in the critical assets that support its resource security.

When we look at New Zealand's position from this perspective we find that it is very fortunate in several respects. As an isolated country with no land borders and few (if any) enemies, it has a high degree of physical security from terrorism. As a country with a small population and much fertile land, ample water, a temperate climate, and an offshore exclusive economic zone which is one of the largest in the world, food security at national level is high and likely to remain so. As a country that generates almost three-quarters of its base-load power from renewable resources, it has high energy security (but not so in relation to transport fuels). New Zealand has opportunities to become much more self-sufficient in sustainable energy resources if it chooses to.

On the other hand New Zealand continues to run down its environmental quality. Clean air remains abundantly available, as does clean water despite rises in aquatic pollution due to intensive land use and in particular pastoral farming. Severe soil erosion on steep hill country continues to denude regions of topsoil, clog waterways and undermine productive potential. As already noted in Chapter 8, New Zealand has one of the worst records in the world for natural biodiversity loss, a reproach redoubled by the fact that New Zealand was one of the last countries in the world to be settled by humans. In late 2013 the iconic kea was added by DOC to the list of nationally endangered species. The New Zealand Biodiversity Strategy, originally launched in 2000, evidently needs more teeth and more action to support it.

Biosecurity and the threat of pathogenic disease vectors to New Zealand flora and fauna (including humans) remains one of New Zealand's most serious ongoing concerns, particularly given the dependence of the economy on primary production. While the Ministry for Primary Industries maintains a rigorous biosecurity programme, biological threats are extremely difficult to control as they may emerge from international trade, travel, tourism, or even the effects of wind and ocean currents. The most critical visible biosecurity threat to New Zealand's economic life and well-being is posed by foot and mouth disease, a highly contagious disease that affects cattle, sheep, pigs, goats and deer. It has never occurred in New Zealand, but a 2001 outbreak of the disease in the UK was overcome at a cost of £4–6bn and the killing of 8.5m sheep and cattle. Outbreaks of the disease occurred in eastern China in 2005, the UK in 2007, and in Japan and South Korea 2010–11. In 2013 a contained outbreak was recorded in southern India. According to government estimates, an outbreak of the disease in New Zealand on the scale of that suffered by the UK in 2001 would result in a NZ$10bn loss in export earnings and a drop in living standards of 25 per cent.[34] Another very serious threat is posed by the Queensland fruit fly, a native of Australia where it is considered the country's most serious insect pest for fruit and vegetable crops. In two recent incidents in 2014, a single male fruit fly was detected in Whangarei, and the incidents controlled.[35] Less successful biosecurity episodes in recent years have resulted in the introduction of the plant pathogen PSA into New Zealand kiwifruit, and the varroa mite into honey-bee populations: both extremely damaging invasions. Biosecurity threats provide a moral of applicability to economic and social issues more generally: if the maintenance of an economic or social value is of sufficient importance to New Zealand, then *barriers* will be required as safeguard against its loss.

New Zealand's economic security is underpinned on the human side by a well-educated and resourceful population and remarkably innovative attitudes among its farmers and entrepreneurs. The era of neoliberal economic policies in New Zealand has, as in other countries of similar experience, exposed the country to greater economic fluctuations and lesser financial security than otherwise would have been the case, crowned by the global financial crisis of 2007–08. Governments in the US and the EU are now proposing to introduce (or re-introduce) regulatory controls on bank activities, and New Zealand should do the same. International financial flows should also be brought under control, so that they reflect more the motive of long-run investment rather than short-term speculation and opportunism. New Zealand should advocate in favour of an international financial transactions (Tobin) tax, as Germany already does.[36] And New Zealand should continue to support the OECD Base Erosion and Profit Sharing Project designed to identify and rectify tax avoidance practices by multinational companies.

A more resilient economy in the future will be underpinned by increased economic diversity. A more robust and vital manufacturing sector would provide a bulwark against serious failure in agriculture – from whatever cause. Increasing value-added processing of primary products, particularly timber, would also aid diversity. Trade arrangements are commercial exchanges. Traditionally these have involved the exchange of goods at borders, but since the advent of the WTO they have become invasive of wide tracts of domestic economies, attempting to restructure them in trade-facilitating form. They harbour dangers for a small country's independence and security. With regard to the TPP in particular, it is difficult to foresee conditions under which New Zealand should sign such an agreement if it involves accepting the proposed ISDS procedure or the degradation of PHARMAC.

New Zealand's long-term economic security will also be enhanced by the acceptance of the reality of global warming and climate change, and the need to respond emphatically and imaginatively to the challenges they pose. The reduction in the level of GHG emissions is evidently a priority. In the case of CO_2 emissions from energy production, the search for and support of more energy-efficient means, and alternative energy technologies, appear as obvious opportunities.

The introduction of a tax on carbon would assert this country's determination to face the problem in a principled manner. Reducing the output of methane from agriculture will however not be so easily achieved. Planning for adaptation to the unpreventable effects of climate change, in both its economic and social aspects, should also be advanced, as is being done in international organizations such as the World Bank, and in individual countries elsewhere.

Economic security in New Zealand requires a significant role for government, not only to ensure an equitable and stable society, and as custodian of our shared values, but to provide a buttress against the malign influences of global forces be they economic or natural. This is a role that can be adequately played only if the government possesses assets. The experience of the Christchurch earthquakes provides a morality tale in this regard. The devastation caused by these events was immense by New Zealand standards: the total economic cost estimated at about US$33bn is equivalent to 20 per cent of the country's GDP, far larger relatively than the cost to Japan of the 2011 Tohoku earthquake and tsunami (3.5–4.0 per cent GDP) or the cost to the US of Hurricane Katrina (1.0 per cent GDP).[37] The need to sell state assets to finance Christchurch reconstruction is both recognition of this important lesson and a repudiation of earlier state asset sales undertaken for more frivolous and ideologically based reasons. The Christchurch earthquakes may not represent the largest or the most protracted economic and social problem to which this country will be exposed in the decades ahead. It is important therefore to give careful consideration to how best to respond in the future to large-scale problems and emergencies, particularly given the randomness with which they will strike and the unpredictability as to whom among us will suffer misfortune when they do.

As for social security, New Zealand is fortunate in having a stable democracy, established social infrastructure, and professional health and welfare services. However this security has started to fray at the edges in recent decades. The changing distribution of costs and benefits within New Zealand society has increasingly called into question what New Zealanders mean by a just society.[38] Declines in voting in general elections, in public service broadcasting, in social participation, not to mention the unreliable conduct of politicians, tear at the fabric of New Zealand's democracy and social security. Efforts need to be made to reverse these trends. It would seem imperative to enshrine not only in law but also in civic life a more encompassing view of social justice, before the widespread and random changes that will accompany climate change, and the essential changes required in the transition to a sustainable economy, reach our hearths.

And cutting across all of these issues of security is that of ownership and the ability to control the levers of policy. Power resides with the owner, not the tenant. New Zealand's transit across the twenty-first century is likely to be far more difficult if it is as tenant on someone else's estate.

The purpose of this book has been to argue for a change of paradigm – a change in the way we think about and act in the economy and in society – as essential for an adequate response to the problems that confront, and will confront, New Zealand in the twenty-first century. When it is said that natural resource availability is declining, that climate change is a problem, or that economic growth is inadequate, and the problems are located somewhere out there in the objective world, we are in fact speaking half-truths. For it can fairly be said that the source of the problems lie not in our environment but in our own attitudes, and assumptions, and behaviours. As Shakespeare had Cassius urge Brutus in the play *Julius Caesar*: 'the fault, dear Brutus, is not in our stars, but in ourselves'[39]. Change in our own behaviour is likely to be the last and greatest resource we can bring to bear to ensure our future well-being and the sustainability of our society.

Addendum: A List of Resources

Economics - General

Kenneth Galbraith and Nicole Salinger, *Almost Everyone's Guide to Economics*, Boston: Houghton Mifflin, 1978. Still a valuable and entertaining read.

Robert Costanza and others, *An Introduction to Ecological Economics*, Boca Raton, FL: St. Lucie Press, 1997.

Herman Daly, *Steady-State Economics: Second Edition with New Essays*, Washington, DC: Island Press, 1991.

Herman Daly and John Cobb, *For the Common Good*, Boston, MA: Bacon Press, 1994.

George Soros, *The Crisis of Global Capitalism*, London: Little Brown & Co., 1998.

Joseph Stiglitz, *The Price of Inequality: How Today's Divided Society Endangers our Future*, New York: W.W. Norton, 2012.

Economics and Politics - New Zealand

Rick Boven, Dan Bidois and Catherine Harland, 'A Goal is not a Strategy: Focusing Efforts to Improve New Zealand's Prosperity', Discussion Paper 2010/1, The New Zealand Institute, Auckland, 2010.

Bryan Gould, *Rescuing the New Zealand Economy: What Went Wrong and How We Can Fix It*, Nelson: Craig Potton, 2008.

Nicky Hager, *The Hollow Men: A Study in the Politics of Deception*, Nelson: Craig Potton, 2006.

Tim Hazledine, *Taking New Zealand Seriously: The Economics of Decency*, Auckland: Harper Collins, 1998.

Jane Kelsey (ed.), *No Ordinary Deal: Unmasking the Trans-Pacific Partnership Free Trade Agreement*, Wellington: Bridget Williams Books, 2010.

Max Rashbrooke (ed.), *Inequality: A New Zealand Crisis*, Wellington: Bridget Williams Books, 2013.

Environment/Climate Change/Sustainability

Neil Adger and Andrew Jordan (eds), *Governing Sustainability*, Cambridge: Cambridge University Press, 2009.

Geoff Bertram and Simon Terry, *The Carbon Challenge: New Zealand's*

Emissions Trading Scheme, Wellington: Bridget Williams Books, 2010.

Rob Dietz and Dan O'Neill, *Enough is Enough: a Sustainable Economy in a World of Finite Resources*, Abingdon, Oxon: Routledge.

International Panel on Climate Change (IPCC), various reports at: http://www.ipcc.ch/publications_and_data/publications_and_data_reports.shtml

Jim Salinger (ed.), *Living in a Warmer World: How a Changing Climate will Affect our Lives*, Auckland: Bateman, 2013. An Australian and New Zealand perspective.

The Royal Society, *People and Planet*, London: The Royal Society, 2012.

Worldwatch Institute, *State of the World 2103: Is Sustainability Still Possible?* Washington: Island Press, 2013.

Democracy

Robert Dahl, *On Democracy*, New Haven: Yale University Press, 1998.

James Fishkin, *Democracy and Deliberation: New Directions for Democratic Reform*, New Haven: Yale University Press, 1991.

John Gastil and Peter Levine (eds), *The Deliberative Democracy Handbook: Strategies for Effective Civic Engagement in the Twenty-First Century*, San Francisco: Jossey-Bass, 2005.

Amy Gutmann and Dennis Thompson, *Democracy and Disagreement*, Cambridge, MA: Harvard University Press, 1996.

Amy Gutmann and Dennis Thompson, *Why Deliberative Democracy?* Princeton: Princeton University Press, 2004.

Uno Svedin and Britt Aniansson, *Sustainability, Local Democracy and the Future: The Swedish Model*, Dordrecht: Kluwer, 2002.

Measuring Performance

Clive Hamilton and Hugh Saddler, 'The Genuine Progress Indicator: a new index of changes in well-being in Australia', Discussion Paper No.14, Australia Institute, Canberra, 1997, http://www.tai.org.au/node/874

Richard Layard, *Happiness: Lessons from a New Science*, 2nd edn, London: Penguin, 2011.

Joseph Stiglitz, Amartya Sen and Jean-Paul Fitoussi, *Report by the Commission on the Measurement of Economic Performance and Social Progress*, 2009.

Philosophy/Politics/Civil Society

Hugh Mercer Curtler, *Ethical Argument*, 2nd edn, New York: Oxford University Press, 2004.

Michael Edwards, *Civil Society*, 2nd edn, Cambridge: Polity Press, 2009.

Bryan Gould, *Myths, Politicians and Money: The Truth behind the Free Market*, Basingstoke, Hants.: Palgrave Macmillan, 2013.

David Marquand, *Decline of the Public: the Hollowing-out of Citizenship*, Cambridge: Polity Press, 2004.

History, film/TV archive - New Zealand

Brian Easton, *The Commercialisation of New Zealand*, Auckland: Auckland University Press, 1997.

Jane Kelsey, *The New Zealand Experiment: A World Model for Structural Adjustment?* Auckland: Auckland University Press and Bridget Williams Books, 1995.

Bruce Jesson, *Only Their Purpose is Mad: The Money Men Take over New Zealand*, Palmerston North: Dunmore Press, 1999.

Alister Barry [writer, director], *Someone Else's Country* [documentary film], Wellington: Community Media Trust/ Vanguard Films, 1996 (NZ Film Archive ref. F30393).

Alister Barry [writer, director], *In a Land of Plenty* [documentary film], Wellington: Community Media Trust/Vanguard Films, 2002 (NZ Film Archive ref. F94530).

Alister Barry [writer, director] *A Civilised Society* [documentary film], 2007 (NZ Film Archive ref. F108218).

Alister Barry, *Hot Air* [documentary film on 20 years of climate change policy], 2014.

Marcia Russell [writer, producer] and John Carlaw [director] *Revolution: Part I - Fortress New Zealand; Part II - The Grand Illusion; Part III - The Great Divide; Part IV - The New Country*, Wellington: Images Ink/Television New Zealand, 1996, http://www.nzonscreen.com/title/revolution-1996/series

Abbreviations and Units

Abbreviations

APEC	Asia-Pacific Economic Cooperation
AUSFTA	Australia-United States Free Trade Agreement
CAFCA	Campaign Against Foreign Control of Aotearoa (NZ)
CBA	cost benefit analysis
CPR	common property resource
DOC	Department of Conservation (NZ)
EC	European Community
ETS	emissions trading scheme
FAO	Food and Agriculture Organization of the United Nations
FDI	foreign direct investment
GATS	General Agreement on Trade in Services
GATT	General Agreement on Tariffs and Trade
GDP	gross domestic product
GNP	gross national product
GFC	global financial crisis (2007–08)
GPI	genuine progress indicator
HDI	human development index
IEA	Institute of Economic Affairs (UK)
IMF	International Monetary Fund
IP	intellectual property
IPCC	Intergovernmental Panel on Climate Change
ISDS	investor-state dispute settlement
IUCN	International Union for Conservation of Nature
LULUCF	land use, land-use change and forestry
MAF	Ministry of Agriculture and Forestry (NZ)
NAFTA	North American Free Trade Agreement
NGO	non-governmental organisation
NIWA	National Institute of Water & Atmospheric Research (NZ)

NZIER	New Zealand Institute of Economic Research
OECD	Organisation for Economic Co-operation and Development
OIO	Overseas Investment Office (NZ)
PHARMAC	Pharmaceutical Management Agency (NZ)
PhRMA	Pharmaceutical Research and Manufacturers of America (US)
RMA	Resource Management Act 1991 (NZ)
SNA	System of National Accounts (UN)
SOE	State-Owned Enterprise (NZ)
SWG	Savings Working Group (NZ)
TPP	Trans-Pacific Partnership
TRIMs	Agreement on Trade-Related Investment Measures
TRIPS	Agreement on Trade-Related Aspects of Intellectual Property Rights
UNDP	United Nations Development Programme
UNEP	United Nations Environment Programme
UNFCCC	United Nations Framework Convention on Climate Change
USTR	United States Trade Representative (Office of)
WBCSD	World Business Council for Sustainable Development
WMO	World Meteorological Office
WTO	World Trade Organization
WWF	World Wildlife Fund

Units

million (m) = 1,000,000; billion (bn) = 1,000,000,000

tonne(t) = 1,000 kilograms (kg); million tonnes (Mt)

dollar ($) = US dollar; other currencies so-indicated e.g. AU$, NZ$, €, etc.

Appendices

Appendix 1: Foreign Direct Investment

In economics, investment is the process of creating and/or combining productive assets (including land, buildings, machinery, technology, energy, human knowhow) in order to produce goods and services for consumption. In matters of finance, the emphasis is on the money involved in this process. Here reference can be made to either the *flow* of money into investment (per year, say) or the accumulated stock of money that has flowed into investment (at the end of a decade, say). When foreign investors make money available for investment in New Zealand, it can be either in the form of *debt* through the purchase of bonds or debentures (on which the investor receives specified and fixed repayments), or in the form of *equity* through the purchase of productive assets or of shares in a New Zealand company (with the expectation of receiving a return in the form of profit, dividends or capital appreciation).

Foreign direct investment (FDI) refers to funds invested from overseas which are used to acquire an ongoing management interest in a New Zealand company, and thereby a measure of control. Statistics New Zealand identifies FDI as those cases in which the foreign investor acquires at least 10 per cent of the ordinary shares or voting power in a New Zealand company. Where a foreign investor holds less than 10 per cent, the holding is referred to as a *portfolio* investment. (The Overseas Investment Office uses a 25 per cent criterion.)

In the national statistics the *balance of payments current account* sets out the money values of the flows of New Zealand's exports and imports of goods and services, inward and outward investment incomes, and transfers with the rest of the world, during a specified period (commonly three months or one year). A deficit on the current account indicates that the value of the funds outflow from New Zealand exceeds the value of the funds inflow. *The balance of payments financial account* sets out the values of the flows of financial transactions between New Zealand and the rest of the world that involve direct investment, portfolio investment, and 'reserves' (as held by the Reserve Bank). The *net international investment position* (NIIP) shows the level of the stock of New Zealand's international assets and liabilities at a point in time, including both debt (borrowings and lendings) and equity (investment in shares and physical assets).

Appendix 2: 'Capitals' in Economics

Capital refers to the stock of all those things which when combined with labour produce the flow of goods and services in the economy. In orthodox economics the consideration of capital was commonly restricted to manufactured capital such as machinery, equipment, buildings, although land was a key asset for earlier economists such as Ricardo and Malthus. In recent decades, particularly under the influence of ecological economists, a range of 'capitals' which contribute directly or indirectly to economic output have become acknowledged. A key distinction is that between man-made capital and natural capital.

Man-made capital

Manufactured capital is 'built capital' including machinery, equipment, buildings, physical infrastructure; *human capital* is the stock of knowledge, competencies and personal attributes that can be applied to the production of economic and social value; *social capital* is the resource that is embodied in relationships between and among people (and particularly important in relation to social stability and democracy).

Natural capital

Refers to the planet's stocks of water, land, air, and renewable and non-renewable resources. These provide flows of 'ecosystem services', many of which are critical for human survival and well-being. *Renewable natural capital* consists of plants and animal species, fish, micro-organisms, forests, which can all provide flows of services as inputs to human activity indefinitely, if used sustainably. Similar flows of services from natural capital are provided by the absorption and detoxification of wastes. Radiant energy from the sun, and wind, are elements of renewable natural capital. *Non-renewable natural capital* is natural capital that can only be used at the cost of its depletion, such as minerals including coal, natural gas, and petroleum. Arable soils are non-renewable natural capital within a timespan of hundreds of years.

Financial capital

Money or money equivalents that can be applied to economically productive use (see Appendix 1).

Appendix 3. Part II, Resource Management Act 1991, No. 69 (as enacted)

PURPOSE AND PRINCIPLES

5. Purpose – (1) The purpose of this Act is to promote the sustainable management of natural and physical resources.

(2) In this Act, "sustainable management" means managing the use, development, and protection of natural and physical resources in a way, or at a rate, which enables people and communities to provide for their social, economic, and cultural wellbeing and for their health and safety while-

(a) Sustaining the potential of natural and physical resources (excluding minerals) to meet the reasonably foreseeable needs of future generations; and

(b) Safeguarding the life· supporting capacity of air, water, soil, and ecosystems; and

(c) Avoiding, remedying, or mitigating any adverse effects of activities on the environment.

6. Matters of national importance – In achieving the purpose of this Act, all persons exercising functions and powers under it, in relation to managing the use, development, and protection of natural and physical resources, shall recognise and provide for the following matters of national importance:

(a) The preservation of the natural character of the coastal environment (including the coastal marine area), wetlands, and lakes and rivers and their margins, and the protection of them from inappropriate subdivision, use, and development:

(b) The protection of outstanding natural features and landscapes from inappropriate subdivision, use, and development:

(c) The protection of areas of significant indigenous vegetation and significant habitats of indigenous fauna:

(d) The maintenance and enhancement of public access to and along the coastal marine area, lakes, and rivers:

(e) The relationship of Maori and their culture and traditions with their ancestral lands, water, sites, waahi tapu, and other taonga.

7. Other matters – In achieving the purpose of this Act, all persons exercising functions and powers under it, in relation to managing the use, development, and protection of natural and physical resources, shall have particular regard to-

(a) Kaitiakitanga:

616 Resource Management 1991, No. 69

(b) The efficient use and development of natural and physical resources:

(c) The maintenance and enhancement of amenity values:

(d) Intrinsic values of ecosystems:

(e) Recognition and protection of the heritage values of sites, buildings, places, or areas:

(f) Maintenance and enhancement of the quality of the environment:

(g) Any finite characteristics of natural and physical resources:

(h) The protection of the habitat of trout and salmon.

8. Treaty of Waitangi – In achieving the purpose of this Act, all persons exercising functions and powers under it, in relation to managing the use, development, and protection of natural and physical resources, shall take into account the principles of the Treaty of Waitangi (Te Tiriti 0 Waitangi).

Source: http://www.nzlii.org/nz/legis/hist_act/toc-1991.html

Appendix 4: Elements of a Genuine Progress Indicator (GPI)

GPI (dollars) =

+ Personal consumption weighted by an income distribution index

+ Value of household work and parenting

+ Value of higher education

+ Value of volunteer work

+ Services of consumer durables

+ Services of highways and streets

- Cost of crime

- Loss of leisure time

- Cost of unemployment

- Cost of consumer durables

- Cost of commuting

- Cost of household pollution abatement

- Cost of automobile accidents

- Cost of water pollution

- Cost of air pollution

- Cost of noise pollution

- Loss of wetlands

- Loss of farmland

-/+ Loss of forest area and damage from logging roads

- Depletion of nonrenewable energy resources

- Carbon dioxide emissions damage

- Cost of ozone depletion

+/- Net capital investment

+/- Net foreign borrowing

Source: Wikipedia, 'Genuine progress indicator'.

Bibliography and Notes

Chapter 1 Free Market Economies

[1] P. Krugman, *The Return of Depression Economics and the Crisis of 2008*, New York: Norton, 2008; J. Stiglitz, *Freefall: Free Markets and the Sinking of the Global Economy*, London: Allen Lane, 2010; J. Quiggin, *Zombie Economics*, Princeton: Princeton University Press, 2010; see also Wikipedia, various entries.

[2] Financial Crisis Inquiry Commission, *Final Report of the National Commission on the Causes of the Financial and Economic Crisis in the United States*, Washington, DC: Government Printing Office, 2011.

[3] R. Skidelsky, *Keynes: The Return of the Master*, London: Allen Lane, 2009; see also Wikipedia, '2008-09 Keynesian resurgence'.

[4] 'Financial services' include banks, insurance companies, pension funds and other asset management companies, stock exchanges, foreign exchange brokers, and credit card companies. These institutions are often referred to as 'financial intermediaries'.

[5] W.L. Megginson, *The Financial Economics of Privatization*, Oxford: Oxford University Press, 2005, p. 28.

[6] D. Harvey, *A Brief History of Neoliberalism*, Oxford: Oxford University Press, 2005; Megginson, op. cit.

[7] At its inception in 1961 the OECD had 20 Member countries. Japan joined in 1964, Finland in 1969, Australia in 1971, New Zealand in 1973. Six further states joined in the 1990s, and a further four in 2010 to a current total of 34.

[8] OECD, *OECD Economic Outlook No.67*, Paris: OECD, 2000, pp. 173-92; OECD, 'Growth in GDP per capita', *OECD Factbook 2009*, pp. 54-5.

[9] OECD, *OECD Unemployment Outlook* (various years).

[10] OECD, *Divided We Stand: Why Inequality Keeps Rising*, Paris: OECD, 2011. Main findings at: http://www.oecd.org/els/soc/49499779.pdf

[11] World Commission on the Social Dimension of Globalization, *A Fair Globalization: Creating Opportunities for All*, Geneva: International Labour Organization, 2004, p. 43.

[12] F.G. Castles and S. Dowrick, 'The impact of government spending levels

on medium-term economic growth in the OECD, 1960-85', *Journal of Theoretical Politics* 2(2), 1990, 173-204.

[13] P.H. Lindert, *Growing Public: Social Spending and Economic Growth since the Eighteenth Century*, Cambridge: Cambridge University Press, 2004.

[14] Skidelsky, op. cit., pp. 116-26.

[15] D. Rodrik, 'Rethinking growth strategies', WIDER Annual Lecture 8, United Nations University, Helsinki, 2005.

[16] T. Persson, and G. Tabellini, 'Is inequality harmful for growth?' *American Economic Review*, 84(3), 1994, 600-21.

[17] G. Esping-Andersen, 'Welfare states and the economy', in N.J. Smelser, and R. Swedberg (eds.) *The Handbook of Economic Sociology*, 1st edn, Ewing, NJ: Princeton University Press, 1994, pp. 711-32.

[18] Sh.-Y. Wu, J.-H. Tang and E.S. Lin, 'The impact of government expenditure on economic growth: How sensitive to the level of development?' *Journal of Policy Modelling* 32(6), 2010, 804-17; see further: B. Moreno-Dodson, 'Assessing the impact of public spending on growth', Policy Research Working Paper 4663, The World Bank, 2008.

[19] J.D. Ostry, A. Berg and C.G. Tsangarides, 'Redistribution, Inequality, and Growth', IMF Report IMF/SDN/14/02, 2014.

[20] P. Krugman, 'Inequality and redistribution', in N. Serra and J.E. Stiglitz (eds), *The Washington Consensus Reconsidered*, Oxford: Oxford University Press, 2008, pp. 31-40.

[21] J.K. Galbraith, 'Recession economics', *New York Review of Books*, 04/02/1982.

[22] G. Bertram, 'The New Zealand economy: 1900-2000', in G. Byrnes (ed.), *The New Oxford History of New Zealand*, Auckland & Melbourne: Oxford University Press, 2009, pp. 537-72.

[23] New Zealand was not the first country to be subjected to free market 'shock therapy'. It had been applied in Chile in 1975 under the dictatorship of Pinochet by Friedman and Chicago-trained Chilean economists.

[24] *New Zealand Official Yearbook 2010*, p. 327.

[25] D. Henderson, 'The revival of economic liberalism: Australia in an international perspective', *Australian Economic Review*, 28(1), 1995, 59-85.

[26] Several books have examined aspects of this transformation. See: J. Kelsey, *The New Zealand Experiment: A World Model for Structural*

Adjustment?, Auckland: Auckland University Press, 1995; B. Easton, *The Commercialisation of New Zealand*, Auckland: Auckland University Press, 1997; T. Hazledine, *Taking New Zealand Seriously: The Economics of Decency*, Auckland: Harper Collins, 1998.

[27] New Zealand Treasury, 'Living Standards: A Short Guide to "Economic Growth"', 2013, http://www.treasury.govt.nz/abouttreasury/higherlivingstandards/hls-ag-econgrow-jan13.pdf

[28] R.G. Gregory, 'Labour market outcomes in the UK, NZ, Australia and the US: Observations on the impact of labour market and economic reforms', Discussion Paper No. 401, Economics Program, RSSS, ANU, 1999. Published also in S. Bell (ed.), *The Unemployment Crisis: Which Way Out?*, Cambridge: Cambridge University Press, 1999.

[29] M. Reddell and C. Sleeman, 'Some perspectives on past recessions', *Reserve Bank of New Zealand Bulletin*, 71(2), 2008, 5-21 (p. 8); *New Zealand Official Yearbook 2010*, p. 284.

[30] D. O'Dea, 'The Changes in New Zealand's Income Distribution', Treasury Working Paper 00/13, 2000.

[31] O. Aziz et al., 'The effect on household income of government taxation and expenditure in 1988, 1998, 2007 and 2010', *Policy Quarterly*, 8(1), 2012, 29-38.

[32] OECD, 2011, op. cit.

[33] M. Fletcher and M. Dwyer, *A Fair Go for All Children: Actions to Address Child Poverty in New Zealand*, Report to the Children's Commissioner and Barnardos, 2008. Note that this provides a relative measure of poverty rather than an absolute one. Statistics New Zealand does not have a definition of poverty and does not publish poverty statistics.

[34] Expert Advisory Group on Solutions to Child Poverty, *Solutions to Child Poverty in New Zealand: Evidence for Action*, Wellington: Families Commission, 2013, p. vi.

[35] L. Evans, A. Grimes and B. Wilkinson, 'Economic reform in New Zealand 1984-95: the pursuit of efficiency', *Journal of Economic Literature*, 34(4), 1996, 1856-902.

[36] D.T. Brash, 'New Zealand's Remarkable Reforms', Fifth Hayek Memorial Lecture, IEA, London, 1996, http://www.rbnz.govt.nz/research_and_publications/speeches/1996/0031201.html

[37] K. Rankin, 'New Zealand 1995: A Miracle Economy?', Policy Discussion Paper No.19, Economics Department, University of Auckland, 1995.

[38] T. Hazledine, 'Agency Theory meets Social Capital: the Failure of the New Zealand Economic Revolution of 1984-91', Economics Working Papers, Economics Department, Auckland University, 2000; P. Dalziel, 'New Zealand's economic reform programme was a failure', 1999, http://jtc.blogs.com/dalziel-1999.pdf

[39] P. Dalziel, 'New Zealand's economic reforms: an assessment', *Review of Political Economy*, 14(1), 2002, 31-46.

[40] W. Smith and H. Montgomery, 'Revolution or evolution? New Zealand agriculture since 1984', *GeoJournal*, 59, 2003, 107-18.

[41] T. Hazledine and J. Quiggin, 'No more free beer tomorrow? Economic and policy outcomes in Australia and New Zealand since 1984', *Australian Journal of Political Studies*, 41(2), 2006, 145-59.

[42] Gregory, op. cit.

[43] Hazledine and Quiggin, op.cit.

[44] Easton, op.cit.

Chapter 2 Liberalism, Economics, and Ethics

[1] J. Bentham, *An Introduction to the Principles of Morals and Legislation*, J.H. Burns and H.L.A. Hart (eds), London: Athlone Press, 1970 [1789], pp. 11-13.

[2] J.S. Mill, 'Considerations on Representative Government', in J.M. Robson (ed.), *Collected Works of John Stuart Mill, Vol.19: Essays on Politics and Society*, Toronto: University of Toronto Press, 1977 [1861], p. 412.

[3] In 1960 Hayek published the more substantial *The Constitution of Liberty* (Chicago University Press), generally considered the high point of twentieth century libertarian political theorising.

[4] The importance of Nozick's book for the emergent neoliberalism is recorded by *Economist*, 'Robert Nozick', 31/01/2002, http://www.economist.com/node/965401

[5] R. Cockett, *Thinking the Unthinkable: Think-Tanks and the Economic Counter-Revolution 1931-1983*, London: Harper Collins, 1994.

[6] Cockett, op.cit., p. 158.

[7] For an account of the influence of conservative think tanks in the US

see: J. Stefancic and R. Delgado, *No Mercy: How Conservative Think Tanks and Foundations Changed America's Social Agenda*, Philadelphia: Temple University Press, 1996.

[8] Atlas Economic Research Foundation, http://atlasnetwork.org/. From New Zealand, The New Zealand Initiative and the Maxim Institute are both listed in the Atlas global directory (at 27/04/2014).

[9] D. Harvey, *A Brief History of Neoliberalism*, Oxford: Oxford University Press, 2005.

[10] J. Rawls, *A Theory of Justice*, Oxford: Oxford University Press, 1972, p. 302.

[11] Rawls, op.cit., p. 277. For 'social capital' and 'externalities' see further Chapter 6.

[12] A. Sen, *Commodities and Capabilities*, Oxford: Oxford University Press, 1999; A. Sen, *Development as Freedom*, New York: Alfred A. Knopf, 1999.

[13] M.C. Nussbaum, 'Capabilities and human rights', *Fordham Law Review*, 66(2), 1997, 273-300; M.C. Nussbaum, *Women and Human Development: The Capabilities Approach*, Cambridge: Cambridge University Press, 2000.

[14] The discussion here is about distributive (social) justice, not retributive (criminal) justice. Distributive justice concerns the apportionment in society of things such as income, wealth, power, opportunity, respect. For a comprehensive discussion: J. Lamont and C. Favor, 'Distributive justice', in E.N. Zalta (ed.), *The Stanford Encyclopedia of Philosophy*, Spring 2013 edn (online).

[15] As for Adam Smith, it is difficult to ascertain what his political views actually were. See D. Winch, *Adam Smith's Politics*, Cambridge: Cambridge University Press, 1978, pp. 170-1.

[16] R. Nozick, *Anarchy, State and Utopia*, New York: Basic Books, 1974, p. 219.

[17] F.A. Hayek, *Law, Legislation and Liberty. Vol. 2: The Mirage of Social Justice,* London: Routledge and Kegan Paul, 1976, p. 97.

[18] M.J. Sandel, *What Money Can't Buy: The Moral Limits of Markets*, New York: Farrar, Straus and Giroux, 2012.

[19] Mill, op. cit., p. 412.

Chapter 3 The Consequences of Neoliberalism in New Zealand

[1] The amount of money raised between 1984 and 1999 was NZ$19.1bn. See: NZ Treasury, 'Income from State Asset Sales as at 30 September 1999', at: http://www.treasury.govt.nz/government/assets/saleshistory (NZ$19.1bn represents about one third of GDP at year 2000).

[2] E.g. A. Hawkins, *The Hawk: Alan Hawkins tells the Equiticorp Story*, Mission Bay, Auckland: Four Star Books, 1989; TV3-Media3, 'For the Public Good, Revisited', April 2013, http://www.tv3.co.nz/MEDIA3-Season-2-Ep-10/tabid/3692/articleID/92011/MCat/3134/Default.aspx

[3] At one time almost half of the SOE directors were members of the New Zealand Business Roundtable: J. Kelsey, *The New Zealand Experiment: A World Model for Structural Adjustment?*, Auckland: Auckland University Press, 1995, p. 76.

[4] C. Barton, 'Telecom jackpot: How privatization made fortunes', *New Zealand Herald*, 03/08/2012.

[5] A list of public assets privatised up until 1999, including sale prices, is available at: http://www.treasury.govt.nz/government/assets/saleshistory

[6] Kelsey, op. cit.; B. Silverstone, A. Bollard and R. Lattimore (eds) *A Study of Economic Reform: The Case of New Zealand*, Amsterdam: Elsevier, 1996, pp. 389-424; B. Easton, *The Commercialisation of New Zealand*, Auckland: Auckland University Press, 1997; B. Jesson, *Only their Purpose is Mad: The Money Men take over New Zealand*, Palmerston North: The Dunmore Press, 1999; B. Rosenberg, 'Issues in privatization - Costs and Benefits', New Zealand Fabian Society, 06/10/2010, http://www.fabians.org.nz/

[7] The story of Tranz Rail can be followed at Wikipedia, 'Tranz Rail'.

[8] G. Bertram, 'New Zealand since 1984', *GeoJournal*, 59, 2004, 93-106.

[9] Commerce Commission, *Investigation into New Zealand Electricity Markets – May 2009*, Wellington: Commerce Commission.

[10] S. Watson, 'Mixed-ownership model warrants closer look', *New Zealand Herald*, 11/06/2013.

[11] J. Wilson, 'A short history of post-privatisation in NZ' (Treasury 1982752v1), paper attached as annexe to Crown Ownership Monitoring Unit 'Privatisation in New Zealand: An assessment of a series of company experiences' (T2010/2642), 2010. The nine companies considered were:

Ports of Auckland, Bank of New Zealand, Air New Zealand, Auckland International Airport, Telecom, Tranz Rail, Trustpower, Contact Energy, and Forest Corporation of New Zealand. http://www.comu.govt.nz/resources/pdfs/mixed-ownership-model/t2010-2642.pdf

[12] E.g. S. Domberger and J. Piggott, 'Privatization policies and public enterprise: a survey', *The Economic Record*, 62(2), 1986, 145-62; S.R. Letza, C. Smallman and X. Sun, 'Reframing privatization: deconstructing the myth of efficiency', *Policy Sciences*, 37(2), 2004, 159-83.

[13] A monopoly exists where a specific enterprise is the only supplier of a particular commodity or service. A natural monopoly is one in which economic efficiency of the enterprise increases with enterprise scale. This is often the case in industries with high capital costs, such as in defence industries, and in public utilities such as water services and electricity provision.

[14] R. Birchfield and I. Grant, *Out of the Woods: The Restructuring and Sale of New Zealand's State Forests*, Wellington: GP Books, 1993, p. 163.

[15] B. Rosenberg, 2010, op. cit.

[16] B. Easton, 'Economy: Light regulation has failed', *New Zealand Listener*, no. 3751, 31/03/2012; New Zealand Fabian Society, 'Light-handed Regulation. Four presentations on work safety, finance, energy and building sectors', 2012, available at: http://www.fabians.org.nz; H. Armstrong, *Your Life or your Job: New Zealand Rail Safety 1974–2000*, Wellington: Hazel Armstrong Law, 2013.

[17] A.B. Atkinson and A. Leigh, 'The Distribution of Top Incomes in New Zealand', Discussion Paper No. 503, Centre for Economic Policy Research, Australian National University, 2005.

[18] J. Savage and A. Leask, 'How super-rich Kiwis dodge tax', *New Zealand Herald*, 01/06/2013.

[19] J.K. Galbraith and N. Salinger, *Almost Everyone's Guide to Economics*, Boston: Houghton Mifflin, 1978, p. 41.

[20] R. Douglas, *Unfinished Business*, Auckland: Random House, 1993, p. 3.

[21] T. Hazledine and J. Siegfried, 'How did the wealthiest New Zealanders get so rich?', *New Zealand Economic Papers*, 31(1), 1997, 35-47; B. Edwards, 'Is NZ run by a power elite?', *National Business Review*, 13/02/2014.

[22] Anon, 'Roundtable and NZ Institute morph into new libertarian think

tank', *National Business Review*, 04/04/2012, http://www.nbr.co.nz/printer/115751

[23] The New Zealand Initiative, http://nzinitiative.org.nz/About+Us/Membership.html

[24] See N. Hager, *The Hollow Men: A Study in the Politics of Deception*, Nelson: Craig Potton Publishing, 2006, pp. 212-32.

[25] N. Hertz, *The Silent Takeover: Global Capitalism and the Death of Democracy*, New York: The Free Press, 2001, p. 86.

[26] R. Finkelstein, *Report of the Independent Inquiry into the Media and Media Regulation,* Report to the Minister for Broadband, Communications and the Digital Economy, Canberra: Australian Government, 2012.

[27] Some advertising was carried on these TV channels.

[28] This section has benefitted particularly from B. Rosenberg, *News Media Ownership in New Zealand,* 2008, http://canterbury.cyberplace.org.nz/community/CAFCA/publications/Miscellaneous/mediaown.pdf ; see also M. Myllylahti and W. Hope, 'Global capital and media communication ownership in New Zealand', *Pacific Journalism Review,* 17(2), 2011, 188-209.

[29] Wikipedia, 'Television New Zealand'.

[30] Rosenberg, 2008, op. cit., p. 61.

[31] In an interview with Colin Peacock of *Media Watch* on this issue in relation to radio, Jeremy Irwin, former chief executive of the Association of New Zealand Advertisers said: '... the companies are there to enhance and or protect their brand ... and the medium itself has a much greater responsibility to ensure the delivery of the advertising is done in an appropriate manner and if it is not they must suffer the consequences' (Radio New Zealand National, *Media Watch*, 17/11/2013).

[32] T. Dunleavy, P. Thompson and others, 'An Open Letter from Media Academics on TVNZ7 and Public Broadcasting', 14/04/2011, http://www.scoop.co.nz/stories/ED1104/S00053/media-academics-open-letter-tvnz7-and-public-broadcasting.htm

[33] D. Cheng, 'Axe falls on last public service channel', *New Zealand Herald*, 07/04/2011.

[34] P. Norris and B. Pauling, *NZ On Air: An Evaluative Study 1989-2011*, NZ On Air, 2012, pp. 59-67.

[35] Radio New Zealand National, *Media Watch*, 10/11/2013.

[36] UNESCO, *Public Broadcasting: Why? How?* Paris: UNESCO, 2001.

[37] B. Wilkinson, *New Zealand's Global Links: Foreign Ownership and the Status of New Zealand's International Investment*, Wellington: The New Zealand Initiative, 2013, p. xxiv.

[38] D. Steenkamp, 'New Zealand's imbalances in a cross-country context', Reserve Bank of New Zealand, *Bulletin* 73(4), 2010, 37-49.

[39] Wilkinson, op. cit., p. xxiii-xxiv.

[40] P. Conway and L. Meehan, 'Productivity by the Numbers: The New Zealand Experience', Research Paper, New Zealand Productivity Commission, 2013.

[41] Statistics New Zealand, 'Productivity statistics 1978-2011', released 15/03/2012.

[42] For example: C. Fons-Rosen et al., 'Quantifying productivity gains from foreign investment', NBER Working Paper No. 18920, National Bureau of Economic Research, Cambridge, MA, 2013; L. Alfaro, S. Kalemli-Ozcan and S. Sayek, 'FDI, productivity and financial development', *The World Economy*, 32(1), 2009, 111-35; C. Hale and C. Long, 'Are there productivity spillovers from FDI in China?' Working Paper, Federal Reserve Bank of San Francisco, 2007; H. Gorg and D. Greenaway, 'Much ado about Nothing? Do domestic firms really benefit from FDI?', *The World Bank Research Observer*, 19(2), 2004, 171-97.

[43] There are some New Zealand studies done at enterprise level using interview techniques which identify benefits flowing to New Zealand-based affiliates of foreign companies, but the evidence must be judged weak, both on account of small sample sizes involved, and because of potential bias of foreign firms 'cherry-picking' more productive firms for takeover or self-selecting into more productive industries.

[44] N. Blakely et al., 'International Connections and Productivity: Making Globalisation Work for New Zealand', Productivity Paper 09/01, NZ Treasury, 2009; Ministry of Business, Innovation and Employment, 'Business Growth Agenda', http://www.mbie.govt.nz/what-we-do/business-growth-agenda

[45] R. Boven, D. Bidois and C. Harland, 'A Goal is not a Strategy: Focusing Efforts to Improve New Zealand's Prosperity', Discussion Paper 2010/1,

Wellington: The New Zealand Institute, 2010.

[46] House of Representatives, *Manufacturing: The New Consensus. A Blueprint for Better Jobs and Higher Wages,* Wellington: House of Representatives, 2013.

[47] The Real Economy, 'Manufacturing inquiry – act or deny', 19/06/2013, http://www.realeconomy.co.nz/352-manufacturing_inquiry_act_or_d.aspx

[48] M. Berry, 'Opposition manufacturing inquiry report released', 17/06/2013, http://www.stuff.co.nz/national/politics/8805482

[49] G. Wheeler, 'Manufacturing decline not just a dollar story', Speech to the New Zealand Manufacturers and Exporters Association, Auckland, 20/02/2013, http://www.rbnz.govt.nz/research_and_publications/speeches/2013/5150125.html

[50] Savings Working Group, *Saving New Zealand: Reducing Vulnerabilities and Barriers to Growth and Prosperity.* Final Report to the Minister of Finance, 2011.

[51] In passing, the report was able to identify that although national wealth has increased significantly in the last two decades, this has been largely due to increases in the prices of houses and farms, and that more than half of private-sector debt was now in housing loans.

[52] Income distribution is often described by means of tenths or deciles. Individuals (or households) are arranged in the order of their income and divided into ten groups of equal size. The first income decile contains the lowest income tenth and the tenth decile the highest income tenth.

[53] R.A. Dahl, *On Democracy,* New Haven: Yale University Press, 1998.

[54] Dahl, op. cit., pp. 173, 176; R.A. Dahl, 'Why free markets are not enough', *Journal of Democracy,* 3(3), 1992, 82-9.

[55] G. McLauchlan, *The Big Con: The Death of the Kiwi Dream*, Wellington: GP Publications, 1992, p. 1.

[56] Hager, op. cit.

[57] NZ Electoral Commission, 'Results of the 2013 citizen initiated referendum', http://www.elections.org.nz/events/2013-citizens-initiated-referendum

[58] NZ Electoral Commission, *Report of the Electoral Commission on the Review of the MMP Voting System*, Wellington: NZ Electoral Commission, 2012.

[59] The Insider, 'Open secret', *New Zealand Herald*, 21/02/2014.

[60] NZ Electoral Commission, 'General elections 1853–2011 – dates and turnout', http://www.elections.org.nz; K. Blechynden, 'Low local body vote 'due to lack of issues', 14/10/2013, http://www.stuff.co.nz

[61] D. Beetham et al. (eds), *The State of Democracy: Assessments in Eight Nations around the World*, The Hague: Kluwer Law International, 2002, pp. 55-6.

[62] R. Miller quoted by T. O'Connor, 'Maori Party "biggest in the country"', *New Zealand Herald*, 29/05/2005.

[63] I. Marsh and R. Miller, *Democratic Decline and Democratic Renewal: Political Change in Britain, Australia and New Zealand*, Cambridge: Cambridge University Press, 2012.

[64] D. Marquand, *Decline of the Public*, Cambridge: Polity Press, 2004, p. 4.

[65] R.D. Putnam, R. Leonardi and R.Y. Nanetti, *Making Democracy Work: Civic Traditions in Modern Italy*, Princeton: Princeton University Press, 1994.

[66] M. Lyons and G. Nowland-Foreman, 'Civil society and social capital in Australia and New Zealand', in H. Anheier and S. Toepler (eds), *International Encyclopedia of Civil Society*, Springer Reference, New York, 2009, pp. 213-18.

[67] S. Grey and C. Sedgwick, 'The contract state and constrained democracy', *Policy Quarterly*, 9(3), 2013, 3-10.

[68] E.g D. Chisholm, 'Science for sale?', *North & South*, April 2014, pp. 48-56.

[69] OECD, *Society at a Glance 2014*, Paris: OECD, 2014.

[70] E. Learmonth and J. Tabakoff, *No Mercy: True Stories of Disaster, Survival and Brutality*, Melbourne: Text Publishing, 2013.

[71] J. Gray, *False Dawn*, London: Granta Books, 1998; J.R. Saul, *The Collapse of Globalism*, London: Atlantic Books, 2005; B. Gould, *The Democracy Sham: How Globalisation Devalues your Vote*, Nelson: Craig Potton, 2006; R. Reich, *Supercapitalism*, New York, Vintage Books, 2007; J.E. Stiglitz, *The Price of Inequality: How Today's Divided Society Endangers Our Future*, New York: W.W. Norton, 2012.

[72] M. Thompson, 'Davos elite: Inequality corroding democracy', *CNN Money*, 25/01/2014, http://money.cnn.com/2014/01/24/news/economy/inequality-politics-democracy/

[73] J.R. Saul, *The Unconscious Civilization*, Harmondsworth, Mddx: Penguin, 1997, p. 76.

Chapter 4 'Free Trade' – Theory and Practice

[1] For a broad-based approach to the economics of trade, see: D.M. Hausman and M.S. McPherson, *Economic Analysis, Moral Philosophy, and Public Policy*, 2nd edn, Cambridge: Cambridge University Press, 2006, p. 68-72 ; for an orthodox and enthusiastic introduction to free trade: D.A. Irwin, *Free Trade under Fire*, 3rd edn, Princeton: Princeton University Press, 2009. For an introductory overview: Wikipedia, 'Free trade'.

[2] For further discussion: A.V. Deardorff, 'How robust is comparative advantage?' *Review of International Economics*, 13(5), 2005, 1004-16; A. Shaikh, 'The economic mythology of neoliberalism', in A. Saad-Filho and D. Johnston (eds), *Neoliberalism: A Critical Reader*, London: Pluto Press, 2005, pp. 41-9.

[3] The Corn Laws were trade laws designed to protect cereal producers in Britain and Ireland against competition from foreign imports.

[4] H.-J. Chang, *Kicking Away the Ladder: Development Strategies in Historical Perspective*, London: Anthem Press, 2002. See also: H.-J. Chang, *Bad Samaritans: The Myth of Free Trade and the Secret History of Capitalism*, London: Bloomsbury, 2008.

[5] The 'infant industry' argument says that, particularly during the early stages of a country's industrialisation, key industries may not have the capacities to survive and prosper against well-established competitors from other countries, and therefore require protection until they become established. The argument is also relevant to New Zealand's current stage of industrial development.

[6] 'Services' include such activities as communication, consultancy, finance, transport and distribution, education, tourism and travel, recreation, culture and sport.

[7] P. Krugman, 'What should trade negotiators negotiate about?' *Journal of Economic Literature*, 35(1), 1997, 113-20 (p. 114).

[8] R.H. Steinberg, 'In the shadow of law or power? Consensus-based bargaining and outcomes in the GATT/WTO', *International Organization*, 56(2), 2002, 339-74.

[9] Steinberg, op. cit., pp. 359-60.

[10] J.M. Finger and J.J. Nogues, *The Unbalanced Uruguay Round Outcome*, World Bank Policy Research Paper 2732, Washington, DC: The World Bank, 2001.

[11] S. Ostry, 'The Uruguay Round North-South grand bargain: implications for future negotiations', in D.L. Kennedy and J.D. Southwick (eds), *The Political Economy of International Trade Law,* Cambridge: Cambridge University Press, 2002, p. 288; J.M. Finger, 'Comment: The Uruguay Round North-South bargain: will the WTO get over it?', *ibid*, p. 301.

[12] In December 2013 the WTO agreed a 'Bali Package' of measures covering a small fraction of the Doha programme, concerned mainly with eliminating red tape.

[13] J.E. Stiglitz, *The Price of Inequality,* New York: W.W. Norton, 2012, p. 324, n25; also A. Hubbard, 'Clinton's economist warns NZ off US trade deal', *Sunday Star-Times* (Auckland), 09/03/2008, p. A13.

Chapter 5 'Free Trade' – the TPP and Other Trade Deals

[1] Change 'at the margin' in economics refers to small or incremental changes in markets which do not significantly alter the quantities or prices of goods exchanged.

[2] In March 2014 it was announced that New Zealand and the EU would take preliminary steps to explore a free trade pact.

[3] The website Infojustice.org maintains a resource library on the TPP containing leaked texts and analyses, white papers, presentations, letters from Congress, news and blogs and other materials related to the TPP. See: http://infojustice.org/resource-library/tpp#

[4] J. Aguilar, 'Twenty years later, Nafta remains a source of tension', *New York Times*, 07/12/2012.

[5] Office of the USTR, http://www.ustr.gov/trade-agreements/free-trade-agreements/north-american-free-trade-agreement-nafta

[6] E. Zepeda, T.A. Wise and K.P. Gallagher, *Rethinking Trade Policy for Development: Lessons from Mexico under NAFTA*, Washington DC: Carnegie Endowment for International Peace, 2009; T.A. Wise and K.P. Gallagher, 'NAFTA: A cautionary tale', Global Affairs Commentary - Foreign Policy in Focus, 24/10/2002.

[7] G.C. Hufbauer and J.J. Schott, *NAFTA Revisited*, Washington DC: Institute for International Economics, 2005.

[8] M. Weisbrot, S. Lefebvre and J. Sammut, 'Did NAFTA help Mexico? An Assessment after 20 Years', Washington DC: Center for Economic Policy and Research, 2014.

[9] The Council of Canadians, 'Canadians to Harper: Renegotiate NAFTA with Obama', news release, 13/02/2009.

[10] Hufbauer and Schott, op. cit.

[11] R.E. Scott, C. Salas and B. Campbell, 'Revisiting NAFTA: Still Not Working for North America's Workers', Briefing Paper 171, Economic Policy Institute, Washington, DC, 2006.

[12] Pew Research Center, 'Americans are of Two Minds on Trade', press release, 09/11/2010, http://www.pewresearch.org/2010/11/09/americans-are-of-two-minds-on-trade

[13] Angus Reid Public Opinion, 'Americans and Canadians Feel they have Lost Out with NAFTA', 2012, http://www.angus-reid.com/wp-content/uploads/2012/05/2012.05.17_NAFTA.pdf

[14] In November 2013 South Korea expressed interest in joining the negotiations, but by March 2014 had yet to do so.

[15] P.A. Petri, M. Plummer and F. Zhai, *The Trans-Pacific Partnership and Asia-Pacific Integration: A Quantitative Assessment*, Washington: Peterson Institute for International Economics (with East-West Center, Hawaii), 2012, pp. 15-19.

[16] http://tinyurl.com/tppinvestment

[17] See further: D. Ikenson, 'Eight reasons to purge investor-state dispute settlement from trade agreements', *Forbes*, 03/04/2014, http://www.forbes.com/sites/danikenson

[18] Coverage of all ISDS cases pursued against Canada under NAFTA can be found at the Government of Canada website: http://www.international.gc.ca/trade-agreements-accords-commerciaux/topics-domaines/disp-diff/gov.aspx?lang=eng&view=d; and for the US, at PublicCitizen,'Table of Foreign Investor-State Cases and Claims under NAFTA and other U.S. Trade Deals' (February 2014), http://www.citizen.org/documents/investor-state-chart1.pdf

[19] J. Rankin, 'Court supports EU decision on fuel additive', *EuropeanVoice.com*, 09/07/2010.

[20] Lone Pine Resources Inc., 'Lone Pine Resources Inc. (Investor) v. The Government of Canada (Party): Notice of Intent to Submit a Claim to Arbitration under Chapter Eleven of the North American Free Trade Agreement', 08/11/2012, http://www.italaw.com/sites/default/files/case-documents/italaw1156.pdf

[21] It's Our Future, 'The TPPA and the New Zealand Environment', http://www.itsourfuture.org.nz/th_gallery/nzenvironment

[22] For an analysis of the TPP Investment chapter see: J. Kelsey, 'Implications of the TPP Investment Chapter for New Zealand', Research Note, Faculty of Law, University of Auckland, 14/06/2011.

[23] WikiLeaks, 'Secret Trans-Pacific Partnership Agreement (TPP) - Environment Consolidated Text', https://wikileaks.org/tpp-enviro/

[24] I.F. Ferguson and B. Vaughn, *The Trans-Pacific Partnership Agreement: Report for Congress*, Washington: Congressional Research Service, 2011.

[25] The USTR is part of the Executive Office of the President and is responsible for developing and coordinating US international trade, commodity and direct investment policy, and for overseeing negotiations with other countries.

[26] Comments by the NMPF to the OSTR concerning the proposed Trans-Pacific Partnership Trade Agreement, docket number: USTR-2009-0041, 25/01/2010, http://www.nmpf.org/files/file/NMPF%20TPP%20FTA%20Comments_012509.pdf

[27] American Farm Bureau Federation and Others, Letter to Ambassador Siddiqui and Under Secretary Miller, 11/05/2010. See 'Agricultural Community Offers Advice on TPP Trade Deal', posted 19/05/2010 at www.farmpolicyfacts.org

[28] US Dairy Export Council (USDEC) and NMPF, 'Trans-Pacific Partnership Trade Agreement: Position Paper', 2013, http://usdec.files.cms-plus.com/PDFs/TradePolicy/Dairy%20TPP%20Backgrounder_0713.pdf

[29] See further: A.M. Pollock and D. Price, 'Rewriting the regulations: How the WTO could accelerate privatisation in health-care systems', *The Lancet*, 356, 2000, 1995-2000; A.M. Pollock and D. Price, 'The public health implications of world trade negotiations on the general agreement

on trade in services and public services', *The Lancet*, 362, 2003, 1072-5; S. Sinclair and J. Grieshaber-Otto, *Facing the Facts: A Guide to the GATS Debate*, Ottawa: Canadian Centre for Policy Alternatives, 2002.

[30] PHARMAC, *Operating Policies and Procedures of the Pharmaceutical Management Agency (PHARMAC)*, 3rd edn, 2006.

[31] J. Cumming, N. Mays and J. Daube, 'How New Zealand has contained expenditure on drugs', *British Medical Journal*, BMJ; 340:c2441, 18/05/2010.

[32] US Embassy, Wellington, 'Subject: Drug industry sees possible salve to its pain in New Zealand', Cable to Washington, DC, 13/01/2006, http://cables.mrkva.eu/cable.php?id=49664

[33] Pharmaceutical Research and Manufacturers of America (PhRMA), 'Special 301 Submission 2012', 2012, http://www.phrma.org/sites/default/files/304/phrmaspecial301submission2012.pdf (no longer publicly accessible at this site).

[34] Ambassador Ronald Kirk, *2012 Special 301 Report*, Washington, DC: OSTR, 2012, http://www.ustr.gov/sites/default/files/2012%20Special%20301%20Report_0.pdf

[35] J.R. Smith and J.H. Birnbaum, 'Drug bill demonstrates lobby's pull', *Washington Post*, 12/01/2007.

[36] M. Angell, *The Truth about the Drug Companies: How they Deceive Us and What to do about It*, New York: Random House, 2005, and summary in M. Angell, 'The truth about the drug companies', *New York Review of Books*, 15/07/2004; B. Goldacre, *Bad Pharma: How Drug Companies Mislead Doctors and Harm Patients*, London: Harper Collins, 2012; J. Abraham, 'The pharmaceutical industry as a political player', *The Lancet*, 360, 2002, 1498-502.

[37] Angell, 2005, op. cit., pp. 229-34.

[38] Trans-Pacific Partnership, Transparency Chapter – Annex on Transparency and Procedural Fairness for Healthcare Technologies, 22/06/2011, http://www.citizenstrade.org/ctc/wp-content/uploads/2011/10/TransPacificTransparency.pdf; for commentary see: http://www.citizenstrade.org/ctc/blog/2011/10/22/leaked-trans-pacific-fta-texts-reveal-u-s-undermining-access-to-medicine/; for New Zealand commentary see: http://www.itsourfuture, 'The TPPA and access to medicines' and

'The TPPA and public health: Tobacco and Alcohol'.

[39] Anon, 'No TPP deal unless dairy and Pharmac are in - Key', *New Zealand Herald*, 26/11/2012.

[40] M. McNicholas, 'Farm lobby retreat boosts TPP chances', *Country Wide*, http://agrihq.co.nz/article/farm-lobby-retreat-boosts-tpp-chances?p=71, 25/10/2013.

[41] Anon, 'No need to worry about TPP – Groser', *National Business Review*, 13/10/2013.

[42] PublicCitizen, 'US pharmaceutical corporation uses NAFTA foreign investor privileges regime to attack Canada's patent policy', March 2013, http://www.citizen.org/eli-lilly-investor-state-factsheet

[43] P. Drahos with J. Braithwaite, *Information Feudalism: Who Owns the Knowledge Economy?*, New York: The New Press, 2002, p. 89.

[44] Knowledge Ecology International, Trans-Pacific Partnership Agreement, texts of intellectual property rights chapter (dated February 2011, and August 2013), http://keionline.org/tpp

[45] Productivity Commission, *Restrictions on the Parallel Importation of Books*, Canberra: Commonwealth of Australia, 2009.

[46] See in particular Electronic Frontier Foundation, 'Trans Pacific Partnership Agreement', undated, https://www.eff.org/issues/tpp, and downloads from this site also available at: http://www.itsourfuture.org.nz

[47] P. Pilcher, 'Software patent stoush could have huge impact', *New Zealand Herald*, 05/02/2013.

[48] S. Flynn et al., *Public interest analysis of the US TPP Proposal for an IP Chapter*, PIJIP Research Paper Series, Paper 21, Program on Information Justice and Intellectual Property, Washington, DC, 2011.

[49] Bank of International Settlements, *Triennial Central Bank Survey: Report on Global Foreign Exchange Market Activity in 2010*, Basel: BIS, 2010 (and earlier editions).

[50] B. Muchhala (ed.), *Ten Years After: Revisiting the Asian Financial Crisis*, Washington, DC: Woodrow Wilson International Center, 2007.

[51] J.E. Stiglitz, *Globalization and its Discontents*, New York: W.W. Norton, 2002, p. 101; A. Caliari and M.V. Stichele, 'Memorandum: Issues and concerns for consideration by workshop participants', Workshop on Trade in Financial Services and Development, WTO Committee on Trade in

Financial Services, 26/06/2012, https://www.coc.org/files/Download%20 Memorandum.pdf

[52] Global Development and Environment Institute, Tufts University, press release, 'Economists Issue Statement on Capital Controls and the Trans-Pacific Partnership Agreement', 28/02/2012, http://www.ase.tufts.edu/gdae/policy_research/TPPAletter.html

[53] IMF, *The Liberalization and Management of Capital Flows: An Institutional View*, Geneva: IMF, 2012. For commentary see: A. Beattie, 'IMF drops opposition to capital controls', *Financial Times*, 03/12/2012.

[54] Petri et al., op. cit.

[55] NZIER, *Review of the Estimated Economic Benefits of TPP: NZIER Report to NZ-US Council*, Wellington: NZIER, 2012.

[56] Pharmaceutical Management Agency, 'Introduction to PHARMAC', undated, http://www.pharmac.health.nz/ckeditor_assets/attachments/374/infosheet-01-intro-2013.pdf

[57] J. Quiggin, 'Lessons from the Australia-US Free Trade Agreement', in J. Kelsey (ed.), *No Ordinary Deal: Unmasking the Trans-Pacific Partnership Free Trade Agreement*, Wellington: Bridget Williams Books, 2010, p. 103.

[58] M. Priestley, 'Australia's free trade agreements: background note', Canberra: Australian Parliamentary Library, 2008.

[59] P. Ranald, 'The politics of the TPPA in Australia', in Kelsey, 2010, op. cit., p. 43.

[60] USTR, 'Australia', http://www.ustr.gov/countries-regions/southeast-asia-pacific/Australia

[61] Productivity Commission, *Bilateral and Regional Trade Agreements: Research Report*, Canberra, p. xx, 2010.

[62] New Zealand Parliament, Questions for Written Answer, 2013, no. 13710.

[63] G. Bertram and S. Terry, *Economic Gains and Costs from the TPP*, Report for the Sustainability Council of New Zealand, 2014.

[64] J. Kelsey, '"Treaty-making 101" for Ministers, bloggers and lobbyists', press release, 4/12/2012, http://www.scoop.co.nz/stories/PO1212/S00035/treaty-making-101-for-ministers-bloggers-and-lobbyists.htm

[65] Wikipedia, 'Ratification'.

[66] Another aspect of 'free trade', that does not appear in the agendas of free trade agreements such as those discussed in this chapter, relates to the international flows of labour i.e. migration.

[67] A. Hubbard, 'Clinton's economist warns NZ off US trade deal', *Sunday Star-Times*, 09/03/2008, p. A13.

Chapter 6 Public Goods and the Common Good

[1] George Soros, Interview with Mark Schapiro, 5/9/2000: http://www.simulconference.com/clients/sowf/interviews/interview3.html

[2] Goods are called public not because they are or may be provided by government, but because they are publicly available.

[3] The 'marginal cost' is the dollar cost of producing one extra unit: here of pollution abatement, or of pollution damage.

[4] For a detailed description see: M. Common, *Sustainability and Policy: Limits to Economics*, Cambridge: Cambridge University Press, 1995, pp. 147-150.

[5] G. Hardin, 'The tragedy of the commons', *Science*, 162 (3859), 1968, 1243-8; and further: G. Hardin, 'Extensions of "The Tragedy of the Commons"', *Science*, 280 (5364), 1998, 682-3.

[6] G. Marwell and R.E. Ames, 'Economists free ride, does anyone else?' *Journal of Public Economics*, 15(3), 1981, 295-310; H. Gintis et al. (eds), *Moral Sentiments and Material Interests*, Cambridge, MA: MIT Press, 2005.

[7] Elinor Ostrom shared the 2009 Nobel Prize in Economics for her work in this area: E. Ostrom, *Governing the Commons: The Evolution of Institutions for Collective Action*, New York: Cambridge University Press, 1990; E. Ostrom, *Understanding Institutional Diversity*, Princeton: Princeton University Press, 2005.

[8] A. Weinberg, 'Science and trans-science', *Minerva*, 10, 1972, 209-222; M. Faber, R. Manstetten and J.R. Proops, 'Humankind and the environment: an anatomy of surprise and ignorance', *Environmental Values*, 1, 1992, 217-241; see also B. Wynne, 'Uncertainty and environmental learning', *Global Environmental Change*, 2, 1992, 111-127.

[9] It is known that even very simple, non-random dynamic systems can show very complicated behaviours in which they evolve along paths that

are extremely sensitive to small differences in initial conditions, and are thus unpredictable in principle.

[10] C.S. Holling, 'Resilience and stability of ecological systems', *Annual Review of Ecology and Systematics*, 4, 1973, 1-23 (p.18).

[11] United Nations, 'Report of the United Nations Conference on Environment and Development. Annex I. Rio Declaration on Environment and Development', Doc. A/CONF.151/26 (Vol.1), 1992.

[12] A. Stirling, 'Risk at a turning point?', *Journal of Risk Research*, 1(2), 1998, 97-109; A. Stirling, 'Participation, precaution and reflexive governance for sustainable development', in W.N. Adger and A. Jordan (eds) *Governing Sustainability*, Cambridge: Cambridge University Press, 2009.

[13] P.C. Stern and H.V. Fineberg (eds), *Understanding Risk: Informing Decisions in a Democratic Society*, Washington, DC: National Academies Press, 1996, p. 3.

[14] M. Oborne, 'Emerging Risks in the 21st Century: An OECD International Futures Project', Paris: OECD, 2003.

[15] A.E. Kahn, 'The tyranny of small decisions: market failures, imperfections, and the limits of economics', *Kyklos*, 19(1), 1966, 23-47.

[16] W.E. Odum, 'Environmental degradation and the tyranny of small decisions', *BioScience*, 32(9), 1982, 728-9.

[17] For a technical discussion see: N. Barr, *Economics of the Welfare State*, 5th edn, Oxford: Oxford University Press, 2012.

[18] D. Marquand, *Decline of the Public*, Cambridge: Polity Press, 2004, pp. 26-29.

[19] A. Gutmann and D. Thompson, *Democracy and Disagreement*, Cambridge, MA: Harvard University Press, 1996; J. Bohman and W. Rehg (eds), *Deliberative Democracy: Essays on Reason and Politics*, Cambridge, MA: MIT Press, 1997; A. Gutmann and D. Thompson, *Why Deliberative Democracy?* Princeton: Princeton University Press, 2004.

[20] D. Miller, 'Deliberative democracy and social choice', in D. Held (ed.), *Prospects for Democracy: North, South, East, West*, Cambridge: Polity Press, 1993, pp. 74-92.

[21] B. Kasemir et al. (eds), *Public Participation in Sustainability Science: A Handbook*, Cambridge: Cambridge University Press, 2003; S. Stoll-Kleeman and M. Welp (eds), *Stakeholder Dialogues in Natural Resource Management:*

Theory and Practice, Berlin: Springer, 2006; J. Gastil and P. Levine (eds), *The Deliberative Democracy Handbook: Strategies for Effective Civic Engagement in the Twenty-First Century*, San Francisco: Jossey-Bass, 2005; J.S. Fishkin, *When the People Speak: Deliberative Democracy and Public Consultation*, Oxford: Oxford University Press, 2011.

[22] G. Soros, quoted in I. Kaul et al. (eds), *Providing Global Public Goods: Managing Globalization*, New York: United Nations Development Programme, 2003, p. viii.

Chapter 7 The Twenty-first Century – Climate Change

[1] That part of global warming due to human activity is referred to as 'anthropogenic' or 'enhanced' global warming.

[2] No scientific body of national or international standing maintains a formal opinion dissenting from the main facts about global warming and climate change: see Wikipedia 'Scientific opinion on climate change'.

[3] IPCC, *Climate Change 2007: The Physical Science Basis* [S.D. Solomon et al. (eds)], Cambridge: Cambridge University Press, 2007, p. 3.

[4] IPCC, *Climate Change 2007: Impacts, Adaptation and Vulnerability* [M. Parry et al. (eds)], Cambridge: Cambridge University Press, 2007, pp. 508-40; see also: Office of the Chief Scientific Advisor, *New Zealand's Changing Climate and Oceans: The Impact of Human Activity and Implications for the Future* (Gluckman Report), PM's Scientific Advisory Committee, Auckland, 2013.

[5] As a footnote to these projections, it can be added that 2013 was New Zealand's second hottest year since records began in 1861, with winter temperatures almost 1.3°C above average.

[6] IPCC, 'Fifth Assessment Report (AR5)', 2014, interim reports available at: http://www.ipcc.ch

[7] A. Rosencranz, 'US Climate Change Policy under G.W. Bush', *Golden Gate University Law Review*, 32(4), 2002, 479-91.

[8] J. Kluger, 'A climate of despair', TIME, 01/04/2001, http://www.time.com/time/printout/0,8816,104596,00.html

[9] D. Zabarenko, 'US Climate scientists allege White House pressure', Reuters, 30/01/2007, http://www.commondreams.org/cgi-bin/print.

cgi?file=/headlines07/0130-10.htm; written testimony by Dr Francesca Grifo: http://www.ucsusa.org/assets/documents/scientific_integrity/ftg-written-testimony.pdf; see also R. Piltz written testimony: Rick Piltz testimony, http://www.climatesciencewatch.org/2007/01/30/climate-science-watch-testimony-at-house-oversight-hearing

[10] N. Lawson, 'The economics and politics of climate change: an appeal to reason', lecture at the Centre for Policy Studies, London, 01/11/2006, http://ac.matra.free.fr/FB/NLawson1.pdf; see also: N. Lawson, *An Appeal to Reason: A Cool Look at Global Warming*, New York: The Overlook Press, 2008.

[11] G. Pearse, *High and Dry: John Howard, Climate Change and the Selling of Australia's Future*, Melbourne: Viking Penguin, 2007.

[12] T. Abbott, 'A realist's approach to climate change', speech 27/07/2009; S. Rintoul, 'Town of Beaufort changed Tony Abbott's view on climate change', *The Australian*, 12/12/2009.

[13] S. Goldenberg, 'US "dark money" funds sceptics', *Guardian Weekly*, 22-28/02/2013.

[14] See Wikipedia, 'The Heartland Institute'.

[15] Including in New Zealand. See: Gareth, 'Puppets on a string: US think tank funds NZ sceptics', 24/01/2012, http://hot-topic.co.nz/puppets-on-a-string-us-think-tank-funds-nz-sceptics

[16] J. Hoggan, *Climate Cover-Up: The Crusade to Deny Global Warming*, Vancouver: Greystone Books, 2009; J.L. Powell, *The Inquisition of Climate Science*, New York: Columbia University Press, 2011; M.E. Mann, *The Hockey Stick and the Climate Wars*, New York: Columbia University Press, 2012.

[17] R. Repetto, 'Cap and trade is better climate policy than a carbon tax', 2013, http://energyfuturecoalition.org/editorsblog/Examining-Cap-and-Trade-vs-Carbon-Tax-Climate-Policy

[18] N.H. Stern, *The Economics of Climate Change: The Stern Review*, Cambridge: Cambridge University Press, 2007, p. 27.

[19] Stern, op. cit..

[20] Stern, op. cit., pp. 218- 220.

[21] Stern, op. cit., p. xv.

[22] International Energy Agency, *World Energy Outlook 2011*, Paris: IEA, 2011.

[23] World Meteorological Office, *The Global Climate 2001-2010: A Decade of Climate Extremes*, Geneva: WMO, 2013.

[24] H. Stewart and L. Elliott, 'Nicholas Stern: I got it wrong on climate change - it's far, far worse', *Guardian* (UK), 26/01/2013, http://www.theguardian.com/environment/2013/jan/27/nicholas-stern-climate-change-davos

[25] S. Connor, 'Fears of faster rising global sea levels', *Independent* (UK), 19/03/2014.

[26] S. Gupta et al., 'Chapter 13: Policies, instruments and co-operative arrangements', in IPCC, *Climate Change 2007: Mitigation* [B. Metz et al. (eds)], Cambridge: Cambridge University Press, 2007.

[27] Repetto, op. cit..; R.N. Stavins, *A US Cap-and-Trade System to Address Global Climate Change*, Hamilton Project, Brookings Institute, Washington DC, 2007; G.E. Metcalf, *A Proposal for a U.S. Carbon Tax Swap: An Equitable Tax Reform to Address Global Climate Change, Discussion Paper 2007-12, Hamilton Project, Brookings Institute, 2007; G.* Mankiw, 'One answer to global warming: a new tax', *New York Times*, 16/09/2007.

[28] Anon, 'Exxon supports carbon tax', *Calgary Herald*, 09/01/2009, http://www.canada.com/calgaryherald/news/calgarybusiness/story.html?id=e8aecbbb-16c6-412d-8054-7e64e2b176ef. See also: 'A least-worst tax: a levy on carbon is an idea whose time has come', *Financial Times*, 15/03/2013; G. Wynn, 'COLUMN: Australia is another nail in cap and trade', 11/09/2013, http://www.reuters.com/article/2013/09/11/column-wynn-australia-co-idUSL5N0H622720130911

[29] L. Lohmann, 'A licence to carry on polluting?', *New Scientist*, 2580, 05/12/2006, http://www.thecornerhouse.org.uk/resource/carry-polluting

[30] Reuters, 'IMF, World Bank leaders engage finance ministers to tackle climate change', 11/04/2014, http://in.reuters.com/article/2014/04/11/climatechange-money-idINL2N0N31GT20140411

[31] Anon, 'ETS, RIP?', *Economist*, 20/04/2013.

[32] UNFCCC, Compilation and Synthesis of Fifth National Communications: Executive Summary, FCCC/SBI/2011/INF.1, 20/05/2011.

[33] As of 2013 the US has not ratified the Protocol and Canada renounced the Protocol in 2012. Other states not party to the Protocol are Andorra, South Sudan, Palestine and Vatican City.

[34] Gupta, loc. cit., pp.775-6.

[35] Climate Change Information New Zealand, http://www.climatechange.govt.nz/reducing-our-emissions/government-policies.html

[36] This section has benefitted in particular from: G. Bertram and S. Terry, *The Carbon Challenge: New Zealand's Emissions Trading Scheme*, Wellington: Bridget Williams Books, 2010.

[37] UNFCCC, op. cit..

[38] I. Davison, 'Groser defends ditching of Kyoto', *New Zealand Herald*, 04/12/2012, http://www.nzherald.co.nz/nz/news/article.cfm?c_id=1&objectid=10851772

[39] Membership of the Coalition is given in Bertram and Terry, op. cit., p. 49, n101.

[40] Anon, 'Carbon tax announcement stirs up a storm', *National Business Review*, 04/05/2005.

[41] Greenhouse Policy Coalition, 'Submission on Implementing the Carbon Tax', 2005, p. 3.

[42] The NZ Emissions Trading Scheme, http://www.climatechange.govt.nz/emissions-trading-scheme/about; see also: Wikipedia, 'New Zealand Emissions Trading Scheme'.

[43] R. Garnaut, *The Garnaut Climate Change Review*, Cambridge: Cambridge University Press, 2008, section 14.3; see also: P. Cramton and S. Kerr, 'Tradable carbon permit auctions: how and why to auction not grandfather', Discussion Paper 98-34, Resources for the Future, Washington, DC, 1998.

[44] For example: Parliamentary Commissioner for the Environment, 'Submission to the Finance and Expenditure Select Committee on the Climate Change Response (Moderated Emissions Trading) Bill', 13/10/2009.

[45] C. Chauvel, 'ETS debate speech', speech to third reading of Climate Change Response (Moderated Emission Trading) Amendment Bill, New Zealand Labour, 25/11/2009, http://www.scoop.co.nz/stories/PA0911/S00383.htm

[46] Ministry for the Environment, *The Framework for a New Zealand Emissions Trading Scheme*, Wellington, 2007, p. 5.

[47] Ministry for the Environment, 'New Zealand's net position under the Kyoto Protocol', 2013, http://www.mfe.govt.nz/issues/climate/greenhouse-gas-emissions/net-position

[48] T. Groser, 'New Zealand commits to 2020 climate change target', 16/08/2013, http://beehive.govt.nz/release/new-zealand-commits-2020-climate-change-target

[49] See: T. Groser, 'Tim Groser: It's time to move past Kyoto agreement', *New Zealand Herald*, 20/12/2012, http://www.nzherald.co.nz/business/news/article.cfm?c_id=3&objectid=10855149

[50] REN21, *Renewables 2013: Global Status Report*, Paris, REN21, 2013, p. 76.

[51] Ministry of Economic Development, *New Zealand Energy Data File 2011*, Wellington: MED, 2012, p.108.

[52] 'Audrey Young: Helen Clark – NZ & GCSB Spys', *New Zealand Herald*, 04/08/2013, http://www.nzherald.co.nz/national/news/video.cfm?c_id=1503075&gal_cid=1503075&
gallery_id=134630

[53] J. Kerry, 'Remarks on Climate Change', Jakarta, Indonesia, 16/02/2014, http://www.state.gov/secretary/remarks/2014/02/221704.htm

Chapter 8 The Twenty-first Century – Natural Resources

[1] UN Population Division, *World Population Prospects – The 2010 Revision*, New York: United Nations, 2011.

[2] S. Chen and M. Ravallion, 'The developing world is poorer than we thought, but no less successful in the fight against poverty', Policy Research Working Paper No. WPS 4703, Washington, DC: World Bank, 2008.

[3] A. Prüss-Üstün et al., *Safer Water, Better Health*, Geneva: WHO, 2008.

[4] FAO, 'World must double food production by 2050: FAO chief', Statement by Jacques Diouf, Director General of FAO, Agence France Presse, 26/01/2009.

[5] P. Pinstrup-Andersen, *Global Food Trends: Prospects for Future Food Security*, Washington, DC: IFPRI, 1994; P.H. Glieck, 'Misuse of food and climate data at *Forbes*', *Huffington Post*, 07/01/2011.

[6] P.M. Vitousek et al., 'Human appropriation of the products of photosynthesis', *BioScience*, 36(6), 1986, 368-73; P.M. Vitousek et al., 'Human domination of earth's ecosystems', *Science*, 277(5325), 1997, 494-9.

[7] B. Ewing et al., *The Ecological Footprint Atlas 2010*, Oakland, CA: Global Footprint Network, 2010.

[8] D.E. McCormack and W.E. Larson, 'A values dilemma: standards for soil quality tomorrow', in W.E. Jeske (ed.), *Economics, Ethics, Ecology: Roots of Productive Conservation*, Ankeny, Iowa: Soil Conservation Society of America, 1981.

[9] World Resources Institute (with UNDP, UNEP and World Bank), *A Guide to World Resources 2000–2001: People and Ecosystems: The Fraying Web of Life*, Washington, DC: WRI, 2000.

[10] D. Pimentel, 'Soil erosion: a food and environmental threat', *Environment, Development and Sustainability*, 8(1), 2006, 119-37.

[11] UN Convention to Combat Desertification, 'Desertification, land degradation and drought - some global facts and figures', undated, http://www.unccd.int/Lists/SiteDocumentLibrary/WDCD/DLDD%20Facts.pdf

[12] S.L. Postel, G.C. Daily and P.R. Ehrlich, 'Human appropriation of renewable fresh water', *Science*, 271(5250), 1996, 785-8.

[13] R.A. Myers and B. Worms, 'Rapid worldwide depletion of predatory fish communities', *Nature*, 423, 2003, 280-3; see also: C. Clover, *The End of the Line: How Over-Fishing is Changing the World and What We Eat*, London: Ebury Press, 2004.

[14] IUCN, *IUCN Red List of Threatened Species: Version 2013.2*, 2013, http://www.iucnredlist.org

[15] UN Convention on Biological Diversity Secretariat, *Global Biodiversity Outlook 2*, Montreal: CBDS, 2006.

[16] L.R. Brown, *Full Planet, Empty Plates: The New Geopolitics of Food Scarcity*, New York: W.W. Norton, 2012, p. 37.

[17] Brown, op.cit., p. 13.

[18] Wikipedia, 'Peak oil'; International Energy Agency, *Key World Energy Statistics – 2013*, Paris, IEA, 2013; idem, *World Energy Outlook 2013*, Paris, IEA.

[19] R.G. Miller and S.R. Sorrell, 'Introduction' in R.G. Miller and S.R. Sorrell (eds), 'The future of oil supply', special edition, *Philosophical Transactions of the Royal Society A*, 372 (2006), January 2014; see also: Sorrell, S.R. et al., *Global Oil Depletion: An Assessment of the Evidence*, UK Energy Research Centre, 2009.

[20] Millennium Ecosystem Assessment, *Ecosystems and Human Well-being: Synthesis*, Washington, DC: Island Press, 2005, p. 1.

[21] A. Steiner, 'Preface', in C. Nellemann and E. Corcoran (eds), *Dead Planet, Living Planet: Biodiversity and Ecosystem Restoration for Sustainable Development*, Geneva: UNEP, 2010.

[22] Environmental Protection Agency (US), 'What is sustainability?', http://www.epa.gov/sustainability/basicinfo.htm

[23] R. Kates, 'Population and consumption: what we know, what we need to know', *Environment*, 42(3), 2000, 10-19; M.R. Chertow, 'The IPAT equation and its variants', *Journal of Industrial Ecology*, 4(4), 2001, 13-29.

[24] R. Repetto, *Natural Resource Accounting for Countries with Natural Resource-based Economies*, Report to the Ministry of Planning and Environment, Victoria, Australia, 1986.

[25] Actually Stern included a small positive adjustment to this figure to take account of the small chance of 'catastrophe risk' that humans may not exist at some time in the future.

[26] Landcare Research (NZ), 'Lifestyle blocks and the loss of New Zealand's productive soils', press release, 20/12/2011.

[27] Ministry for the Environment, *Environment New Zealand 2007*, Wellington: MfE, 2007.

[28] D. Ballantine et al., *Analysis of National River Water Quality Data for the Period 1998-2007*, NIWA report for Ministry for the Environment, Christchurch, 2010.

[29] Parliamentary Commissioner for the Environment, *Water Quality in New Zealand: Land Use and Nutrient Pollution*, Wellington, 2013.

[30] J. Alder et al., 'Aggregate performance in managing marine ecosystems of 53 maritime countries', *Marine Policy*, 34, 2010, 468-76; see also: L.J. Wood et al., 'Assessing progress towards global marine protection targets: shortfalls in information and action', *Oryx*, 42(03), 2008, 340–51.

[31] L. Milich, 'Resource management versus sustainable livelihoods: the

collapse of the Newfoundland cod fishery', *Society and Natural Resources*, 12, 1999, 625-42.

[32] D. Robertson, 'Comments on Chapter 6: Fisheries', in Science Media Centre, *WWF Report Assesses NZ's Environmental Record - Experts Respond* , 2012, http://www.sciencemediacentre.co.nz/2012/05/28/

[33] Combined Ministries, 'Current state of New Zealand's biodiversity', http://www.biodiversity.govt.nz/picture/biodiversity/state

[34] NIWA, *Water and Atmosphere*, Issue 7, 2013, p.42-3.

[35] Ministry for Economic Development, *New Zealand Energy Quarterly*, Issue 18, 2012 (March).

[36] Cf. Environmental Defence Society, 'Our Place: State of the Environment 2013', conference proceedings, http://www.edsconference.com/2013_conference.cfm

[37] The particular issues raised by the Crown Minerals Act 1991 are not considered here.

[38] G. Palmer, 'Sustainability – New Zealand's resource management legislation', in M. Ross and J.O. Saunders (eds), *Growing Demands on a Shrinking Planet: Managing Resource-Use Conflicts*, Calgary: Canadian Institute of Resources Law, 1992, pp. 408-28. See also: Wikipedia, 'Resource Management Act 1991'.

[39] Hon. S. Upton, H. Atkins and G. Willis, 'Section 5 re-revisited: a critique of Skelton and Memon's analysis', *Resource Management Journal*, 10(3), 2002, 10-22; also available at: http://www.arcadia.co.nz/rm/section5.htm

[40] S. Upton, 'Purpose and principle in the Resource Management Act', *Waikato Law Review*, 3, 1995, 17-56.

[41] Ministry for the Environment, 'Improving our Resource Management System: A Discussion Document', Wellington: Ministry for the Environment, 2013.

[42] Sir G. Palmer, 'Memorandum to Bryce Johnson, Chief Executive, Fish and Game New Zealand on the matter of Government Reforms to the Resource Management Act 1991', 2013.

[43] 3News, 'RMA not economic tool – watchdog', 01/03/2013, http://www.3news.co.nz/RMA-not-economic-tool---watchdog/tabid/1607/articleID/288609/Default.aspx; also 3News, 'Watchdog renews criticism of RMA changes', 03/04/2013.

[44] Parliamentary Commissioner for the Environment, 'Improving our resource management system: a discussion document', Submission to the Minister for the Environment', 02/04/2013.

[45] MSN News, 'Govt hits back at RMA "scaremongering"', 01/03/2013, http://news.msn.co.nz/nationalnews/8619153/rma-not-economic-tool-watchdog

[46] See for example: G. Taylor, 'An environmental agenda for action', presentation at national conference, Environmental Defence Society, Auckland, 06-07/08/2013, http://www.edsconference.com/content/docs/2013_presentations/Taylor%2C%20Gary%20130808.pdf

[47] Ministry for the Environment, *Summary of Submissions: Improving our Resource Management System*, 2013.

[48] New Zealand Government, *Resource Management: Summary of Reform Proposals 2013*, August 2013.

[49] New Zealand Government, *Report of the Advisory Group on the Review of the Centre*, Report to the Ministers of State Services and Finance, 2001, http://www.ssc.govt.nz/roc; also State Services Commission, *Review of the Centre One Year On*, Wellington: SSC, 2002, http://www.ssc.govt.nz/roc-one-year-on

[50] E.g. Canadian Centre for Management Development, *Using Horizontal Tools to Work Across Boundaries: Lessons Learned and Signposts for Success*, CCMD Roundtable on the Management of Horizontal Initiatives, 2002, http://publications.gc.ca/collections/Collection/SC94-90-2002E.pdf

[51] Stewardship land is a category of conservation land that comprises about one third of all land managed by DOC, and over which only weak legal protection exists. See: Parliamentary Commissioner for the Environment, *Investigating the Future of Conservation: The Case of Stewardship Land*, Wellington, 2013.

[52] Ministry for the Environment, 'About the Ministry for the Environment', http://www.mfe.govt.nz/about/about.html (contents as at 02/05/2014), and 'Statement of Intent 2013-2016', http://www.mfe.govt.nz/publications/about/soi/2013/index.html

[53] Ministry for the Environment, 'Sustainability: a definition', http://www.mfe.govt.nz/issues/sustainable-industry/tools-services/definition.php (contents as at 02/05/2014)

[54] M. Britton, 'Mine plan adds to plateau's struggle', 17/01/2012, http://www.stuff.co.nz/the-press/opinion; Anon, 'DOC advice showed it opposed Denniston mine', 27/05/2013, http://www.stuff.co.nz/nelson-mail/news/8720484/DOC-advice-showed-it-opposed-Denniston-mine

[55] E.g. M. White, 'Does the Department of Conservation need saving?' *North & South*, March 2012, pp. 52-61; Dame A. Salmond, 'Dame Anne Salmond: Help steer us away from disaster', *New Zealand Herald*, 27/06/2013; G. Nixon, 'The DOC revolution', *FMC Bulletin*, No.193, August 2013, pp. 22-5.

[56] It should be noted that John Locke, the founding father of classical liberalism to whom neoliberals pay deep obeisance, was opposed to the foreign ownership of land.

[57] D. Boswell, 'The Crafar farm sale: are there new hurdles for overseas investors in "sensitive land"?' *Bell Gully Update: Corporate*, May 2012.

[58] CAFCA, 'Foreign investment in Aotearoa/New Zealand: decisions of the OIC and OIO', 2013, http://canterbury.cyberplace.co.nz/community/CAFCA/OIC.html

[59] New Zealand First, 'Loss of more New Zealand land to foreign interests a betrayal', press release, 13/09/2013.

[60] Federated Farmers of New Zealand, 'Foreign ownership of farmland', press release, 23/04/2012.

[61] The OECD regulatory restrictive index calculations which purport to show that New Zealand is very restrictive to FDI relative to other countries, should be given little credence. The highest restrictiveness index score by sector is for fisheries, but as this is a CPR it demands management not free entry; the highest restrictiveness index score by type of measure is for 'screening and approval' because this exists in New Zealand for investments of less than US$100m - an unrealistically high figure for small countries; and the index calculation takes no cognisance of the level of implementation of the regulatory regime. See: B. Kalinova, A. Palerm and S. Thomsen, 'OECD's FDI Restrictiveness Index: 2010 Update', *OECD WorkingPapers on International Investment*, 2010/03, Paris: OECD.

[62] C. Anderson and K. Johnston, 'New Zealand: 98.5% pure', *Sunday Star Times*, 08/07/2012, pp. A1-3.

[63] NZCTU, 'Overseas ownership of farmland far above PM's claim', press release, 20/04/2012.

[64] ONE News (TVNZ), 'Poll suggests opposition to Crafar sale remains', 19/03/2012, http://tvnz.co.nz/business-news/poll-suggests-opposition-crafar-sale-remains-4784379; for details on Crafar Farms see Wikipedia, 'CraFarms'.

[65] New Zealand Parliament, *Hansard (Debates)*, v.682, p.4421 (15/08/2012).

[66] W. Berry, *Essays by Wendell Berry: What are People For?*, San Francisco: North Point Press, 1990, p. 115.

Chapter 9 New Zealand – Retrospect and Prospect

[1] The assumption is made in this book that greater democratic involvement of citizens will entail support for a sustainability principle. It is also an assumption that liberal democracy itself is resilient enough to respond successfully in the future to the facts as they are and will be.

[2] Rt Hon Sir Kenneth Keith, *On the Constitution of New Zealand: An Introduction to the Foundations of the Current Form of Government*, Cabinet Manual, Wellington, 2008, http://www.cabinetmanual.cabinetoffice.govt.nz/node/68

[3] The exceptions are set out in section 268 of the Electoral Act 1993.

[4] Rt Hon Sir Kenneth Keith, 'New Zealand's Constitution – Is it brilliant or odd?', Address, 20th Anniversary Seminar, Law Commission, 25/08/2006.

[5] Following the general election of 2008 and under a prior commitment by the National Party government to its Maori Party partners in coalition, a constitutional advisory panel was established to carry out widespread consultation in the community on constitutional issues and to recommend constitutional changes. The Panel produced its report in November 2013: *New Zealand's Constitution: A Report on a Conversation*, Wellington: New Zealand Government.

[6] C.G. Weeramantry, 'Separate Opinion of Vice-President Weeramantry', International Court of Justice: Case Concerning the Gabcikovo-Nagymaros Project, 1997, I.C.J. Rep. 7, 1997 WL 1168556 (I.C.J.). Weeramantry opinion available directly at: http://www.icj-cij.org/docket/files/92/7383.pdf

[7] H. Shue, *Basic Rights*, 2nd edn, Princeton: Princeton University Press, 1996; C.D. Beitz and R.E. Goodin (eds), *Global Basic Rights*, Oxford: Oxford University Press, 2009.

[8] Earthjustice (M. Mollo et al.), *Environmental Rights Report: Human Rights and the Environment*, Oakland, CA: Earthjustice, 2005.

[9] For jurisprudence see: C.M. Abraham, *Environmental Jurisprudence in India*, The Hague: Kluwer Law International, 1999.

[10] B. Ackerman and J.S. Fishkin, 'Deliberation Day' in J.S. Fishkin and P. Laslett (eds) *Debating Deliberative Democracy*, Oxford: Blackwell, 2003; J. Gastil, *By Popular Demand*, Berkeley: University of California Press, 2000; J. Gastil and P. Levine (eds), *The Deliberative Democracy Handbook: Strategies for Effective Civic Engagement in the Twenty-First Century*, San Francisco: Jossey-Bass, 2005.

[11] New Zealand Medical Association, *Code of Ethics*, Wellington: NZMA, 2008.

[12] Aristotle, *Nicomachean Ethics*, R. Crisp (tr. and ed.), Cambridge: Cambridge University Press, 2000, Bk I, 1096a.

[13] R. Layard, *Happiness: Lessons from a New Science*, 2nd edn, London: Penguin, 2011.

[14] H.E. Daly and J.B. Cobb, *For the Common Good*, 2nd edn, Boston: Beacon Press, 1994; see also C. Hamilton, 'The genuine progress indicator: methodological developments and results from Australia', *Ecological Economics*, 30, 1999, 13-28.

[15] Two issues of importance need to be borne in mind when considering these index calculations: the extent to which individual indices are based on objective or subjective (i.e. personal) measures; and whether the individual indices are combined to provide a single overall index, or are kept separate as individual indices (the 'dashboard' approach).

[16] J.E. Stiglitz, A. Sen and J.-P. Fitoussi, *Report by the Commission on the Measurement of Economic Performance and Social Progress*, 2009, p. 12, http://www.stiglitz-sen-fitoussi.fr/en/index.htm

[17] OECD, *How's Life? Measuring Well-Being*, Paris: OECD, 2013. New Zealand scores comparatively well on the OECD indices.

[18] United Nations General Assembly, 'Happiness: towards a holistic approach to development', Resolution 65/309, adopted 19/07/2011.

[19] J. Helliwell, R. Layard and J. Sachs (eds), *World Happiness Report: A Report Commissioned for the United Nations Conference on Happiness*, New York: Earth Institute, Colombia University, 2012.

[20] K. Ura et al., 'A short guide to gross national happiness index', Centre for Bhutan Studies, Thimphu, Bhutan, 2012, http://www.grossnationalhappiness.com

[21] G. O'Donnell, 'Using well-being as a guide to policy', in Helliwell et al. (eds), *World Happiness Report 2013*, pp. 98-111, http://unsdsn.org/resources/publications/world-happiness-report-2013

[22] R. Inglehart and H.-D. Klingemann, 'Genes, culture, democracy, and happiness', in E. Diener and E.M. Suh (eds), *Culture and Subjective Well-Being*, Cambridge, MA: MIT Press, 2000, p. 168; R. Inglehart et al., 'Development, freedom, and rising happiness', *Perspectives on Psychological Science*, 3(4), 2008, 264-85; R. Inglehart, *Modernization and Postmodernization: Cultural, Economic, and Political Change in 43 Societies*, Princeton, NJ: Princeton University Press, 1997.

[23] In similar manner the New Zealand General Social Survey of 2010 found that although satisfaction with life increased with household income, the largest increase was between the two lowest household income groups, with higher income groups showing progressively smaller increases.

[24] World Wildlife Fund, *Living Planet Report 2006*, Gland, Switzerland: WWF, 2006, p. 19.

[25] R. Costanza and H.E. Daly, 'Natural capital and sustainable development', *Conservation Biology*, 6(1), 1992, 37-46.

[26] Royal Society, *People and the Planet*, London: Royal Society, 2012; R. Beddoe et al., 'Overcoming systemic roadblocks to sustainability: the evolutionary redesign of worldviews, institutions, and technologies', *Proceedings of the National Academy of Sciences*, 106(8), 2009, 2483-9; R. Costanza et al., 'Principles for sustainable governance of the oceans', *Science*, 281, 1998, 198-9.

[27] WBCSD, *Vision 2050: The New Agenda for Business*, Geneva: WBCSD, 2010.

[28] Sustainable Business Council, *Vision 2050: 2012 New Zealand Edition*, Wellington: Sustainable Business Council, 2012.

[29] J. Elkington, *Cannibals with Forks: The Triple Bottom Line of 21st Century Business*, Gabriola Is., BC: New Society Publishers, 1998.

[30] R. Chapman and M.J. Milne, 'The triple bottom line: How New Zealand companies measure up', Accountancy Working Paper Series,

School of Business, University of Otago, 2003, http://otago.ourarchive.ac.nz/handle/10523/1547; URS New Zealand, 'Corporate sustainability reporting in New Zealand', research paper prepared for the Parliamentary Commissioner for the Environment, 2006.

[31] D. Marquand, *Decline of the Public*, Cambridge: Polity Press, 2004, p. 27.

[32] The B Team, http://bteam.org/about/vision

[33] Statistics New Zealand, 'Key findings on New Zealand's progress using a sustainable development approach: 2010', Wellington: Statistics New Zealand.

[34] Controller and Auditor-General, *Ministry of Agriculture and Forestry: Management of Biosecurity Risks*, Wellington: The Audit Office, 2002, p. 14.

[35] In March 2014 it was announced that government funding for the Bio-Protection Research Centre at Lincoln University was to be eliminated. *Radio New Zealand News*, 03/04/2014.

[36] Wikipedia, entries on: 'Tobin tax', 'Financial transaction tax', 'Reaction to the Tobin tax'; S. Griffith-Jones, 'Germany wants the Robin Hood tax - and Europe's voters do too', *Guardian* (UK), 30/10/2013.

[37] G. Wheeler, 'The building blocks of the economic expansion', Speech delivered to Canterbury Employers' Chamber of Commerce, Christchurch, 31/01/2014.

[38] Rt Hon Sir Edmund Thomas, 'Reducing inequality: a strategy for a cause', 2013 Bruce Jesson Lecture, University of Auckland, 30/10/2013, http://www.livingwagenz.org.nz/files/2013%20Bruce%20Jesson%20Lecture%20EW%20Thomas.pdf

[39] *Julius Caesar*, Act I, Scene 2, 140-1.

Index

Made in the USA
Monee, IL
04 November 2026

67381922R00154